As this appalling ocean surrounds the verdant land,
so in the soul of man there lies one insular Tahiti,
full of peace and joy, but encompassed by
all the horrors of the half-known life.
God help thee! Push not off from that isle,
thou canst never return.

—Herman Melville

TAHITI
-POLYNESIA
HANDBOOK

DIANA LASICH HARPER

TAHITI
-POLYNESIA
HANDBOOK

DAVID STANLEY

MOON
PUBLICATIONS INC.

TAHITI-POLYNESIA HANDBOOK

Published by
Moon Publications, Inc.
722 Wall Street
Chico, California 95928, U.S.A.

Printed by
Colorcraft Ltd.

Library of Congress Cataloging in Publication Data

Stanley, David/
    Tahiti-Polynesia Handbook / David Stanley. —2nd ed.
        p.   cm.
    Includes bibliographical references (p. 198) and index.
    ISBN 0-918373-87-5 : $11.95
    I. French Polynesia—Description and travel.   I. Title
DU870.S73   1992
996.2—dc20   92-22632
                          CIP

Printed in Hong Kong

Cover photograph courtesy of Douglas Peebles

A German translation of this book is published by Verlag Gisela E. Walther, Oppenheimerstr. 26, 2800 Bremen 44, Germany.

Please send all comments,
corrections, additions,
amendments, and critiques to:

DAVID STANLEY
c/o MOON PUBLICATIONS, INC.
722 WALL STREET
CHICO, CA 95928, U.S.A.

Printing History
  1st edition—September 1989
    Reprinted—June 1991
  2nd edition—November 1992

CONTENTS

LIST OF MAPS

MAP SYMBOLS

——— MAIN ROAD   ▲   MOUNTAIN

——— SECONDARY ROAD

– – – FOOT TRAIL   REEF

○   TOWN

○ ■   POINT OF INTEREST   WATER

LIST OF CHARTS

ABBREVIATIONS

4WD—four-wheel drive
A$—Australian dollars
a/c—air conditioned
B.P.—Boîte Postale
C—centigrade
C$—Canadian dollars
cm—centimeter
d—double
EC—European Community
EEZ—Exclusive Economic Zone
f.—CFP (Pacific francs)
km—kilometer
kph—kilometers per hour
LDS—Latter-day Saints (Mormons)
min.—minutes
mm—millimeters

MV—motor vessel
no.—number
NZ—New Zealand
OW—one way
PK—point kilométrique
pp—per person
RT—roundtrip
s—single
SPF—South Pacific Forum
t—triple
tel.—telephone
U.S.—United States
US$—U.S. dollars
WW I—World War One
WW II—World War Two
YHA—Youth Hostel Association

IS THIS BOOK OUT OF DATE?

Travel writing is like trying to take a picture out the side of *le truck:* time frustrates the best of intentions. Things change fast—you'll understand how hard it is for us to keep up. So if something in *Tahiti-Polynesia Handbook* seems out of date, please let us know about it. Did anything lead you astray or inconvenience you? In retrospect, what sort of information would have made your trip easier? Please share your discoveries with us and we'll share them with others. Everything will be carefully field-checked, but your lead could help us zero in on some fascinating aspect which might otherwise be overlooked. Please be as precise and accurate as you can, however. Notes made on the scene are far better than later recollections. Write comments into your copy of *Tahiti-Polynesia Handbook* as you go along, then send us a summary when you get home. If this book helped you, please help us make it even better. Address your letters to:

David Stanley
c/o Moon Publications
722 Wall Street
Chico, CA 95928 U.S.A.

ACKNOWLEDGEMENTS

Thanks to "coconut time" editor Anne-Marie Nicoara for picking out the little inconsistencies, to editor-in-chief Taran March for putting her magic marker away (for now), to Bob Race for correcting the maps, to Anne Hikido for laying out the book and pasting it up, and to Robert Kolb for bouncing it back and forth between Chico, Amsterdam, and Hong Kong.

Many of the antique engravings included in this book were taken from M.G.L. Domeny de Rienzi's classic three-volume work *Oceanie ou Cinquième Partie du Monde* (Paris: Firmin Didot Freres, 1836).

Special thanks to Hyacinthe Cao and Pierre Fredj of the Tahiti Tourist Promotion Board for updating information, to Tjalling Terpstra of Amber Travel Agency, Amsterdam, for help in checking Pacific air routes, to Banque Socredo for current exchange rates, to Margaret Argue of the South Pacific Peoples Foundation of Canada for a big box of resources, to Madame Jacques Brel for kind permission to reproduce *Les Marquises*, to Bill Weir for getting my computer operational, and to Ria for providing the support I needed to continue updating this book.

I'm deeply grateful to Bengt Danielsson of Papehue, Tahiti, who read and corrected the entire manuscript. Dr. Danielsson arrived in Tahiti-Polynesia in 1947 aboard Thor Heyerdahl's famous raft, *Kon Tiki*. During the next ten years, he and his French wife, Marie Thérèse, carried out anthropological field work in the Tuamotu, Marquesas, and Society islands. Later Bengt served as director of Sweden's National Museum of Ethnology before returning to Tahiti for good in 1971. Some of his numerous publications are listed in the "Booklist" herein, and in Dec. 1991 the Danielssons were awarded the "alternative Nobel Prize" by the Right Livelihood Foundation for their scientific studies and antinuclear actions. If *Tahiti-Polynesia Handbook* displays any historical accuracy it's due to the very thorough check Bengt did of both the first and second editions; remaining inadequacies are the responsibility of the author.

Thanks too to the following readers who took the trouble to write us letters about their trips: Jan Van Aerschot, Charlie Appleton, Audrey Beavin, Amy Best, Nick Bischoff, Dolores Blalock, Dr. Alex Brunnendorfer, Norm Buske, Hendrikje Buss, Kathy Cox, Dorothy Culley, Miguel DaSilva, Malcolm Easton, Alvin H. Grobmeier, Doug & Fran Hubbard, Albert Hsu, Wayne S. Johnson, Andrea Kaluzny, Johannes Keintzel, David Kitching, Michael Langer, Rolf Lasa, Real Leboeuf, Joseph F. Lewis, Steffan Liebscher, Hermann Litwin, Rick Luttmann, Beate Lutzebäck, Edward R. Meili, David Miles, Dr. Albrecht Moll, Amy L. Perkins, Ulrich Piesker, Rainer Reichelt, Markus Reichl, Gudrun and Robert Schmid, Margitta Schneider-Wist, Jürg M. Sprenger, Robert Leger Teitelbaum, Sänke Thiesen, Verne Valentine, Jochem Wadsack, Marianne Wenthaus, Andreas Wolf, Curt Zaumeyer, Mag. Martin Zausner, and Dr. Waltraud Zausner. You can have your own name included here next edition for the price of a postage stamp.

Attention Hotel Keepers, Tour Operators, Divemasters:

The best way to keep your listing in *Tahiti-Polynesia Handbook* up to date is to send us current information about your business. There's never any charge or obligation for a mention. Thanks to the following tourism workers and government officials who *did* write in: Mrs. Amouy B., Edwina Arnold, Jean-Paul Aromaiterai, Alicia Baldwin, A.K. Braden, Jacques Briquet, Wendy Brooks, Bambi Bryant, Jill Church, Colleen E. Condon, Kirsten Corbett, Mary Crowley, Charles Durand, Pierre Florentin, Val Gavriloff, Brad Hoopes, Roger Hoskins, Gabrielle Hunt, Rozita Ibrahim, Richard Johnson, Walter Kamm, Folke von Knobloch, Pascal A. Le Cointre, William Leeteg, Leslie G. Lewis, Charles Mardiks, Marie-Isabelle, Philippe Molle, Jean-Paul Perea, Marie-France Philip, C. Gregory Posey, Henri Poulíquen, Al Prince, Miss Raywadee A., Elaine Schultz, Claude Sibani, Pascale Siu, Kay and Gerald Teriierooiterai, Jean-Luc Untz, and Gérard Warti.

While out researching my books I find it cheaper to pay my own way and nothing in this book is designed to repay favors from hotels, tour operators, or airlines. I prefer to arrive unexpected and uninvited, and to experience things as they really are. On the road I seldom identify myself to anyone. The companies and organizations included in this book are there for information purposes only and a mention in no way implies an endorsement.

FOREWORD

"All my life I had longed to go to the South Seas. These very words had magic in them, conjuring up primordial memories of palms and coral reefs and sun-drenched sands, of fruits and flowering trees, of women warm in welcome, of peace and isolation, and of a shore where the struggle for existence is unknown."

Thus writes Cecil Lewis, an ordinary, average American, who before the Second World War managed to realize his dream and consequently published an enthusiastic account of the happy months he spent in Tahiti and the other Society Islands.

The dream is not dead. But as most South Sea travelers today will sadly discover, the "native" villages they find along their crowded paths are often human zoos, where the athletic guitar players and graceful hula dancers are paid performers, professional natives so to say, with a bank account, a car, and a TV set at home.

So there is a general belief that there is nothing left of the "real" South Seas. Fortunately, this is not altogether true. During the forty years I have lived in Tahiti, I have received a steady stream of visitors, who are all appalled by the traffic jams, concrete buildings, and frantic life in and around Papeete, and therefore eager to learn the exact location of the primitive, unspoiled island paradises they have been dreaming of, and which do exist in the remote archipelagoes of Tahiti-Polynesia, or French Polynesia, as the colony is officially named.

It has always surprised me that none of the previous guidebooks have supplied this badly needed information, and I am very happy to see that my friend David Stanley has at long last filled this gap and has thus taken a heavy burden off my shoulders. Fortunately, this does not mean, however, that there is nothing in this new-style up-to-date handbook about the central, more sophisticated islands, like Tahiti, Moorea, Raiatea, and Bora Bora.

Actually, this blend of old and new, Polynesian and European cultural elements found today in varying degrees in the majority of the 118 islands is as interesting

Bengt Danielsson

and fascinating as the "pure" traditional life-style in the outer islands. Whereas few other travel guides take notice of these changes, the readers of this handbook will also find much information about all these social, economic, and political consequences due to the long exposure of a stone-age people with a simple subsistence economy and strong family and community solidarity to our Western type of individualistic and commercial civilization.

There are also pertinent notices about the regional differences in French Polynesia which, in fact, consists of five distinct archipelagoes, inhabited by native peoples, speaking separate Polynesian tongues and having different cultural traditions.

The last but not the least important feature of this unique handbook is the complete, detailed, and accurate practical information it offers the user about where to stay and what to pay—as well as equally useful advice about how to avoid being overcharged for goods and services.

With sincere congratulations for your fortunate choice of handbook, I guarantee you a happy sojourn, wish you a warm welcome to my islands, and extend to you the traditional greeting, corresponding to a Hawaiian aloha, which in Tahitian is pronounced

AROHA
Papehue, Tahiti
Bengt Danielsson

INTRODUCTION

Tarita co-starred with Marlon Brando in the 1962 MGM film Mutiny on the Bounty *the Tahitian fleet preparing to attack Moorea, 1774 (after William Hodges)*

INTRODUCTION

Legendary Tahiti, isle of love, has long been the vision of "la Nouvelle Cythère," the earthly paradise. Explorers Wallis, Bougainville, and Cook told of a land of spellbinding beauty and enchantment, where the climate was delightful, hazardous insects and diseases unknown, and the islanders, especially the women, among the handsomest ever seen. Rousseau's "noble savage" had been found! A few years later, Fletcher Christian and Capt. Bligh acted out their drama of sin and retribution here.

The list of famous authors who came and wrote about these islands reads like a high-school literature course: Herman Melville, Robert Louis Stevenson, Pierre Loti, Rupert Brooke, Jack London, W. Somerset Maugham, Charles Nordhoff and James Norman Hall (the Americans who wrote *Mutiny on the Bounty*), among others. Exotic images of uninhibited dancers, fragrant flowers, and pagan gods fill the pages. Here, at least, life was meant to be enjoyed.

The most unlikely PR man of them all was a once-obscure French painter named Paul Gauguin, who transformed the primitive color of Tahiti and the Marquesas into powerful visual images seen around the world. When WW II shook the Pacific from Pearl Harbor to Guadalcanal, rather than bloodcurdling banzais and saturation bombings, Polynesia got a U.S. serviceman named James A. Michener, who added Bora Bora to the legend. Marlon Brando arrived in 1961 on one of the first jets to land in Polynesia and, along with thousands of tourists and adventurers, has been coming back ever since.

Trouble In Paradise
In the early 1960s, President Charles de Gaulle transferred France's atomic testing program from Algeria to Polynesia. Since then over 175 nuclear explosions, 44 of them in the atmosphere, have rocked the Tuamotus, spreading contamination as far as Peru and New Zealand.

The official French attitude to its Pacific colonies has changed little since 1842 when Admiral Du Petit-Thouars sailed into Papeete harbor and forced young Queen Pomare IV to sign a request for a French protectorate. In the 1960s-70s, as independence blossomed across the South Pacific, France tightened its strategic grip on Tahiti-Polynesia.

New mineral wealth has been discovered on the seabed and, despite the collapse of the Cold War, the arms race is far from over. In late 1991 French Defense Minister Pierre Joxe announced France would continue nuclear testing as long as it had nuclear weapons! Deadly radiation could already be leaking into the sea from dumps and cracks at the French facilities on Moruroa. If you've never visited a *colony* before, here's your chance.

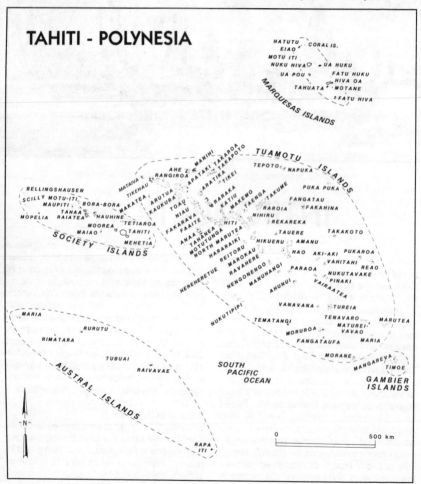

TAHITI - POLYNESIA

THE LAND

Tahiti-Polynesia consists of five great archipelagos, the Society, Austral, Tuamotu, Gambier, and Marquesas islands. The Society Islands are subdivided into the Windwards or Îles du Vent (Tahiti, Moorea, Maiao, Tetiaroa, and Mehetia), and the Leewards or Îles Sous le Vent (Huahine, Raiatea, Tahaa, Bora Bora, Maupiti, Tupai, Maupihaa/Mopelia, Manuae/Scilly, and Motu One/Bellingshausen). Together the 35 islands and 83 atolls of Tahiti-Polynesia total only 3,543 square km in land area, yet they're scattered over 5,030,000 square km of the southeastern Pacific, from the Cook Is. in the west to Pitcairn in the east. Though Tahiti-Polynesia is only half the size of Corsica in land area, if Papeete were Paris then the Gambiers would be in Romania and the Marquesas near Stockholm.

There's a wonderful geological diversity to these islands midway between Australia and South America—from the dramatic, jagged volcanic outlines of the Society and Marquesas islands to the 400-meter-high hills of the Australs and Gambiers and the low coral atolls of the Tuamotus. All of the Marquesas are volcanic islands, while the Tuamotus are all coral islands or atolls. The Societies and Gambiers include both volcanic and coral types.

Tahiti, just over 4,000 km from both Auckland and Honolulu, is not only the best known and most populous of the islands, but also the largest (1,045 square km) and highest (2,241 meters). Bora Bora and Maupiti are noted for their combination of high volcanic peaks within low coral rings. Rangiroa is one of the world's largest coral atolls while Makatea is an uplifted atoll. In the Marquesas, precipitous and sharply crenelated mountains rise hundreds of meters, with craggy peaks, razor-back ridges, plummeting waterfalls, deep fertile valleys, and dark broken coastlines pounded by surf. Compare them to the pencil-thin strips of yellow reefs, green vegetation, and white beaches enclosing the transparent Tuamotu lagoons. In all, Tahiti-Polynesia offers some of the most varied and spectacular scenery in the entire South Pacific.

Darwin's Theory Of Atoll Formation

The famous formulator of the theory of evolution surmised that atolls form as high volcanic islands subside into lagoons. The original island's fringing reef grows into a barrier reef as the volcanic portion sinks. When the last volcanic material finally disappears below sea level, the coral rim of the reef/atoll remains to indicate how big the island once was.

POLYNESIA AT A GLANCE

	Population (1988)	Area (hectares)
WINDWARD ISLANDS	140,341	118,580
Tahiti	131,309	104,510
Moorea	8,801	12,520
LEEWARD ISLANDS	22,232	38,750
Huahine	4,479	7,480
Raiatea	8,560	17,140
Tahaa	4,005	9,020
Bora Bora	4,225	1,830
Maupiti	96	31,140
AUSTRAL ISLANDS	6,509	14,784
Rurutu	1,953	3,235
Tubuai	1,846	4,500
TUAMOTU ISLANDS	11,7547	2,646
Rangiroa	1,305	7,900
Manihi	429	1,300
GAMBIER ISLANDS	620	4,597
MARQUESAS ISLANDS	7,358	104,930
Nuku Hiva	2,100	33,950
Hiva Oa	1,671	31,550
TAHITI-POLYNESIA	188,814	354,287

CROSS SECTION OF AN OCEAN PLATE

CONTINENTAL PLATE — TRENCH — OCEANIC PLATE — RIDGE

HIGH ISLAND

ATOLLS

SUBMARINE VOLCANO   RIDGE VOLCANO

DIRECTION OF PLATE MOVEMENT

HOT SPOT

SEVERAL THOUSAND KILOMETERS

Of course, all this takes place over thousands, perhaps millions, of years, but deep down below every atoll is the old volcanic core, as any nuclear tester worth his contamination knows. Darwin's theory is well illustrated at Bora Bora, where a high volcanic island remains inside the rim of Bora Bora's barrier reef; this island's volcanic core is still sinking imperceptibly at the rate of one cm a century. Return to Bora Bora in about 25 million years and all you'll find will be a coral atoll like Rangiroa or Manihi.

Plate Tectonics
High or low, all of the islands have a volcanic origin best explained by the "Conveyor Belt Theory." A crack opens in the sea floor and volcanic material escapes upward. A submarine volcano builds up slowly until the lava finally breaks the surface, becoming a volcanic island. The Pacific Plate moves northwest approximately 10 cm a year; thus, over geologic eons the volcano disconnects from the hot spot or crack from which it emerged. As the old volcanoes disconnect with the crack, new ones appear to the southeast, and the older islands are carried away from the cleft in the earth's crust from which they were born.

The island then begins to sink under its own weight, perhaps only one cm a century, but ero-

sion also cuts into the volcano, by this time extinct. In the warm clear waters a living coral reef begins to grow along the shore. As the island subsides, the reef continues to grow upward. In this way a lagoon forms between the reef and the shoreline of the slowly sinking island. This barrier reef marks the old margin of the original island.

As the hot spot shifts southeast, in an opposite direction to the sliding Pacific Plate (and shifting magnetic pole of the earth), the process is repeated, time and again, until whole chains of islands ride the blue Pacific. Weathering is most advanced on the composite islands and atolls at the northwest ends of the Society, Austral, Tuamotu, and Marquesas chains. Maupiti and Bora Bora with their exposed volcanic cores are the oldest of the larger Society Islands. The Tuamotus have eroded almost to sea level; the Gambier Islands originated out of the same hot spot and volcanic peaks remain inside a giant atoll reef. In every case, the islands at the southeast end of the chains are the youngest.

By drilling into the Tuamotu atolls, scientists have proven their point conclusively: the coral formations are about 350 meters thick at the southeast end of the chain, 600 meters thick at Hao near the center, and 1,000 meters thick at Rangiroa near the northwest end of the Tuamotu Group. Clearly Rangiroa, where the volcanic rock is now a kilometer below the surface, is many millions of years older than the Gambiers, where a volcanic peak still stands 482 meters above sea level.

Island-building continues at an active undersea volcano called MacDonald 50 meters below sea level at the southeast end of the Australs. The crack spews forth about a cubic mile of lava every century and someday MacDonald too will poke its smoky head above the waves. The theory of plate tectonics, or the sliding crust of the earth, seems proven in Tahiti-Polynesia.

Life Of An Atoll

A circular or horseshoe-shaped coral reef bearing a necklace of sandy, slender islets *(motus)* of debris thrown up by storms, surf, and wind is known as an atoll. Atolls can be up to 100 km across, but the width of dry land is usually only 200-400 meters from inner to outer beach. The central lagoon can measure anywhere from one to 50 km in diameter; huge Rangiroa Atoll is 77 km long. Entirely landlocked lagoons are rare; passages through the barrier reef are usually found on the leeward side. Most atolls are no higher than four to six meters.

A raised or elevated atoll is one that has been pushed up by submarine volcanic activities to become a coral platform. Raised atolls have steep oceanside cliffs and are often known for their huge sea caves. The only raised atoll in Tahiti-Polynesia is crescent-shaped Makatea in the northwestern corner of the Tuamotu group. It is 100 meters high, seven km long, and 4 km wide.

Soil derived from coral is extremely poor in nutrients, while volcanic soil is known for its fertility. Dark-colored beaches are formed from volcanic material; the white beaches of travel brochures are entirely coral-based. The black beaches are cooler and easier on the eyes, enabling plantlife to grow closer, giving patches of shade; the white beaches are generally safer for swimming as visibility is better.

A new danger facing the atolls of Oceania is the "greenhouse effect," a gradual warming of earth's environment due to fuel combustion and the widespread clearing of rainforests. In the past 20 years the concentration of carbon dioxide in the atmosphere has increased 25%. As in-

frared radiation from the sun is absorbed by the gas, the trapped heat causes the expansion of sea water and the melting of glaciers and polar ice caps. Water levels could rise by one meter in 50 years, three meters by the year 2100. Not only will this reduce the supply of drinking water and the growing area for food crops, but rising sea levels will mean salt water intrusion into ground water supplies—a horrifying prospect during droughts. In time entire populations could be forced to evacuate, and eventually whole archipelagos like the Tuamotus may be flooded. And if that's not enough, the greenhouse effect may also lead to a dramatic increase in hurricanes in the eastern Pacific.

CORAL REEFS

To understand how a basalt volcano becomes a limestone atoll, it's necessary to know a little about the growth of coral. Coral reefs cover some 200,000 square km worldwide, between 35° N and 32° S latitude. A reef is created by the accumulation of millions of tiny calcareous skeletons left by long generations of tiny coral polyps. Though the skeleton is usually white, the living polyps are of many different colors.

They thrive in clear salty water where the temperature never drops below 18° C. They must also have a base not over 50 meters from the surface on which to form. The coral colony grows slowly upward on the consolidated skeletons of its ancestors until it reaches the low-tide mark, after which development extends outward on the edges of the reef. Sunlight is critical for coral growth. Colonies grow quickly on the ocean side due to clearer water and a greater abundance of food. A strong healthy reef can grow four to five cm a year. Fresh or cloudy water inhibits coral growth, which is why villages and ports all across the Pacific are located at the reef-free mouths of rivers.

Polyps extract calcium carbonate from the water and deposit it in their skeletons. All reef-building corals also contain limy encrustations of microscopic algae within their cells. The algae, like all green plants, obtain their energy from the sun, and contribute this energy to the growth of the reef's skeleton. As a result, corals behave (and look) more like plants than animals, competing for sunlight just as terrestrial plants do. Many polyps are also carnivorous, and supplement their energy by capturing tiny planktonic animals and organic particles at night with minute stinging tentacles. A small piece of coral is a colony composed of thousands of polyps.

Coral Types

Corals belong to a broad group of stinging creatures which includes polyps, soft corals, stony corals, sea anemones, sea fans, and jellyfish. Only those types with hard skeletons and a single hollow cavity within the body are considered true corals. Stony corals such as brain, table, staghorn, and mushroom corals have external skeletons and are important reef builders. Soft corals, black corals, and sea fans have internal skeletons. The fire corals are recognized by their smooth, velvety surface and yellowish-brown color. The stinging toxins of this last group can easily penetrate the human skin and cause swelling and painful burning that can last up to an hour. The many varieties of soft, colorful anemones gently waving in the current might seem inviting to touch, but beware! Many are also poisonous.

The corals, like most other forms of life in the Pacific, colonized the ocean from the fertile seas of Southeast Asia. Thus the number of species declines as you move east. Over 600 species of coral make their home in the Pacific, compared to only 48 in the Caribbean. The diversity of coral colors and forms is endlessly amazing. This is our most unspoiled environment, a world of almost indescribable beauty.

Exploring A Reef

Until you've explored a good coral reef, you haven't experienced one of the greatest joys of nature. While one cannot walk through pristine forests due to the lack of paths, it's quite possible to swim over untouched reefs—the most densely populated living space on earth. Dive shops throughout the region rent scuba and snorkeling gear, so do get into the clear, warm waters around you. Be careful, however, and know the dangers. Practice snorkeling in the shallow water; don't head into deep water until you're sure you've got the hang of it. Breathe easily; don't hyperventilate.

When snorkeling on a fringing reef, beware of deadly currents and undertows in channels which drain tidal flows. Observe the direction the water is flowing before you swim into it. If you feel yourself being dragged out to sea through a reef passage, try swimming across the current rather than against it. If you can't resist the pull at all, it may be better to let yourself be carried out. Wait till the current diminishes, then swim along the outer reef face until you find somewhere to come back in. Or use your energy to attract the attention of someone on shore. Most beach drownings occur in such situations, so try not to panic.

Snorkeling on the outer edge or drop-off of a reef is thrilling for the variety of fish and corals, but only attempt it on a very calm day. Even then it's best to have someone on shore or standing on the edge of the reef (at low tide) to watch for occasional big waves which can take you by surprise and smash you into the rocks. Also, beware of unperceived currents outside the reef—you may not get a second chance.

A far better idea is to limit your snorkeling to the protected inner reef and leave the open waters to the scuba diver. Guides know their waters and are able to show you the most amazing things in perfect safety. Dive centers are operating on Tahiti, Moorea, Tetiaroa, Huahine, Raiatea, Bora Bora, Rangiroa, and Manihi. Rangi-

BOB HALSTEAD

roa and Manihi offer the best diving, followed by Bora Bora and Moorea. Diving is possible year-round, with marinelife most profuse from July to November. Divers should bring their certification card, buoyancy compensator, and regulator. Many of the scuba operators listed in this book offer resort courses for beginning divers. The main constraint is financial: snorkeling is free, while scuba diving varies from f.4000-7000 a dive.

Conservation

Coral reefs are one of the most fragile and complex ecosystems on earth, providing food and shelter for countless species of fish, crustacea (shrimps, crabs, and lobsters), mollusks (shells), and other animals. Hard corals grow only about 10 to 25 mm a year and it can take 7,000 to 10,000 years for a coral reef to form. Though corals look solid they're easily broken; by standing on them, breaking off pieces, or carelessly dropping anchor you can destroy in a few minutes what took so long to form. Once a piece of coral breaks off it dies, and it may be years before the coral reestablishes itself and even longer before the broken piece is replaced. Sometimes the damage is permanent, and when this happens over a wide area the diversity of marinelife declines dramatically.

We recommend that you not remove seashells, coral, plantlife, or marine animals from the sea. In a small way, you are upsetting the delicate balance of nature, and coral is much more beautiful underwater anyway! This is a particular problem along shorelines frequented by large numbers of tourists who can completely strip a reef in very little time. If you'd like a souvenir, content yourself with what you find on the beach. Also think twice about purchasing jewelry or souvenirs made from coral or seashells. Genuine traditional handicrafts which incorporate shells are one thing, but by purchasing unmounted seashells or mass-produced coral curios you are contributing to the destruction of the marine environment.

There's an urgent need for stricter government regulation of the seas and in many places coral reefs are already protected by law. Exhortations such as the one above have only limited impact. As consumerism spreads, once-remote areas become subject to the problems of

PAPEETE'S CLIMATE

ANNUAL AVERAGE 77.7°F / 25.4°C

ANNUAL 73.74 in 1873 mm

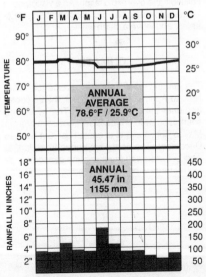

ATUONA'S CLIMATE

ANNUAL AVERAGE 78.6°F / 25.9°C

ANNUAL 45.47 in 1155 mm

a waterspout during a tropical cyclone or hurricane

near the equator, which then flow toward the poles at high altitude. Cooler air drawn toward the vacuum is deflected to the west by the rotation of the earth. Tahiti-Polynesia's proximity to the intertropical convergence zone (5° north and south of the equator) or "doldrum zone"—where the most heated air is rising—explains the seasonal shift in the winds from northeast to southeast. The trade winds cool the islands and offer clear sailing for mariners, making May to Oct. the most favorable season to visit.

Hurricanes are relatively rare, although they do hit the Tuamotus and occasionally Tahiti. From Nov. 1980 to May 1983 an unusual wave of eight hurricanes and two tropical storms battered the islands. A hurricane would only inconvenience a visitor staying at a hotel, though campers and yachties might get blown into oblivion. The days immediately following a hurricane are clear and dry. Tahiti-Polynesia enjoys some of the cleanest air on earth—air that hasn't blown over a continent for weeks.

Rainfall is greatest in the mountains and along the windward shores of the high islands. The Societies are far damper than the Marquesas. In fact, the climate of the Marquesas is erratic: some years the group experiences serious drought, other years it could rain the whole time you're there. The low-lying Tuamotus get the least rainfall of all. Tahiti-Polynesia encompasses such a vast area that latitude is an important factor: at 27° S latitude Rapa Iti is far cooler than Nuku Hiva (9° S).

Winds from the southeast *(maramu)* are generally drier than those from the northeast or north. The northeast winds often bring rain: Papenoo on the northeast side of Tahiti gets twice as wet as rain-shadowed Punaauia. The annual rainfall is extremely variable but the humidity is generally high, reaching 98%. In the evening the heat of the Tahiti afternoons is replaced by soft, fragrant mountain breezes called *hupe,* which drift down to the sea.

pollution and overexploitation. As a visitor, don't hesitate to practice your conservationist attitudes, and leave a clean wake.

CLIMATE

The hot and humid summer season runs from Nov. to April. The climate is somewhat cooler and drier the rest of the year. The refreshing southeast trade winds blow consistently from May to Aug., varying to easterlies from Sept. to December. The northeast trades from Jan. to April coincide with the hurricane season.

The trade winds are caused by hot air rising

FLORA AND FAUNA

FLORA

The variety of floral species encountered in the Pacific islands declines as you move away from the Asian mainland. Although some species may have spread across the islands by means of floating seeds or fruit, wind and birds were probably more effective. The microscopic spores of ferns, for example, can be carried vast distances by the wind. In the coastal areas of Tahiti most of the plants now seen have been introduced by man.

Here in Polynesia the air is sweet with the bouquet of tropical blossoms such as bursting bougainvillea, camellia, frangipani, ginger, orchids, poinsettia, and pitate jasmine. The fragrant flowers of the Polynesian hibiscus *(purau)* are yellow, not red or pink as on the Chinese hibiscus. A useful tree, the soft wood of the hibiscus is used for house and canoe construction, the bast fiber to make cordage and mats. The national flower, the delicate, heavy-scented tiare Tahiti *(Gardenia tahitiensis)*, can have anywhere from six to nine white petals. It blooms year-round, but especially from Sept. to April. In his *Plants and Flowers of Tahiti* Jean-Claude Belhay writes: "The tiare is to Polynesia what the lotus is to India: a veritable symbol." Follow local custom by wearing this blossom or a hibiscus behind your left ear if you're happily taken, behind your right ear if you're still available.

Tahiti-Polynesia's high islands support a great variety of plantlife, while the low islands are restricted to a few hardy, drought-resistant species such as coconut and pandanus palm. On the atolls taro, a root vegetable with broad heart-shaped leaves, must be cultivated in deep organic pits. Rainforests fill the valleys and damp windward slopes of the high islands, while brush and thickets grow in more exposed locations. *Mape* (Tahitian chestnut) grows along the streams. Other trees you'll encounter include almond, candlenut, Casaurina (ironwood), flamboyant, barringtonia, *purau* (wild hibiscus), pistachio, and rosewood. Mountain bananas *(fei)* grow wild in the high country. Along the coast fruits such as avocado, banana, custard apple, guava, grapefruit, lime, lychee, mango, orange, papaya, pineapple, watermelon, and a hundred more are cultivated.

Mangroves can occasionally be found along some high-island coastal lagoons. The cable roots of the saltwater-tolerant mangroves anchor in the shallow upper layer of oxygenated mud, avoiding the layers of hydrogen sulfide below. The tree provides shade for tiny organisms dwelling in the tidal mudflats—a place for birds to nest and fish or shellfish to feed and spawn. The mangroves also perform the same task as land-building coral colonies along the reefs. As sediments are trapped between the roots, the trees extend farther into the lagoon—creating a unique natural environment.

MARINELIFE

Polynesia's richest store of life is found among the fish of the lagoons and open sea, including angelfish, bonito, butterflyfish, eels, groupers, harpfish, jacks, mahimahi, mullets, parrotfish, sharks, soldierfish, stingrays, surgeonfish, swordfish, trumpetfish, tuna, and countless more. It's believed that most Pacific marine organisms evolved in the triangular area bounded by New Guinea, the Philippines, and the Malay Peninsula. This "Cradle of Indo-Pacific Marinelife" includes a wide variety of habitats and has remained stable through several geological ages. From this cradle the rest of the Pacific was colonized.

Dolphins

While most people use the terms dolphin and porpoise interchangeably, a porpoise lacks the dolphin's beak (although many dolphins are also beakless). There are 62 species of dolphins, and only six species of porpoises. Dolphins leap from the water, and many legends tell of their saving humans, especially children, from drowning (the most famous concerns Telemachus, son of Odysseus). Because dolphins are often found in the vicinity of schools of tuna, many drown in purse-seine nets off the coast of Central and South America.

Sharks

The danger from sharks has been greatly exaggerated. Of some 300 different species, only 28 are known to have attacked humans. Most dangerous are the white, tiger, hammerhead, and blue sharks. Fortunately, all inhabit deep water, far from the coasts. Sometimes, however, attracted by wastes thrown overboard, they follow ships into port and create problems. An average of 50 shark attacks a year occur worldwide, so considering the number of people who swim in the sea, your chances of being involved are pretty slim. In Tahiti-Polynesia shark attacks are extremely rare.

Sharks are not dangerous where food is abundant, but they can be very nasty far offshore. You're always safer if you keep your head underwater (with a mask and snorkel), and don't panic if you see a shark—you might attract it. Even if you do, usually they're only curious, so look them straight in the eye, and slowly back off. Sharks are attracted by shiny objects (a knife or jewelry), bright colors (especially yellow and red), urinating, spearfishing, blood, and splashing: divers should ease themselves into the water. Sharks have poor eyesight and often mistake the white palms and soles of a bather's hands and feet for small fish.

Never swim alone if you suspect the presence of sharks. If you see one, get out of the water calmly and quickly, and go elsewhere (unless you're with someone knowledgeable). Sharks normally stay outside the reef, but ask local advice. White beaches are safer than dark, and clear water safer than murky. Avoid swimming in places where sewage or edible wastes enter the water, or fish have just been cleaned.

Recent studies indicate that sharks, like most other creatures, are territorial. Thus an attack could be a shark's way of warning someone to get out of his backyard. Over half the victims of these incidents are not eaten, but merely wounded. Let common sense be your guide, not blind fear or carelessness. Actually, many scuba

divers come *looking for* sharks, and local divemasters swim among them with impunity (we certainly aren't suggesting you do this on your own, however).

Sea Urchins

Sea urchins (living pin cushions) are common in tropical waters. The black variety is the most dangerous: their long sharp quills can go right through a snorkeler's fins. Even the small ones, which you can easily pick up in your hand, can pinch you if you're careless. They're found on rocky shores and reefs, never on clear sandy beaches where the surf rolls in.

Most sea urchins are not poisonous, though quill punctures are painful, and can become infected if not treated. The pain is caused by an injected protein which you can eliminate by holding the injured area in a pail of very hot water for about 15 minutes. This will coagulate the protein, eliminating the pain for good. If you can't heat water, soak the area in vinegar or urine for a quarter hour. Remove the quills if possible, but as they are calcium, they'll decompose in a couple of weeks anyway—not much of a consolation as you limp along in the meantime. In some places sea urchins are a favorite delicacy: the orange or yellow meat is delicious with lemon and salt.

The sea urchin feeds on seaweed and uses tubular feet on its underside for locomotion. The long protective spines do not always protect it from hungry snails and fish.

DIANA LASICH HARPER

The highly camouflaged stonefish (Synanceia verrucosa) *rests on reef flats waiting for the chance to strike small fish. The deadly venom in the stonefish's dorsal fins causes excruciating pain and even death to anyone who happens to step on one.*

Others

Although jellyfish, stonefish, crown-of-thorns starfish, cone shells, eels, and poisonous sea snakes are hazardous, injuries resulting from any of these are rare. Gently apply methylated spirit, alcohol, or urine (but not water, kerosene, or gasoline) to areas stung by jellyfish. Harmless sea cucumbers (bêche-de-mer) punctuate the lagoon shallows. Stonefish also rest on the bottom, and their camouflage makes them hard to see; if you happen to step on one, their dorsal fins inject a painful poison which burns like fire in the blood. Treat the wound by holding it, along with an opposite foot or hand, in water as hot as you can stand for 30 minutes (immersing the opposite extremity prevents scalding due to numbness). Fortunately stonefish are not common.

Never pick up a live cone shell; some varieties have a deadly stinger dart coming out from the pointed end. Eels hide in reef crevices by day; most are dangerous only if you inadvertently poke your hand or foot in at them. Of course, never tempt fate by approaching them. The flesh of some types of fish is also poisonous, so ask local advice before eating your catch. The signs of ciguatera (seafood poisoning) are nausea, prickling, itching, and tingling of the face, fingers, and toes. Induce vomiting and take castor oil as a laxative if you're unlucky.

REPTILES

Sea turtles are facing extinction due to over-hunting and the harvesting of eggs. For this reason, importing any turtle product is prohibited in most countries. In Tahiti-Polynesia it's prohibited to capture sea turtles on land in Nov. and at sea from June to January.

Geckos and skinks are small lizards often seen on the islands. The skink hunts insects by day; its tail breaks off if you catch it, but a new one quickly grows. The gecko is nocturnal and has no eyelids. Adhesive toe pads enable it to pass along vertical surfaces, and it changes color to avoid detection. Unlike the skink, which avoids humans, geckos often live in people's homes where they eat insects attracted by electric lights. Its loud ticking call may be a territorial warning to other geckos.

Tahiti-Polynesia has no snakes. This, and the lack of leeches, poisonous plants, and dangerous wild animals, make the country a paradise for hikers. Centipedes exist, but their bite, though painful, is not lethal. The main terrestrial hazards are dogs and mosquitos.

LAND-BASED FAUNA

Island birdlife is more abundant than land-based fauna, but still reflects the decline in variety from west to east. Of the 90 species of birds in Tahiti-Polynesia, 59 are found in the Society Islands, of which 33 are native. Among the seabirds are the white-tailed tropicbirds, brown and black noddies, white and crested terns, petrels, and boobies. The *itatae* (white tern), often seen flying about with its mate far from land, lays a single egg in the fork of a tree without any nest. The baby terns can fly soon after hatching. Its call is a sharp ke-ke-yek-yek. The *oio* (black noddy) nests in colonies, preferably in palm trees, building a flat nest of dead leaves, sticks, and stems. It calls a deep cra-cra-cra. The hopping Indian mynah bird *(Acridotheres tristis)* with its yellow beak and feet was introduced from Indonesia at the turn of the century to control insects. Today these noisy, aggressive birds are ubiquitous, feeding on fruit trees and forcing the native finches and blue-tinged doves out of their habitat.

The Polynesians brought with them chickens, dogs, pigs, and rats. Captain Cook introduced cattle, horses, and goats; Capt. Wallis left behind cats. Whalers dropped more goats off in the Marquesas. Giant African snails *(Achatina fulica)* were brought to Tahiti from Hawaii in the 1960s by a local policeman fond of fancy French food. He tried to set up a snail farm, but some escaped, multiplied, and now crawl wild, destroying the vegetation. Dogs and roosters add to the sounds of the night.

LOUISE FOOTE

The giant African snail (Achatina fulica). *Each individual has both male and female organs, and can lay up to 500 eggs at a time. This scavenger is considered an agricultural pest and possible carrier of disease. Rats and coconut crabs help control their numbers.*

the double-hulled sailing canoe Hokule'a

HISTORY

THE POLYNESIANS

Discovery And Settlement
Three thousand five hundred years ago the early Polynesians set out from Southeast Asia on a migratory trek which would lead them to make the "many islands" of Polynesia their home. Great voyagers, they sailed their huge double-hulled canoes far and wide, steering with huge paddles and pandanus sails. They navigated by the sun, stars, currents, swells, winds, clouds, and birds. The first Polynesian islands settled were Tonga and Samoa; the oldest known dwelling site on Tongatapu dates from 1200 B.C. Around the time of Christ they pushed out into the eastern half of the Pacific from this primeval area remembered as Havaiki.

About A.D. 300 they reached the Marquesas from Samoa, and somewhere around A.D. 500 they sailed on from the Marquesas to Hawaii and Easter Island. They were on the Society Islands by A.D. 800 and sailed from there to the Cooks and New Zealand around A.D. 1000, completing the occupation of the Polynesian tri-angle. These were planned voyages of colonization carrying all the plants and animals needed to continue their way of life. To show how it was done a group of Hawaiians led by American anthropologist Ben Finney sailed the recreated canoe *Hokule'a* from Hawaii to Tahiti and back in 1976 and 1980, without modern navigational instruments.

Early Culture
The Polynesians lived from fishing and agriculture, using tools made from stone, bone, shell, and wood. The men were responsible for planting, harvesting, fishing, cooking, house and canoe building; the women tended the fields and animals, gathered food and fuel, prepared food, and made tapa clothes and household items. Both men and women worked together in family or community groups, not as individuals. The Polynesians lost the art of pottery making during their long stay in Havaiki and had to cook their food in underground ovens *(umu)*. It was *tapu* for men and women to eat together, so two earth ovens had to be prepared each time. Breadfruit, taro, yams, sweet potatoes, bananas,

DISCOVERY AND SETTLEMENT OF THE PACIFIC

and coconuts were cultivated. Pigs, chickens, and dogs were also kept for food, but the surrounding sea yielded the most important source of protein.

Numerous taboos regulated Polynesian life, such as prohibitions against taking certain plants or fish which were in danger of extinction. Land was collectively owned by families and tribes, and there were nobles and commoners. The chiefly families controlled the land worked collectively by commoners and took its produce, but redistribution customs were well defined. Large numbers of people could be mobilized for public works or war.

Canoes were made of planks stitched together with sennit and caulked with gum from breadfruit trees. Clothing consisted of tapa (bark cloth). Both men and women wore a belt of pandanus leaves or tapa when at work, and during leisure, a skirt that reached to their knees. Ornaments were of feathers, whale or dolphin teeth, and flowers. Both sexes were artfully tattooed using candlenut oil and soot.

For weapons there were clubs, spears, and slings. Archery was practiced only as a game to determine who could shoot farthest. Spear throwing, wrestling, boxing, kite-flying, surfing, and canoe racing were popular sports. Polynesian music was made with nasal flutes and cylindrical sharkskin or hollow slit drums. Their dancing is still appreciated today.

The museums of the world possess many fine stone and wood tikis in human form from the Marquesas Islands where the decorative sense was highly developed. Sculpture in the Australs was more naturalistic and only here were female tikis common. The Tahitians showed less interest in the plastic arts, but excelled in the social arts of poetry, oratory, theater, music, song, and dance. Life on the Tuamotus was a struggle for existence and objects had utilitarian functions. Countless Polynesian cult objects were destroyed in the early 19th century by over-zealous missionaries.

Prior to European contact three hereditary classes structured the Society Islands: high chiefs *(arii)*, lesser chiefs *(raatira)*, and commoners *(manahune)*. A small slave class *(titi)* also existed. The various *arii* tribes controlled wedge-shaped valleys and their authority was

a tattooed Marquesan woman from Dumont d'Urville's Voyage au Sud Pole *(1846)*

DUMONT D'URVILLE

balanced. Noñe managed to gain permanent supremacy over the rest.

Two related forces governed Polynesian life: *mana* and *tapu*. *Mana* was a spiritual power of which the gods and high chiefs had the most and the commoners the least. In this rigid caste system marriage or even physical contact between persons of unequal *mana* was forbidden. Children resulting from sexual relations between the classes were killed. Our word "taboo" originated from the Polynesian *tapu*. Early missionaries would often publicly violate the taboos and smash the images of the gods to show that their *mana* had vanished.

Religion centered around an open air temple called *marae* with a stone altar. Here priests prayed to the ancestors or gods and conducted all the significant ceremonies of Polynesian life. An individual's social position was determined by his family connections, and the recitation of one's genealogy confirmed it. Members of the Raiatea-based Arioi Society traveled through the islands performing ritual copulation and religious rites. The fertility god Oro had descended on a rainbow to Bora Bora's Mount Pahia where he found a beautiful *vahine*. Their child *a chief mourner before a cadaver, 1773 (after William Hodges)*

M.G.L. DOMENY DE RIENZI

was the first Arioi. In their pursuit of absolute *free* love, the Arioi killed their own children and shared spouses. Human sacrifices took place on important occasions on a high chief's *marae*. Cannibalism was rife in the Marquesas, and also practiced in the Tuamotus.

Archaeology

The first archaeological survey of Tahiti-Polynesia was undertaken in 1925 by Professor Kenneth P. Emory of Honolulu's Bernice P. Bishop Museum. Emory's successor, Professor Yosihiko Sinoto of the same museum, has carried out extensive excavations and restorations in the area since 1960. In 1962, at a 9th-century graveyard on Maupiti's Motu Paeao, Emory and Sinoto uncovered artifacts that perfectly matched those of the New Zealand Maoris. A few years later at Ua Huka in the Marquesas, Sinoto discovered a coastal village site dating from A.D. 300, the oldest yet found in Eastern Polynesia. Sinoto was responsible for the restoration of the Maeva *maraes* on Huahine and many historical *marae* on Tahiti, Moorea,

Raiatea, and Bora Bora. During construction of the Bali Hai Hotel on Huahine in 1973-77 Sinoto's student diggers located 10 flat hand clubs of the *patu* model previously considered only to exist in New Zealand, plus a 1,000-year-old sewn double canoe.

EUROPEAN CONTACT

European Exploration

While the Polynesian history of the islands goes back at least 1,700 years, the European period only began in the 16th century when the Magellan expedition sailed past the Tuamotus and Mendana visited the Marquesas. Quiros saw the Tuamotus in 1606, as did the Dutchmen Le Maire and Schouten in 1616 and Roggeveen in 1722. But it was not until 18 June 1767 that Captain Samuel Wallis on the HMS *Dolphin* happened upon Tahiti. He and most of his contemporary explorers were in search of Terra Australis Incognita, a mythical southern landmass thought to balance the northern hemisphere.

At first the Tahitians attacked the ship, but after experiencing European gunfire they decided to be friendly. Eager to trade, they loaded down the Englishmen with pigs, fowl, and fruit. Iron was in the highest demand, and Tahitian women lured the sailors to exchange nails for love. Consequently, to prevent the ship's timbers from being torn asunder for the nails, no man was allowed on shore except in parties strictly for food and water. Wallis sent ashore a landing party which named Tahiti "King George III Island," turned some sod, and hoisted the Union Jack. A year later the French explorer Louis-Antoine de Bougainville arrived on the east coast, unaware of Wallis' discovery, and claimed Tahiti for the King of France.

Wallis and Bougainville only visited briefly, leaving it to Capt. James Cook to really describe Polynesia to Europeans. Cook visited "Otaheite" four times, in 1769, 1773, 1774, and 1777. His first three-month visit was to observe the transit of the planet Venus across the face of the sun. The second and third were in search of the southern continent, while the fourth was to locate a northwest passage between the Pacific and Atlantic oceans. Some of the finest artists and scientists of the day accompanied Capt. Cook. Their explorations added the Leeward Islands, two Austral islands, and a dozen Tuamotu islands to European knowledge. Cook wrote that to the Leewards, "as they lie contiguous to each other, I gave the names of Society Islands." Later the name was extended to the Windward Islands. On Tahiti Cook met a high priest from Raiatea named Tupaia who had an astonishing knowledge of the Pacific and could name dozens of islands. He drew Cook a map which included the Cook Islands, the Marquesas, and perhaps also some Samoan islands!

In 1788 Tahiti was visited for five months by the HMS *Bounty,* commanded by Lieutenant William Bligh, with orders to collect young breadfruit plants for transportation to the West Indies. The famous mutiny did not take place at Tahiti as some travel brochures infer, but in Tongan waters. Bligh, one of the top mariners of the 18th century, managed to navigate 6,500 km to escape to Dutch Timor in an open boat, so in 1791 the HMS *Pandora* came to Tahiti in search of the *Bounty* mutineers, intending to take them to England for trial. They captured 14 survivors of the 16 who had elected to stay on Tahiti when Fletcher Christian and eight others left for Pitcairn. Although glamorized by Hollywood, the mutineers helped destroy traditional Tahitian society by acting as mercenaries for rival chiefs.

By the early 19th century, ruffian British and American whalers were fanning out over the Pacific. Other ships traded with the islanders for sandalwood, bêche-de-mer, and mother-of-pearl, as well as the usual supplies. They brought with them smallpox, measles, influenza, tuberculosis, scarlet fever, and venereal diseases, which devastated the unprepared Polynesians. Slave raids, alcohol, and European firearms did the rest.

Captain Cook and his officers sharing a meal with Tahitians

Kings And Missionaries

In 1797 the ship *Duff* dropped off 18 English missionaries and their wives on Tahiti. By this time Pomare, chief of the area adjoining Matavai Bay, had become powerful through the use of European tools, firearms, and mercenaries. He welcomed the missionaries but would not be converted, and infanticide, sexual freedom, and human sacrifices continued. By 1800 all but five of the original 18 had left Tahiti disappointed.

In 1803 Pomare I died and his despotic son, Pomare II, attempted to conquer the entire island. After initial success he was forced to flee to Moorea in 1808. Missionary Henry Nott went with him and in 1812 Pomare II turned to him for help in regaining his lost power. Though the missionaries refused to baptize Pomare II himself because of his heathen and drunken habits, his subjects on Moorea became nominal Christians. In 1815 this "Christian king" managed to regain Tahiti and overthrow paganism. The eager missionaries then enforced the Ten Commandments and dressed the Tahitian women in "Mother Hubbard" costumes—dresses which covered their bodies from head to toe. Henceforth singing anything but hymns was banned, dancing proscribed, and all customs which offended puritanical sensibilities wiped away. "Morality police" terrorized the confused Tahitians in an eternal crusade against sin. Even the wearing of flowers in the hair was prohibited.

In *Omoo* (1847) Herman Melville comments:

> Doubtless, in thus denationalizing the Tahitians, as it were, the missionaries were prompted by a sincere desire for good; but the effect has been lamentable. Supplied with no amusements, in place of those forbidden, the Tahitians, who require more recreation than other people, have sunk into a listlessness, or indulge in sensualities, a hundred times more pernicious than all the games ever celebrated in the Temple of Tanee.

Omai, a native of Huahine, accompanied Capt. Cook's second expedition to England in 1774 and immediately became the talk of London. For many Europeans he epitomized the "noble savage" but, to those who came to know him, he was a sophisticated man with a culture of his own.

COLONIALISM

The Rape Of Polynesia

Upon Pomare II's death from drink at age 40 in 1821, the crown passed to his infant son, Pomare III, but he passed away in 1827. At this junction the most remarkable Tahitian of the 19th century, Aimata, half-sister of Pomare II, became Queen Pomare IV. She was to rule Tahiti, Moorea, and part of the Austral and Tuamotu groups for half a century until her death in 1877, a barefoot Tahitian Queen Victoria. She allied herself closely with the London Missionary Society (LMS). When two French-Catholic priests, Honoré Laval and François Caret, arrived on Tahiti in 1836 from their stronghold at Mangareva (Gambier Islands), she expelled them promptly.

This affront brought a French frigate to Papeete in 1838, demanding $2000 compensation and a salute to the French flag. Although the conditions were met, the Queen and her chiefs wrote to England appealing for help, but none came. A second French gunboat returned and

M.G.L. DOMENY DE RIENZI

the ceding of Matavai, Tahiti, to English missionaries in 1797

threatened to bombard Tahiti unless its missionaries were given free entry. Back in Mangareva, Laval pushed forward a grandiose building program, which wiped out 80% of the population of the Gambiers from overwork.

A French consul named Moerenhout was appointed to Queen Pomare in 1838. In Sept. 1842, while the Queen and George Pritchard, the English consul, were away, he tricked a few local chiefs into signing a petition asking to be brought under French "protection." This demand was immediately accepted by French Admiral Dupetit-Thouars who was in league with Moerenhout, and on 9 Sept. 1842 they forced Queen Pomare to accept a French protectorate. When the queen tried to maintain her power and kept her red-and-white royal flag, Dupetit-Thouars deposed the queen on 8 Nov. 1843 and occupied her kingdom, an arbitrary act which was rejected by the French king who reestablished the protectorate in 1844. Queen Pomare fled to Raiatea, and Pritchard was deported to England in March 1844, bringing Britain and France to the brink of war. The Tahitians resisted as best they could for three years: old French forts and war memorials recall the struggle.

A French Protectorate

At the beginning of 1847 when Queen Pomare realized that no British assistance was forthcoming, she and her people reluctantly accepted the French protectorate. As a compromise the British extracted a promise from the French not to annex the Leeward Is., so Huahine, Raiatea, and Bora Bora remained independent. The French had taken possession of the Marquesas in 1842, even before imposing a protectorate on Tahiti. French missionaries then attempted to convert the Tahitians to Catholicism, but only in the Marquesas were they successful.

Queen Pomare tried to defend the interests of her people as best she could, but much of her nation was dying: between the 18th century and 1926 the population of the Marquesas fell from 80,000 to only 2,000. In April 1774 Capt. Cook tried to estimate the population of Tahiti by counting the number of men he saw in a fleet of war canoes and ascribing three members to each one's family. Cook's figure was 204,000, but according to Bengt Danielsson the correct number at the time of discovery was about 150,000. By 1829 it had dropped to 8,568 and a low of 7,169 was reached in 1865. The name "Pomare" means "night cough" from *po,* night, plus *mare,* cough, because Pomare I's infant daughter died of tuberculosis in 1792. Pomare V, the final, degenerate member of the line, was more interested in earthly pleasures than the traditions upheld by his mother. In 1880, with French interests at work on the Panama Canal, a smart colonial governor convinced him to sign away his kingdom for a 5000-franc-a-month pension.

tomb of King Pomare V, Tahiti: *Pomare V's mother died in 1877 after reigning for 50 troubled years during which she was exhorted to accept a French protectorate over her Polynesian kingdom. A less heroic figure than his mother, King Pomare V (above left), the fifth and last of his name to hold the throne, took over a luckless dynasty and also took to drink. He was particularly fond of Benedictine and although the distinctive symbol enshrined forever atop his pylon-shaped mausoleum at Arue appears to be a massive Benedictine bottle it is actually a Grecian vase. He died in 1891, an unhappy man.*

Tahiti-Polynesia then became the full French colony it is today, the "Établissements français de l'Océánie." In 1957 the name was changed to "Polynésie Française." The most earthshaking event between 1880 and 1960 was a visit by two German cruisers, the *Scharnhorst* and *Gneisenau*, which shelled Papeete on 22 Sept. 1914. (Both were subsequently sunk by the British at the Battle of the Falkland Islands.) On 2 Sept. 1940 the colony declared its support for the Free French side and the Americans arrived to establish a base on Bora Bora soon after Pearl Harbor. Polynesia remained cut off from occupied metropolitan France until the end of the war, although Tahitians served with the Pacific battalion in North Africa and Italy.

RECENT HISTORY

The early 1960s were momentous times for Polynesia. Within a few years MGM filmed *Mutiny on the Bounty,* an international airport opened on Tahiti, and the French began testing their atomic bombs. After Algeria became independent in July 1962, the French decided to move their Sahara nuclear-testing facilities to the Tuamotus. In 1963, when all local political parties protested the invasion of Polynesia by thousands of French troops and technicians sent to establish a nuclear test center, President Charles de Gaulle simply outlawed political parties. The French set off their first atmospheric nuclear explosion at Moruroa on 2 July 1966. In 1974, 44 bombs later, international protests forced the French to switch to underground tests, which still continue today. Over the years the territorial assembly of Tahiti-Polynesia has adopted numerous resolutions asking the French government to halt the testing, without response.

The spirit of the time is best summed up in the life of one man, Pouvanaa a Oopa, an outspoken WW I hero from Huahine. In 1949 he became the first Polynesian to occupy a seat in the French Chamber of Deputies. In 1957 he was elected vice-president of the Government Council. A dedicated proponent of independence, Pouvanaa was arrested in 1958 on trumped-up charges of arson, eventually sentenced to an eight-year prison term, and exiled by the French government. De Gaulle wanted Pouvanaa out of the way until French nuclear-testing facilities could be established in Polynesia and he was not freed until 1968. In 1971 he won the "French" Polynesia seat in the French Senate, a post he held until his death in

the Tahitian independence leader Pouvanaa a Oopa (1895-1977)

early 1977. Tahitians refer to the man as *metua* (father) and his statue stands in front of Papeete's Territorial Assembly.

Pouvanaa's successors, John Teariki (now deceased) and Francis Sanford (since retired), were also defenders of Polynesian autonomy and opponents of nuclear testing. Their combined efforts convinced the French government to grant Polynesia a new statute with a slightly increased autonomy in 1977.

Greenpeace
In July 1985 French General Directorate for Foreign Security (DGSE) agents planted terrorist bombs on the Greenpeace ship *Rainbow Warrior* as it lay anchored at Auckland, New Zealand. Greenpeace photographer Fernando Pereira drowned in the sinking. Top officials in the French government who ordered the killing and the two agents who actually planted the bombs have never been brought to trial.

By chance two other DGSE agents were captured by New Zealand police, tried, and sentenced to 10 years imprisonment. A year later France tried to block butter and mutton exports to Europe to blackmail New Zealand into allowing the convicted saboteurs, Major Alain Mafart and Captain Dominique Prieur, to serve a three-year term of exile at the French military base on Hao in the Tuamotus in lieu of jail, promising they would stay there until their sentences were complete. French Prime Minister Chirac brought both terrorists home to Paris in 1987, a year before their Tuamotu holiday was over.

The bombing was intended to prevent the ship from sailing to Moruroa to commemorate the 40th anniversary of Hiroshima. The French also feared that the Greenpeace environmentalists intended to carry doctors to Mangareva for a survey which might uncover the serious health problems they have thus far successfully covered up. The French attack couldn't stop a five-boat "peace flotilla" which formed a floating picket line off Moruroa in Oct. 1985. The ketch *Vega,* which deliberately breached the 12-nautical-mile limit, was seized by a French warship.

In Dec. 1990 Greenpeace's *Rainbow Warrior II* attempted to visit Moruroa. Although forbidden to enter the lagoon or tie up to the dock,

NON A LA BOMBE
EN POLYNESIE

radiation expert Norm Buske managed to take plankton samples from the ship's position just outside the atoll's 12-mile exclusion zone while surrounded by French helicopters and destroyers. The samples were found to contain cobalt 60 and cesium 134, proof that radiation is leaking into the sea from Moruroa. Buske and four others then embarked in an inflatable Zodiak and attempted to enter the lagoon to take further samples, but were immediately arrested by the French naval armada and deported to Los Angeles on the first flight out of Papeete (after take-off the plane's crew congratulated the group with a bottle of champagne). Tahitian political leaders are now demanding that the World Health Organization intervene to properly investigate the radiation leaking from Moruroa.

Analysis

Tahiti-Polynesia is part of a worldwide chain of French colonies including Kerguelen, Guyana, Martinique, Guadeloupe, Mayotte, New Caledonia, Wallis and Futuna, Reunion, and St. Pierre and Miquelon, under the DOM-TOM (Ministry of Overseas Departments and Territories). France spends 16 billion French francs a year to maintain this system, a clear indication that it's something totally different from colonial empires of the past, which were based on economic exploitation, not investment. A closer analogy is the American network of military bases around the world, which serve the same purpose—projecting power. What is at stake is French national prestige.

These conditions totally contradict what has happened elsewhere in the South Pacific. Over the past 20 years the British have voluntarily withdrawn from their Pacific colonies as French pretensions to global midsized nuclear power status grew stronger. This digging in has created the anachronism of a few highly visible bastions of white colonialism in the midst of a sea of English-speaking independent nations. When French officials summarily rejected all protests against their nuclear testing and suppression of independence movements, even going to the extreme of employing state terrorism to stop a protest vessel from leaving New Zealand, most Pacific islanders were outraged. Their subsequent boycotts of French goods and anti-French statements have only exacerbated the situation.

What must be accepted is that there's a place for France in the Pacific. It's no longer possible to turn the clock back to 1842 or 1767. In fact, in almost every Pacific micro-state the basis for complete self-reliance simply doesn't exist. In recent years France has come to realize that its interests in the Pacific are as well served by emphasizing social, cultural, and economic matters as by outright political and military domination. French universities have been established on Tahiti and New Caledonia and economic/military aid to the smaller South Pacific countries stepped up. Space-age technology is being used to maintain this empire as never before.

Yet by continuing its nuclear testing, uncontrolled immigration, and military build-ups France risks an independence struggle with the Tahitians. This may well lead to increasing destabilization, plus continuing international condemnation and a black image in the region. By stopping the testing and granting full internal self-government to its colonies, France would quickly be accepted as a good neighbor throughout the Pacific, as it was before 1963 when de Gaulle exported *la bombe*. (The commentary above was inspired in part by Jean Chesneaux's article "France in the Pacific: Global Approach or Respect for Regional Agendas?" in Vol. 18, No. 2, 1986, of the *Bulletin of Concerned Asian Scholars.*)

GOVERNMENT

In 1885 an organic decree created the colonial system of government which remained in effect until the proclamation of a new statute in 1958, making Tahiti-Polynesia an overseas territory. In 1977, when Francis Sanford, Polynesia's representative in the French Parliament, threatened to launch an independence campaign, the French granted the territory partial internal self-government and Sanford was elected premier of "autonomous" Polynesia. A new local-government statute passed by the French parliament and promulgated on 6 Sept. 1984 gave only slightly more powers to the Polynesians; the constitution of the Republic of France remains the supreme law of the land. There have been requests to the United Nations Special Committee of 24 that the territory be reinscribed on its priority list of states awaiting decolonization, as New Caledonia was in 1986.

A Territorial Assembly elects the president of the government, who chooses his 10 ministers. The Territorial Assembly is responsible for public works, sports, health, social services, and primary education. The 41 assembly members are elected from separate districts, with 22 seats from Tahiti/Moorea, eight from the Leeward Islands, five from the Tuamotus and Gambiers, three from the Australs, and three from the Mar-

quesas. One vote in the Tuamotus has the weight of three on Tahiti and many constituencies have been gerrymandered. French soldiers and civil servants can vote in local elections the day they arrive in the territory, and there are thousands of them, including many in the Tuamotus.

The territory is represented in Paris by two elected deputies, a senator, and a social and economic councilor. The French government, through its high commissioner and assisted by a secretary-general of his choice, retains control over defense, foreign affairs, money, justice, immigration, the police, the civil service, foreign trade, TV and radio broadcasting, international communications, secondary education, and the municipal councils. As may be seen, the high commissioner has considerable power. He can also dissolve the Territorial Assembly or refer its decisions to an administrative tribunal.

Tahiti-Polynesia is divided into 48 communes, each with an elected Municipal Council which chooses a mayor from its ranks. These elected bodies, however, are controlled by appointed French civil servants who run the five administrative subdivisions. The administrators of the Windward, Tuamotu-Gambier, and Austral subdivisions are based at Papeete, while the headquarters of the Leeward Is. administration is at Uturoa, and the Marquesas Is. is at Taiohae.

Politics

In 1982 the neo-Gaullist **Tahoeraa Huiraatira** ("Popular Union") won the territorial elections and the pro-nuclear, anti-independence mayor of Pirae, Gaston Flosse, became premier of the local government. In the 1986 territorial elections Flosse's party won a majority of assembly seats, but a year later Flosse resigned as president to devote his full time to the post of French Secretary of State for the South Pacific.

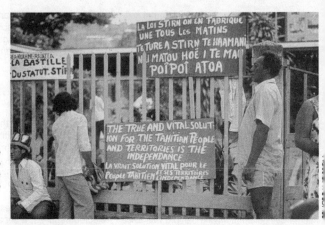

pro-independence
demonstrators at the
High Commissioner's
gate in Papeete

With the defeat of the Chirac government in France in 1988 Flosse found himself out in the cold politically. Flosse's reputation for fixing government contracts while in office earned him the title "Mr. Ten Percent" from the Paris newspaper *Libération*.

After rioting in Papeete and allegations of corruption, Tahoeraa deputy leader Alexandre Léontieff broke with Flosse in Dec. 1987 and formed a coalition government with other Tahoeraa defectors and several smaller parties. In the 1988 elections to select Polynesia's two representatives to the 577-member French National Assembly, Flosse was defeated in the heavily Catholic eastern constituency by Emile Vernaudon, opportunistic leader of the **Ai'a Api** ("New Country") party. The predominantly Protestant western constituency elected the autonomist mayor of Papeete, Jean Juventin, of the **Here Ai'a** ("Patriots' Party") as its deputy. Juventin favors independence in association with France and is mildly opposed to nuclear testing. Daniel Millaud of **Te E'a No Maohi Nui** ("Voice of the Great Maohi"), Tahiti-Polynesia's senator from 1980-1989, is a strong advocate of full internal self-government.

The 17 March 1991 Territorial Assembly elections returned Flosse's Tahoeraa Huiraatira party to power with 18 seats compared to only 14 for **Union Polynesienne**, a coalition of Léontieff's **Te Tiarama** ("The Torch") and Juventin's Here Ai'a. Half of those voting for Flosse's party

were French expatriates, civil servants, and military personnel. Flosse first formed a coalition with Vernaudon's Ai'a Api which won five seats, then dropped Vernaudon and realigned his party with Juventin's Here Ai'a in September. Léontieff's 1987-1991 administration was marked by financial mismanagement and political fence-sitting on the nuclear and independence issues.

The anti-nuclear **Tavini Huiraatira No Te Ao Maohi** ("Polynesian Liberation Front"), formed in 1978 by Faaa mayor Oscar Temaru, doubled its assembly representation from two to four in the 1991 election. Te Ao Maohi favors immediate and complete independence, and Temaru has repeatedly called for a referendum on independence. A second, more moderate pro-independence party, **Ia Mana Te Nunaa** ("Let the People Take the Power"), founded in 1975 to campaign for land redistribution and an independent nuclear-free socialist state, lost its three seats. Support for Ia Mana Te Nunaa declined as a result of party secretary-general Jacqui Drollet's decision to serve as Minister of Health in Léontieff's coalition government.

The most radical of the pro-independence groups, the **Te Taata Tahiti Tiama** ("Free Tahitians' Party") led by Pouvanaa a Oopa's nephew Charlie Ching, is not represented in the assembly. The French have made something of a martyr of Ching by repeatedly jailing him on dubious charges. He was prevented from running in 1991 by the French government, which deprived him of his "civic rights" after he organized a 1985 demonstration in support of Greenpeace. French officials also barred the **Pomare Pati**, headed by descendants of the last king, from running in 1991. The Pomares have angered the French by aggressively squatting on lost ancestral lands. The *indépendentistes* are strongest in Papeete, weakest in the Tuamotus and Marquesas—areas heavily dependent on French aid.

ECONOMY

Government Spending

The inflow of people and money since the early 1960s has substituted consumerism for subsistence. Except for tourism and cultured pearls, the economy of Tahiti-Polynesia is now totally dominated by French government spending. The French government contributes very little to the territorial budget, but it finances departments and services under the direct control of the high commissioner (defense, foreign affairs, police, justice, immigration, information, foreign trade, international communications, labor, finance, postal services, television, higher education, and the 200-nautical-mile Exclusive Economic Zone).

The colonial government spends US$55 million a month in the territory each year, two-thirds of it on the military. Much of the rest goes into inflated salaries for 2,200 expatriate French civil servants. Posts in the colonies are much sought after among French officials for the high salaries and benefits, exotic location, lack of taxation and short working hours. This privileged class is a built-in lobby to perpetuate its own existence.

There's no personal income tax. This is fine for businessmen and civil servants who earn high wages or profits, but hard on everyone else hit by indirect taxes such as Customs duties of 20-200% and licensing fees. In 1985 these taxes accounted for 78% of government revenue, leading to highly inflated prices which hurt the little guy most. There's also a flat 35% levy on businesses, which is simply passed along to consumers. Companies can mark up imports as high as 47%.

Only a third of the population receives any direct benefit from French spending. The rest feel only the effects of soaring inflation, inequalities, and foreign interference. The nuclear-testing program has provoked an influx of 30,000 French settlers, plus a massive infusion of capital which distorted the formerly self-supporting economy into one totally dependent on France. In June 1991 French government auditors reported that the territorial debt stood at US$570 million.

In the early 1960s, many Polynesians left their homes for construction jobs with the *Centre d'Expérimentations du Pacifique* (CEP), the government, and hotel chains. Now that the volume of this work is decreasing, most of them subsist in precarious circumstances on Tahiti, dependent on government spending. Some 2,000 locals are presently employed by the testing program (compared to 10,000 in 1968). The CEP is headquartered at Pirae, just east of Papeete, with a major support base opposite the yacht club at Arue. Some 3,000 persons live and work for the CEP in the Tuamotus (of whom 600 are Polynesian).

Despite protests by almost every Pacific nation, the nuclear tests continue. In fact, this program has become a major incentive for the French government to hold onto their colony, since underground nuclear testing on *their* continent would never be accepted by Europeans, regardless of French assurances that it is "safe." The main objections would come from the population of France itself: any French government that moved the tests to the Massif Central would risk losing millions of votes! Polynesia is far away and the population small: it is expendable.

Trade

Prior to the start of nuclear testing, trade was balanced. Only 25 years later, 1990 imports stood at US$920 million while exports amounted to only US$110 million, one of the highest disparities in the world. Much of the imbalance is consumed by the French administration itself and 28% of imports are related to nuclear testing.

Half the imports come from France, which has imposed a series of self-favoring restrictions. Imports include food, fuel, building material, consumer goods, and automobiles. The main exports from the outer islands are copra and empty Hinano bottles. Copra, the main agricultural product, is crushed into coconut oil and animal feed at the Papeete mill, while cultured pearls from farms in the Tuamotus are the biggest export by far. The vast distances between the islands themselves and the outside world are one reason for the slow commercial development of the territory.

Business
Business is concentrated in a few hands. The Martin family (French/Polynesian) owns the electric company (EDT), Hinano brewery, and a huge commercial center called Fare Tony in Papeete. The French banker Jean Bréaud runs Total (Standard Oil of California), owns vast tracts of real estate, and has an important interest in the Banque de Tahiti. The powerful Sin Tung Hing dynasty controls the local Mobil Oil of Australia, Gaz de Tahiti, the Banque de Polynésie, an insurance company, and auto imports. Aline (Chinese) dominates imports and merchandising. Virtually all shipping and docking, both local and international, is in the hands of the Cowan family (French/Polynesian). This powerful class gets the most out of French rule and is the strongest supporter of its continuation.

Now, with the final integration of the European Community approaching, large corporations in all 12 EC countries may soon get the right to open branch offices in Tahiti-Polynesia and make uncontrolled investments. The Territorial Assembly has strongly condemned this new economic colonialism, which was agreed upon by French officials in Paris and Brussels without even consulting anyone in Tahiti-Polynesia.

Tourism
Tourism only got underway with the opening of Faaa Airport in 1961. Today Tahiti-Polynesia is second only to Fiji as a South Pacific tourist center, with 132,361 visitors in 1990, a third of them from the United States. Earnings from tourism cover 18% of Tahiti-Polynesia's import bill and provide 4,000 jobs. Yet 80% of the things

the cover of an official brochure promoting tourism as a source of income for Tahiti-Polynesia

tourists buy are also imported. Tourism is almost completely in the hands of transnational corporations, either hotel chains, tour companies, or airlines. Top management of the big hotels is invariably French or foreign, as ownership rests with Japanese (Beachcomber Parkroyal, Hyatt Regency, Moana Beach, Kia Ora), French (Sofitel, Club Med), and American (Bali Hai) corporations. Carriers such as Air New Zealand and Qantas only promote Tahiti as a stopover on the way Down Under, limiting many tourists to a few nights in Papeete. This urban tourism has tended to create a bad impression, and the Tahiti Tourist Board is attempting to persuade more visitors to visit the less spoiled outer islands.

In general, two kinds of people make it to Tahiti-Polynesia: packaged tourists on a two-week trip from the States who book all their accommodations in advance, stay at the best hotels, and travel interisland by air; and independent budget travelers (often young Europeans) who have more time, find a place to stay upon arrival, and travel by boat as much as possible. Tahiti, Moorea, Huahine, Raiatea, and Bora Bora are popular among visitors for their combination of beaches, mountain scenery, easy access, and the wealth of budget accommodations. The Society group is closely linked by sea and air, an island-hopper's playground.

Tourism is far less developed than in Hawaii. A single Waikiki hotel could have more rooms than the entire island of Tahiti; Hawaii gets more visitors in 10 days than Tahiti-Polynesia gets in a year. In Tahiti-Polynesia only one tourist is present for every 100 inhabitants at any given time, while overcrowded Hawaii has 11. Distance and reports of high prices have kept Tahiti out of the American mass market, and high local labor costs have hampered development. Since 1987 when the American-Hawaiian cruiseship *Liberté* withdrew from Polynesia and the Hyatt resort on Bora Bora went under, tourism to Tahiti-Polynesia has taken a nosedive. The bankruptcy of Exploration Cruise Lines in 1988 and the closing of Continental Airlines' route through Tahiti in 1989 were other setbacks. This has meant that with so many rooms or tables empty many hotels and restaurants have kept prices steady for the past few years and in some cases things even have gotten cheaper.

Tourism by high-budget Japanese (especially honeymooners) is being vigorously promoted to replace a decline in arrivals from the States. Japan Air Lines buys seats aboard the weekly nonstop Air France Boeing 747 flight from Tokyo to Tahiti. In Sept. 1989 the Japanese corporation Electronic and Industrial Enterprises (EIE) purchased four major hotels, and in 1990 a Tokyo company bought Rangiroa's Kia Ora as the Japanese scramble to recycle their massive foreign exchange surpluses. After paying US$78.5 million for the hotels EIE announced that it planned to spend another US$51 million upgrading the properties to five-star levels. Many Polynesians are rather nervous about all this Japanese-driven development, and in June 1991 voters on Moorea decided against a US$94.3 million Sheraton hotel and championship golf course that Japanese investors had wanted to build on their island. In May 1990 the 200 traditional owners of Tupai, just north of

Bora Bora, blocked its sale to a Japanese corporation which had intended to build a major new resort on the atoll.

Cultured Pearls

Tahiti-Polynesia's cultured-pearl industry, now second only to tourism as a money-earner, originated in 1963 when an experimental farm was established on Hikueru atoll in the Tuamotus. Today dozens of cooperative and private pearl farms operating in Tuamotu-Gambier employ hundreds. The cooperatives sell their production at an auction in Papeete organized by the chamber of commerce each October. The pearls are offered to bidders in mixed lots of a hundred or more for US$10,000 and up. Local jewelers vie with Japanese buyers at these events with some 40,000 black pearls changing hands for about US$5 million. Private producers sell their pearls through independent dealers or plush retail outlets in Papeete. In 1990 black pearl exports were worth US$37 million, with 60% going to Japan. The next-largest agricultural export, coconut oil, brought in only US$1.6 million that year. The 1990 crop of 360,000 pearls is expected to double by 1995.

Unlike the Japanese cultured white pearl, the Polynesian black pearl is created only by the giant blacklipped oyster *(Pinctada margaritifera)* which thrives in the Tuamotu lagoons. Beginning in the 19th century, the oysters were collected by Polynesian divers who could dive up to 40 meters. The shell was made into mother-of-pearl buttons; finding a pearl this way was pure chance. Overharvesting had depleted the slow-growing oyster beds by the middle of this century. Today live oysters are collected only to supply cultured-pearl farms and the shell is a mere byproduct made into decorative items or exported.

It takes around three years for a pearl to form in a seeded oyster. A spherical pearl is formed when the Mississippi River mussel graft is introduced inside the coat; the oyster creates a hemispherical half pearl if the graft goes between the coat and the shell. Half pearls are much cheaper than real pearls and make outstanding rings and pendants.

The relative newness of this gemstone is reflected in wildly varying prices. A brilliant, perfectly round, smooth, and flawless pearl with a good depth of metallic green-gray/blue-gray color can sell for 100 times more than a similar pearl with only one or two defects. Unless you really know your pearls it's intelligent to stick to the cheaper, even "baroque" ones which, mounted in gold and platinum, still make exquisite jewelry. These pearls are now in fashion in Paris, so don't expect any bargains. Quality pearls cost US$1000 and up, but slightly flawed pearls are much cheaper (US$50 is average). Half the fun is in the shopping, so be in no hurry to decide. A reputable dealer will give you an invoice or certificate verifying the authenticity of your pearl.

Agriculture

Labor recruiting for the nuclear-testing program caused local agriculture to collapse in the mid-'60s. Exports of coffee and vanilla had ceased completely by 1965, and coconut products dropped 40% despite massive subsidies. Today about 85% of all food consumed locally is imported. Tahiti-Polynesia does manage to cover three-quarters of its own fruit requirements. Most of the local pineapple and grapefruit crop is consumed by the fruit-juice factory on Moorea. In the 1880s-90s four million oranges a year were ex-

Every part of the coconut tree (Cocos nucifera) can be used. The husk provides cord, mats, brushes, and fuel, the leaves thatch, baskets, and fans, and the trunk building material. Food and oil from the nuts are the greatest prize. A healthy tree will produce 50 nuts a year for over 60 years.

DIANA LASICH HARPER

ported to Australia, New Zealand, and California. The industry was wiped out by a blight at the turn of the century and now only a few trees grow wild.

Local vegetables supply half of local needs, while Tahitian coffee only covers 20% of consumption. Considerable livestock is kept in the Marquesas. Large areas have been planted in Caribbean pine to provide for future timber needs. Aquaculture, with tanks for freshwater shrimp, prawns, live bait, and green mussels, is being developed. Most industry is related to food processing (fruit-juice factory, brewery, soft drinks, etc.) or coconut products.

The coconut tree has long been the mainstay of the outer islanders. A good tree gives nuts for 50 or 60 years (the 29-cm-wide metal bands around the trunk are for protection against rats). The green coconut provides food and drink, while the harder meat from more mature nuts is grated and squeezed to obtain coconut cream used as sauce and in cooking. The oldest nuts are cracked open and the meat dried in the sun to become copra. Schooners collect bags of copra which they carry to a mill beside the interisland wharf at Papeete. Here the copra is pressed into coconut oil used in making vegetable oil, margarine, candles, soap, cosmetics, etc. The world price for copra has been depressed for years, so the government wisely pays a subsidy (more than twice the actual price) to producers to keep them gainfully employed on their home islands.

Vanilla, a vine belonging to the orchid family, is grown on small family plantations. Brought to Tahiti from Manila in 1848, the Tahitensis type, which has a worldwide reputation, originated from a mutation of Fragrans vanilla. The plants must be hand pollinated, then harvested between April and June. The pods are then put out to dry for a couple of months—an exceptionally time-consuming process generally entrusted to the Chinese. Between 1915 and 1933 Tahiti produced 50 to 150 tons of vanilla a year, peaking in 1949 at 200 tons. Production remained high until 1966 when a steady decline began due to the producers leaving for paid in employment in Papeete related to nuclear testing. By 1990 production had fallen to only 39 metric tons, though the territorial government wants to get things going again.

Law Of The Sea

This law has changed the face of the Pacific. States traditionally exercised sovereignty over a three-mile belt of territorial sea along their shores; the high seas beyond these limits could be freely used by anyone. Then on 28 Sept. 1945 President Harry Truman declared U.S. sovereignty over the natural resources of the adjacent continental shelf. Other states followed with similar claims. In 1958 the United Nations convened a Conference on the Law of the Sea at Geneva that accepted national control over shelves up to 200 meters deep. Agreement could not be reached on extended territorial sea limits.

National claims multiplied so much that in 1974 another U.N. conference was convened, leading to the signing of the Law of the Sea convention at Jamaica in 1982. This complex agreement—200 pages, nine annexes, and 320 articles—extended national control over 40% of the world's oceans. The territorial sea was increased to 12 nautical miles and the continental shelf ambiguously defined as extending 200 nautical miles offshore. This 200-nautical-mile belt was declared an Exclusive Economic Zone (EEZ) with the state having full control over all resources, living or nonliving. The French government passed legislation in 1976 which gave it control of this zone, not only along France's coastal waters but also around all her overseas territories and departments.

To date the EEZs have mainly affected fisheries and seabed mineral exploitation. Freedom of navigation within the zones is guaranteed. The Law of the Sea increased immensely the territory of independent oceanic states, giving them real political weight for the first time. The land area of Tahiti-Polynesia comes to only 3,265 square km, while its EEZ totals 5,030,000 square km! It's known that vast mineral deposits are scattered across this seabed awaiting the technology to exploit them. The National Marine Research Center and private firms have already drawn up plans to recover nickel, cobalt, manganese, and copper nodules from depths of over 4,000 meters. The French government has adamantly refused to give the Territorial Assembly any jurisdiction over this tremendous resource, an important indicator as to why they are determined to hold onto their colony at any price.

Fisheries

Tuna is the second-largest commercial fishery in the world (after shrimp and prawns), and 66% of the world's catch is taken in the Pacific. Japanese and Korean fishing boats annually pay around 100 million francs in license fees to the local government, with boat stores and provisions accounting for even greater sums. Tuna is one of the few renewable resources the islanders have—it's bitterly ironic that local fish are sent to American Samoa to be canned, then sold back to islanders at high prices. Most of the tuna fished from the Pacific islands region is taken by around 110 purse seiners, 65 of them affiliated with the American Tunaboat Association, and 32 of them Japanese. Longline vessels are used to supply the Japanese sashimi market. Some Pacific countries have established small pole-and-line fishing industries, but the capital-intensive, high-tech purse-seiner operations carried out by the Americans and Japanese are still beyond their means.

The dolphin fish (Coryphaena hippurus) or dorado is a large, fast-moving fish with a body of luminous purple, green, and gold colors that fade soon after death. Mahimahi (dolphin fish) is a favored food, but the fish has no relation to its namesake mammal dolphin.

THE PEOPLE

The criteria used for defining the racial groups that make up the 1988 population of 188,814 are so unsatisfactory that only an approximate breakdown can be made: 70% Polynesian, 12% European, 10% Polynesian/European, five percent Chinese, and three percent Polynesian/Chinese. All are French citizens. The 1988 population figures for the five administrative subdivisions are Windward Islands 140,341, Leeward Islands 22,232, Austral Islands 6,500, Tuamotu/Gambier Islands 12,374, Marquesas Islands 7,358. About 70% of the total population lives on Tahiti.

The indigenous people of Tahiti-Polynesia are the *maohi* or Eastern Polynesians (as opposed to the Western Polynesians in Samoa and Tonga). The word *colon* formerly applied to Frenchmen who arrived long before the bomb and made a living as planters or traders. Practically all of them married Polynesian women;

ARCHIVES NATIONALES, SECTION OUTRE-MER, FRANCE

a Polynesian woman

most of these *colons* have already passed away. Their descendants are termed *demis* or *afa*. The present Europeans are mostly recently arrived metropolitan French *(faranis)*. Most *faranis* live in urban areas or are involved in the administration or military. Their numbers increased dramatically in the 1960s and 1970s.

Local Chinese *(tinito)* dominate the retail trade throughout the territory. In Papeete and Uturoa entire streets are lined with Chinese stores, and individual Chinese merchants are found on almost every island. During the American Civil War when the supply of cotton to Europe was disrupted, Scotsman William Stewart decided to set up a cotton plantation on the south side of Tahiti. Unable to convince Tahitians to accept the heavy work, Stewart brought in a contingent of 1,010 Chinese laborers from Canton in 1865-66. When the war ended the enterprise went bankrupt, but many of the Chinese managed to stay on as market gardeners or shopkeepers.

In 1964 the French government decided to assimilate the Chinese by granting them citizenship, requiring that they adopt French-sounding names, and closing all Chinese schools. Despite this the Chinese community has remained distinct. Most of the Tahiti Chinese used to be supporters of the Kuomintang regime in Taiwan and fierce anticommunists. But since France recognized mainland China in 1964 the Taiwanese consulate has been closed, and many local Chinese now visit their ancestral country.

From 1976 to 1983 some 18,000 people migrated to the territory, 77% of them from France and another 13% from New Caledonia. Nearly 1,000 new settlers a year continue to arrive. Some 30,000 Europeans are now present in the territory, plus 8,000 soldiers, policemen, and transient officials. Most Tahitians would like to see this immigration restricted, as it is in virtually every other Pacific state. Yet with the integration of the European Community, all 300 million citizens of the 12 EC countries may soon gain the right to live in Polynesia. To protest this threatened "second invasion" (the first, related to nuclear testing, began in 1963) all local political parties boycotted the 1989 elections to the European Parliament.

There's an undercurrent of anti-French sentiment; English speakers are better liked by the Tahitians. Yet inevitably the newcomers get caught up in the Polynesian openness and friendliness—even the surliest Parisian. In fact, the Gallic charm you'll experience even in government offices is a delight. Tahiti-Polynesia really is a friendly place.

The New Class Structure

The creation of the Centre d'Expérimentations du Pacifique (CEP) in the early 1960s upset the economic and social equilibrium, drove up the cost of living, created artificial needs, and led to a migration toward Papeete. In 1962 46% of the labor force was engaged in fishing and agriculture. Since then there's been a massive shift to public and private services, and about 80% of the working population of 58,000 are now employees. Of these, 40% work for the government, 40% in services, 11% in industry, and only eight percent in agriculture.

Civil servants in Tahiti-Polynesia get 84% higher salaries than their counterparts in France and don't have to pay any income tax. There are generous expatriation benefits and six months leave is paid after three years. The minimum monthly wage in the territory is US$1500 in the public sector, but only US$850 in the private sector. Living standards in Tahiti-Polynesia may be far higher than in the surrounding insular countries due to the subsidies, yet this expansion of wealth has created inequalities; also, the number of unemployed or underemployed is increasing. The gap between an affluent foreign clique and the impoverished Tahitian mass has created an explosive situation.

In Oct. 1987 the French High Commissioner used riot police flown in from Paris to suppress a dockworkers' strike, leading to serious rioting in Papeete and US$50 million in damage. The mayor of Papeete, Jean Juventin, accused French officials of deliberately provoking the violence as a way of breaking the union, which handled cargo bound for the nuclear-testing facilities. Most of those eventually convicted of looting were not strikers at all but unemployed Tahitian youths who took advantage of the disturbance to grab consumer goods. Fresh rioting in July 1991 forced the territorial government to cancel tax increases on gasoline, alcohol, and tobacco meant to cover a US$73.4 million budget deficit. The strikers said these levies placed an intolerable burden on Tahitian families and called for the imposition of income tax on salaries over US$3000 a month instead. In the end France agreed to pick up part of the deficit bill to restore calm.

An estimated 20,000 poor, unemployed, and marginalized Tahitians live in *bidonvilles* or slums on the outskirts of Papeete. In the valley shanty towns behind Papeete and Faaa, 10-15 Polynesians are crammed into each neat flower-decked plywood house. Many are children, as a government subsidy of US$50 per month per child encourages big families. Opportunities for young Tahitians with a taste for the consumer society are not adequate. Every year 3,000 young people turn 18 and begin competing for scarce jobs. The present social structure places *farani* officials at the top, followed by *demis* in the lower echelons of business and government, while *maohis* work for wages or subsist at the bottom of the shredded social fabric.

Tahitian Life

For the French lunch is the main meal of the day, followed by a siesta. Dinner may consist of leftovers from lunch. Tahitians traditionally eat their main meal of fish and native vegetables in the evening when the day's work is over. People at home often take a shower before or after a meal and put flowers in their hair. If they're in a good mood a guitar or ukulele might appear. About the only time the normally languid Tahitians go really wild is when they're dancing or behind the wheel of a car.

Tahitians often observe with amusement or disdain the efforts of individuals to rise above the group. In a society where sharing and reciprocal generosity have traditionally been important qualities the deliberate accumulation of personal wealth was always viewed as a vice. Now with the influx of government and tourist money Tahitian life is changing, quickly in Papeete, more slowly in the outer islands. To prevent the

Polynesians from being made paupers in their own country, foreigners other than French are not usually permitted to purchase land here. Most land is still owned by the islanders. A new impoverished class is forming among those who have sold their ancestral lands to recent French immigrants.

The educational curriculum is entirely French. Children enter school at age three and for 12 years study the French language, literature, culture, history, and geography, but not much about Polynesia. The failure rate ranges from 40% to 60% and most of the rest of the children are behind schedule. The best students are given scholarships to continue studying, while many of the dropouts become delinquents. About half the schools are privately run by the churches, but these must teach exactly the same curriculum or lose their subsidies. The whole aim is to transform the Polynesians into "Pacific Frenchmen." In 1987 the Université Française du Pacifique (B.P. 4635, Papeete; tel. 42-16-80) opened on Tahiti with courses in law, arts, and sciences.

Most Tahitians live along the coast because the interior is too rugged and possibly inhabited by *tupapau* (ghosts). Some people leave a light on all night in their home for the latter reason. A traditional Tahitian residence consists of several separate buildings: the *fare tutu* (kitchen), the *fare tamaa* (dining area), the *fare taoto* (bedrooms), plus bathing and sanitary outhouses. Often several generations live together and young children are sent to live with their grandparents. Adoption is commonplace and family relationships complex. Young Tahitians generally go out as groups rather than on individual "dates."

The life-style may be summed up in the words *aita e peapea* (no problem) and *fiu* (fed up, bored).

Sex

Since the days of Wallis and Bougainville, Tahitian women have had a reputation for promiscuity. Well, for better or worse, this is largely a thing of the past, if it ever existed at all. As a short-term visitor your liaisons with Tahitians are likely to remain polite. Westerners' obsession with the sexuality of Polynesians usually reflects their own frustrations. The view that Tahitian

a Polynesian vahine

morality is loose is rather ironic considering that Polynesians have always shared whatever they have, cared for their old and young, and refrained from ostracizing unwed mothers or attaching stigma to their offspring. The good Christian Tahitians of today are highly moral and compassionate.

Polynesia's *mahus,* or third sex, bear little of the stigma attached to female impersonators in the West. A young boy may adopt the female role by his own choice or that of his parents, performing female tasks at home and eventually finding a job usually performed by women such as serving in a restaurant or hotel. Usually only one *mahu* exists in each village or community, proof that this type of individual serves a certain sociological function. George Mortimer of the British ship *Mercury* recorded an encounter with a *mahu* in 1789. Though Tahitians may poke fun at *mahus* they're fully accepted in society, seen teaching Sunday school, etc. Many, but not all, *mahus* are also homosexuals. Today, with money all-important, some transvestites have involved themselves in male prostitution and the term *raerae* has been coined for this category. Now there are even Miss Tane and Miss Male beauty contests! All this may be seen as the degradation of a phenomenon which has always been part of Polynesian life.

LANGUAGE

Tahitian and French are both official languages, but official documents and speeches are as a rule in French and are rarely translated. French is spoken throughout the territory and visitors will sometimes have difficulty making themselves understood in English, although everyone involved in the travel industry speaks English. It's useful to brush up your high school French a little by checking out some "Learn French" language records/tapes from your local library before you arrive. The "Capsule French Vocabulary" at the end of this book may also help you get by. Large Chinese stores often have someone who speaks English, though members of the Chinese community use Hakka among themselves.

Tahitian, or *Maohi,* is one of a family of Austronesian languages spoken from Madagascar through Indonesia, all the way to Easter Island and Hawaii. The related languages of Eastern Polynesia (Hawaiian, Tahitian, Tuamotuan, Mangarevan, Marquesan, Maori) are quite different from those of Western Polynesia (Samoan, Tongan). Today as communications improve, the outer island dialects are becoming mingled with the predominant Tahitian. Among the Polynesian languages the consonants did the changing rather than the vowels. The "k" and "l" in Hawaiian are generally rendered as a "t" and "r" in Tahitian.

Instead of attempting to speak French to the Tahitians, a foreign language for you both, turn to the Tahitian vocabulary at the back of this book and give it a try. Remember to pronounce each vowel separately, "a" as the *ah* in far, "e" as the *ai* in day, "i" as the *ee* in see, "o" as the *oh* in go, and "u" as the *oo* in lulu—the same as in Latin or Spanish. Written Tahitian has only eight consonants: f, h, m, n, p, r, t, v. Two consonants never follow one another and all words end in a vowel. No silent letters exist in Tahitian, but there is a glottal stop often marked with an apostrophe. A slight variation in pronunciation or vowel length can change the meaning of a word completely, so don't be surprised if your efforts produce some unexpected results!

Some of the many English words that have entered Tahitian through contact with early seamen include: *faraipani* (frying pan), *manua* (man of war), *matete* (market), *mati* (match), *moni* (money), *oniani* (onion), *painapo* (pineapple), *pani* (pan), *pata* (butter), *pipi* (peas), *poti* (boat), *taiete* (society), *tapitana* (captain), *tauera* (towel), and *tavana* (governor).

Writer Pierre Loti was impressed by the mystical vocabulary of Tahitian:

> The sad, weird, mysterious utterances of nature: the scarcely articulate stirrings of fancy. . . . *Faa-fano:* the departure of the soul at death. *Aa:* happiness, earth, sky, paradise. *Mahoi:* essence or soul of God. *Tapetape:* the line where the sea grows deep. *Tutai:* red clouds on the horizon. *Ari:* depth, emptiness, a wave of the sea. *Po:* night, unknown dark world, Hell.

RELIGION

Though the old Polynesian religion died out in the early 19th century the Tahitians are still strongly religious people. Protestant missionaries arrived on Tahiti 39 years before the Catholics and 47 years before the Mormons, so about two-thirds of the Polynesians now belong to the Evangelical Church; it's strongest in the Austral and Leeward Islands. Of the 30% of the total population that is Catholic, half are Polynesians from the Tuamotus and Marquesas, and the other half are Frenchmen. Another six percent are Mormons. Seventh-day Adventists and Jehovah's Witnesses are also represented. Some Chinese are Buddhists. It's not unusual to see two or three different churches in a village of 100 people. All the main denominations operate their own schools. Local ministers and priests are powerful figures in the outer-island communities. The Evangelical Church has condemned nuclear testing. One vestige of the pre-Christian religion is a widespread belief in ghosts *(tupapau).*

Protestant church services are conducted mostly in Tahitian; Catholic services are in French. It's often worth sitting through one (one to two hours) just to hear the singing and observe the women's hats. Never wear a *pareu* to church—you'll be asked to leave. Young missionaries from the Church of Latter-day Saints (Mormons) continue to flock to Polynesia from the U.S. for two-year stays. They wear short-sleeved white shirts with ties and travel in pairs—you may spot a couple. There's also a local branch of the so-called Reorganized Church of L.D.S. whose headquarters are in Independence, Missouri, instead of Salt Lake City, Utah.

The most sinister religious development in recent years occurred on Faaite atoll in the Tuamotus in early Sept. 1987. A pair of self-proclaimed fundamentalist crusaders from the "charismatic renewal movement" managed to instill such intense revivalist fervor in the villagers that six people were actually burned to death, some by their own children, to exorcise "devils" that threatened the island with disaster. A radio alert brought the mayor and a Catholic priest to the scene just in time to prevent another four "impure souls" from being sacrificed to the "healing" fire. In 1990 24 Faaite villagers were found guilty of the act and ringleader François Mauati was sentenced to 14 years imprisonment.

ARTS AND CRAFTS

As weaving was unknown in the old days, tapa cloth was made by women from the bark of the paper mulberry, breadfruit, and banyan trees. The boughs were soaked in a river for several days, the outer bark then stripped off and the inner bark separated from it. The softened inner bark was placed on a block of wood and beaten with a mallet. When the tapa was of a uniform thickness it was dried in the sun and dyed. Floral or geometric patterns were printed or painted on.

Early missionaries introduced the Tahitians to quilting, and two-layer patchwork *tifaifai* have now taken the place of tapa (bark cloth). Used as bed covers and pillows by tourists, Tahitians still use *tifaifai* to cloak newlyweds and cover coffins. To be wrapped in a *tifaifai* is the highest honor. Each woman has individual quilt pat-

a contemporary tapa design from Fatu Hiva, Marquesas Islands

terns, which are her trademarks. Bold floral designs are popular, with contrasting colors drawn from nature. A good *tifaifai* can take up to six months to complete and cost US$1000. The French artist Henri Matisse, who in 1930 spent several weeks at the now-demolished Stuart Hotel on Papeete's boulevard Pomare, was so impressed by the Tahitian *tifaifai* that he applied the same technique and adopted many designs for his "gouaches découpees."

Spectacles

Though the missionaries banned dancing completely in the 1820s and the French colonial administration only allowed performances which didn't disturb Victorian decorum, traditional Tahitian dancing is back in a big way. During major festivals troupes of 20-50 dancers and 6-10 musicians participate in thrilling competitions. The big hotels on Tahiti and Bora Bora offer exciting dance shows several nights a week which you may attend for the price of a drink.

The Tahitian *tamure* is a fast, provocative, erotic dance done by rapidly shifting the weight from one foot to the other. The rubber-legged men are almost acrobatic, though their movements tend to follow those of the women closely. The tossing, shell-decorated bast or fiber skirts *(mores)*, the pandanus wands in the hands, and the tall headdresses add to the drama.

Dances such as the *aparima, ote'a,* and *hivinau* reenacted Polynesian legends and each movement told part of a story. The *aparima* is a dance resembling the Hawaiian hula or Samoan *siva* executed mainly with the hands while standing or sitting. The hand movements tell the story that is the subject of the accompanying song. The *ote'a* is a theme dance executed to the accompaniment of drums with great precision and admirable timing by a group of men and/or women arrayed in two columns. The *ute* is a restrained dance based on ancient refrains.

Listen to the staccato beat of the *toere,* a slit tamanu-wood drum, each slightly different in size and pitch, hit with a stick. A split bamboo drum *(ofe)* often provides a contrasting sound. The *pahu* is a more conventional drum made from a hollowed coconut tree trunk with a sharkskin cover. Another traditional Polynesian musical instrument is the bamboo nose flute *(vivo),* though today guitars and ukuleles are more often seen. The ukulele was originally the *braguinha,* brought to Hawaii by Portuguese immigrants a century ago. Homemade ukuleles with the half-shell of a coconut as a sound box emit pleasant tones, while those sporting an empty tin give a more metallic sound.

Traditional Tahitian vocal music was limited to inharmonious chants conveying oral history and customs and the *hymene* or "hymn" sung by large choirs today is based on these ancient chants.

Firewalking, once a part of pagan religious rites, is still performed occasionally. A so-called "high priest" and his ti-leaf-clad assistants parade barefoot twice across a pit full of red-hot volcanic rocks. How the participants escape injury is another mystery of Polynesia! A seldom-used firewalking pit is opposite the Bali Hai Hotel on Raiatea; ask, you may be lucky.

Stone Fishing

This traditional method of fishing is now only practiced on very special occasions in the Leeward Islands. Coconut fronds are tied end to end until a line a half km long is ready. Several dozen outrigger canoes form a semicircle. Advancing slowly together, men in the canoes beat the water with stones tied to ropes. The frightened fish are thus driven toward a beach. When the water is shallow enough the men leap from their canoes, push the leaf line before them, yell, and beat the water with their hands. In this way the fish are literally forced ashore.

TAHITI IN LITERATURE

Over the years the romance of legendary Tahiti has been elaborated by a succession of famous writers who came in search of Bougainville's "Nouvelle Cythere" or Rousseau's "noble savage." Brought to the stage or silver screen, their stories entered the popular imagination alongside Gauguin's rich images. If you can manage to read a couple of the books mentioned below before you come, your trip will be enhanced.

Herman Melville, author of the whaling classic *Moby Dick* (1851), deserted his New Bedford whaler at Nuku Hiva in 1842. *Typee* (1846) describes his experiences there. An Australian whaler carried Melville on to Tahiti where he joined a mutiny on board which landed him in the Papeete *calabooza* (prison). His second Polynesian book *Omoo* (1847) was a result. In both books Melville decries the ruin of Polynesian culture by Western influence.

Pierre Loti's *The Marriage of Loti* (1880) is a sentimental tale of the love of a young French

Robert Louis Stevenson

TAHITIAN DANCE MOVEMENTS

anuanua
rainbow

ao
day

here
to love

maeva
welcome

mana'o
to think

marama
moon

mata'i
wind

nehenehe
nice

no'ano'a
perfumed

ori
to walk

ruperupe
verdant, flourishing

tahiri
to wind

tahua
esplanade

ta'u'ai'a
my father land

midshipman for a Polynesian girl named Rarahu. Loti's naivete is rather absurd, but his friendship with Queen Pomare IV and fine imagery make the book worth reading. Loti's writings influenced Paul Gauguin to come to Tahiti.

From 1888-90 Robert Louis Stevenson, famous author of *Treasure Island* and *Kidnapped,* cruised the Pacific in his schooner, the *Casco.* His book *In the South Seas* describes his visits to the Marquesas and Tuamotus. Stevenson settled at Tautira on Tahiti Iti for a time, but eventually retired at Apia in Samoa which offered the author better mail service.

Jack London and his wife Charmian cruised the Pacific aboard their yacht, the *Snark,* in 1907-09. A longtime admirer of Melville, London found only a wretched swamp at Taipivai in the Marquesas. His *South Sea Tales* (1911) was the first of the 10 books on the Pacific that he wrote. London's story, "The House of Mapuhi," about a Jewish pearl buyer, earned him a costly lawsuit. London was a product of his time and the modern reader is often shocked by his insensitive presentation of the islanders.

In 1913-14 the youthful poet Rupert Brooke visited Tahiti, where he fell in love with Mamua, a girl from Mataiea whom he immortalized in his poem "Tiare Tahiti." Later Brooke fought in WW I and wrote five famous "War Sonnets." He died of blood poisoning at age 28 on a French hospital ship in the Mediterranean in 1915.

W. Somerset Maugham toured Polynesia in 1916-17 to research his novel, *The Moon and Sixpence* (1919), a fictional life of Paul Gauguin. Of the six short stories in *The Trembling of a Leaf* (1921), "The Fall of Edward Barnard"

contrasts the simple island life with the demands of the "real world." Maugham's *A Writer's Notebook* published in 1984, 19 years after his death, describes his travels in the Pacific. On Tahiti Maugham discovered not only material for his books but by chance located a glass door pane with a female figure painted by Gauguin himself, which he bought for 200 francs. In 1962 it sold at Sotheby's in London for $37,400.

American writers Charles Nordhoff and James Norman Hall came to Tahiti after WW I, married Tahitian women, and collaborated on 11 books. Their most famous was the *Bounty* trilogy (1934) which tells of Fletcher Christian's mutiny on the *Bounty,* the escape to Dutch Timor of Capt. Bligh and his *Men Against the Sea,* and the mutineer's fate on *Pitcairn's Island.* Three generations of filmmakers have selected this saga as their way of presenting paradise.

Hall remained on Tahiti until his death in 1951; his house at Arue still stands. His last book, *The Forgotten One,* is a collection of true stories about intellectuals and writers lost in the South Seas. Hall's account of the 28-year correspondence with his American friend Robert Dean Frisbie who settled on Pukapuka in the Cook Islands is touching.

James A. Michener joined the U.S. Navy in 1942 and ended up visiting around 50 South Sea islands, among them Bora Bora. His *Tales of the South Pacific* (1947) tells of the impact of WW II on the South Pacific and the Pacific's impact on those who served. It was later made into the long-running Broadway musical, *South Pacific.* Michener's *Return to Paradise* (1951) is a readable collection of essays and short stories.

Eugene Burdick is best known for his best sellers *The Ugly American* (1958) and *Fail-Safe* (1962). Like Michener, Burdick served in the Pacific during WW II. His 1961 book *The Blue of Capricorn* is a collection of essays and short stories on the area.

Many of the titles mentioned above (or extracts of them) are available in cheap paperback editions in the series "Tales of the Pacific" from Mutual Publishing, 2055 North King St., Suite 201, Honolulu, HI 96819 USA, tel. (808) 924-7732. Write for a complete list. See also the Booklist at the end of this book.

CONDUCT AND CUSTOM

The dress code in Tahiti-Polynesia is very casual—you can even go around barefoot. Cleanliness *is* important, however. Formalwear or jacket and tie are unnecessary (unless you're to be received by the high commissioner!). One exception is downtown Papeete, where scanty dress would be out of place. For clothing tips, see "What To Take."

People usually shake hands when meeting; visitors are expected to shake hands with everyone present. If a Polynesian man's hand is dirty he'll extend his wrist or elbow. Women kiss each other on the cheeks. When entering a private residence it's polite to remove your shoes. It's okay to show interest in the possessions of a host, but don't lavish too much praise on any single object or he/she may feel obligated to give it to you. It's rude to refuse food offered by a Tahitian, but don't eat everything on your plate just to be polite as this will be a signal to your host that you want another helping. Often guests in a private home are expected to eat while the family watches.

All the beaches of Tahiti-Polynesia are public to one meter above the high-tide mark, although some bad watchdogs don't recognize this. Topless sunbathing is completely legal in Tahiti-Polynesia, though total nudity is only practiced on offshore *motus* and floating pontoons. (For information on naturism in Tahiti-Polynesia write: Marcel Arrouet, Relais Naturiste, B.P. 457, Papeete; tel. 42-90-26).

Despite the apparent *laissez faire* attitude promoted in the travel brochures and this book, female travelers should take care: there have been sexual assaults by Polynesian men on foreign women who seemed to project an image of promiscuity by sunbathing topless on a remote beach or even by traveling alone! Women should avoid staying in isolated tourist bungalows or camping outside organized campgrounds. Rape is a less serious offense in Polynesian society than it is in ours.

DIANA LASICH HARPER

TAHITI TOURIST DEVELOPMENT BOARD

a canoe race at Papeete

HOLIDAYS AND EVENTS

The big event of the year is the two-week-long **Heiva i Tahiti,** which runs from the end of June to Bastille Day (14 July). Formerly known as the Tiurai Festival or La Fête du Juillet, it brings contestants and participants to Tahiti from all over the territory to take part in elaborate processions, competitive dancing and singing, feasting, and partying. There are bicycle, car, horse, and outrigger canoe races, petanque, archery, and javelin-throwing contests, firewalkers from Raiatea, sidewalk bazaars, arts and crafts exhibitions, tattooing, games, and joyous carnivals. **Bastille Day** itself, which marks the fall of the Bastille in Paris on 14 July 1789 at the height of the French Revolution, features a military parade in the capital. Ask at the Papeete tourist office about when to see the historical reenactments at Marae Arahurahu, the canoe race along Papeete waterfront, horseracing at the Pirae track, and the traditional dance competitions at the Moorea ferry landing.

The July celebrations on Bora Bora are as good as those on Tahiti, and not as commercial. Note well that all ships, planes, and hotels are fully booked around 14 July, so be in the right place beforehand or get firm reservations, especially if you want to be on Bora Bora that day.

Chinese New Year in Jan. or Feb. is celebrated with dances and fireworks. On Nuclear Free and Independent Pacific Day (1 March), a protest march proceeds from Faaa to Papeete, to commemorate a disastrous nuclear test on Bikini atoll in Micronesia that day in 1954. This is a great opportunity to get to know some local people while showing your concern for the problems of colonialism and militarism in the Pacific. Also watch for public protests on 2 July, the anniversary of the first French nuclear test at Moruroa in 1966. On **All Saints' Day** (1 Nov.) the locals illuminate the cemeteries at Papeete, Arue, Punaauia, and elsewhere with candles. On **New Year's Eve** the Papeete waterfront is beautifully illuminated and there's a seven-km foot race. Ask at the Departement Fêtes et Manifestations in Papeete's Cultural Center (B.P. 1709, Papeete; tel. 42-88-50) about special events, and check the daily papers. In 1995 Tahiti will host the South Pacific Games, the region's most important sporting event.

Public holidays in Tahiti-Polynesia include New Year's Day (1 Jan.), Gospel Day (5 March), Good Friday and Easter Monday (March/April), Labor Day (1 May), Ascension Day (May), Whitsunday and Whitmonday (May/June), Bastille

Day (14 July), Assumption Day (15 Aug.), Internal Autonomy Day (8 Sept.), All Saints' Day (1 Nov.), Armistice Day (11 Nov.), and Christmas Day (25 Dec.). *Everything* will be closed these days (and maybe also the days before and after—ask).

Entertainment

The Tahitian dance shows put on at the hotels are invariably free (no cover charge)—you only pay for the food and drink you consume. Most of the big hotels have a Tahitian show several nights a week, usually accompanied by a barbecue or traditional feast. If the price asked for the meal is too steep, settle for a drink at the bar and enjoy the show. Many of the regular performances are listed in this book, but be sure to call the hotel to confirm the time and date as these do change to accommodate tour groups. The drinking age in Tahiti-Polynesia is officially 18, but it's not strictly enforced.

ACCOMMODATIONS

With *Tahiti-Polynesia Handbook* in hand you're guaranteed a good, inexpensive place to stay on every island. Every hotel in the islands at press time is included herein. We don't solicit freebies from the hotel chains; our only income is from the price you paid when you bought this book. So we don't mind telling you that, as usual, most of the luxury hotels are just not worth the exorbitant prices they charge. Many simply recreate Hawaii at three times the cost, offering far more luxury than you need. Even worse, they tend to isolate you in a French/American environment, away from the Polynesia you came to experience. We list them here for comparison and most are worth visiting as sightseeing attractions, watering holes, or sources of entertainment, but unless you're a millionaire sleep elsewhere.

One of the golden rules of independent travel is "the more you spend the less you experience." Any room you can book from the States over a toll-free number has got to be overpriced. On all the islands are middle-level hotels that charge half what the top end places ask while providing adequate comfort. These are popular weekend destinations for local French. If you really *can* afford US$250 a night and up, you'd do better chartering a skippered or bareboat yacht.

A wise government regulation prohibiting buildings higher than a coconut tree outside Papeete means that most of the hotels are lowrise or consist of small Tahitian *fares.* When choosing a hotel keep in mind that although a thatched bungalow is cooler and infinitely more attractive than a concrete box, it's also more

Guynette's Lodging at Fare, Huahine, is popular among budget travelers.

likely to have insect problems. If in doubt check the window screens and carry mosquito coils and/or repellent. Hopefully there'll be a resident lizard or two to feed on the bugs. As the lagoon waters off the northwest corner of Tahiti become increasingly polluted with raw sewage, hotels like the Beachcomber and Maeva Beach fall back on their swimming pools. On all of the outer islands open to foreign tourists the water is so clear that it makes pools superfluous.

Hotel prices range from f.800 for a dormitory bed all the way up to f.70,000 double with meals. Price wars often erupt between rival hotels and at times you're charged considerably less than the prices given herein! When things are really slow even the luxury hotels sometimes discount their rooms to those who show up at the front desk with advance reservations. If your hotel can't provide running water, electricity, air conditioning, or something similar because of a hurricane or otherwise, ask for a price reduction. You'll easily get 10% off. You usually get what you pay for, so don't feel ripped off unless you're paying top dollar. A seven-percent room tax is usually charged extra at the luxury resorts, but included in the price at the budget places. Many hotels add a surcharge to the bill unless you stay more than one night. Some hotels charge a supplement during the high season (July, August, and at Christmas).

A room with cooking facilities can save you a lot on restaurant meals, and some moderately priced establishments have weekly rates. If you have to choose a meal plan, take only breakfast and dinner (Modified American Plan) and have fruit for lunch. The cheapest hostels expect you to have your own sleeping bag and towel; linen is not usually provided. As you check into your room, note the nearest fire exits. Don't automatically take the first room offered; if you're paying good money look at several, then choose. Single women intending to stay in isolated tourist bungalows should try to find someone with whom to share.

Your best accommodations option is the well-organized homestay program, in which you get a private room or bungalow with a local family. *Logement chez l'habitant* is available on all the outer islands, and even in Papeete itself; the tourist office supplies printed lists. Travel agents abroad won't book the cheaper hotels or lodgings with the inhabitants because no commissions are paid. You must make reservations directly with the owners themselves either by mail or phone. Letters are usually not answered so calling up is best; things change fast and printed listings are often out of date. Most pensions don't accept credit cards and English may not be spoken.

These private guesthouses can be hard to locate. There's usually no sign outside and they don't cater to walk-in clients who show up unexpectedly. Also, the limited number of beds in each may all be taken. Sometimes you'll get airport transfers at no additional charge if you call ahead. Don't expect a lot of privacy or hot water in the bath. Sometimes cooking facilities or meals are included (often seafood); the provision of blankets and towels may depend on the price. The family may loan you a bicycle and generally can be helpful in arranging tours, etc. It's a great way to meet the people while finding a place to stay.

In remote areas residents are often very hospitable and may offer to put you up. Try to find some tangible way to show your appreciation, such as paying for the groceries or giving a gift. It wouldn't hurt to offer cash payment if a stranger helps you when you're in a jam. Once you get home, don't forget to mail prints of any photos you've taken. If you do make friends on one island, ask them to write you a letter of introduction to their relatives on another.

A tent saves the budget traveler a lot of money and proves very convenient to fall back on. The Polynesians don't usually mind if you camp, and quite a few French locals also have tents. Regular campgrounds exist on Tahiti, Moorea, and Bora Bora, catering to the growing number of camper-tourists. On Huahine, Raiatea, and Rangiroa it's possible to camp at certain small hotels (listed herein). On the outer islands camping should be no problem, but ask permission of the landowner, or pitch your tent well out of sight of the road. Ensure this same hospitality for the next traveler by not leaving a mess. Make sure your tent is water- and mosquito-proof. Never pitch a tent directly below coconuts hanging from a tree or a precariously leaning trunk.

FOOD AND DRINK

Restaurants are expensive but you can bring the price way down by ordering only a single main dish. Fresh bread and cold water come with the meal. Avoid appetizers, alcohol, and desserts. No taxes or service charges are tacked on and tipping is unnecessary. So it's really not as expensive as it looks! US$10 will get you through an excellent no-frills lunch of fried fish at a small French restaurant. The same thing in a five-star hotel dining room will be only a few dollars more. Even the finest places are affordable if you order this way.

Most restaurants post their menu in the window. If not, have a look at it before sitting down. Check the entrees as that's all you'll need to take. If the price is right, the ambience congenial, and local French are at the tables, sit right down. In Tahiti-Polynesia it's actually hard to get a bad meal! Sure, food at a snack bar would be half as much, but your Coke will be extra. In the end it's smart to pay a little more to enjoy excellent cuisine once in awhile. Steer clear of restaurants where you see a big plastic bottle of mineral water on every table as this will add a couple of hundred francs to your bill. Also beware of set meals designed for tourists: if you can't order á la carte, walk back out the door.

Local restaurants offer French, Chinese, Vietnamese, Italian, and, of course, Tahitian dishes. The *nouvelle cuisine Tahitienne* is a combination of European and Oriental recipes with local seafoods and vegetables, plus the classic *maa Tahiti*. The French are famous for their sauces, so try something exotic. Lunch is the main meal of the day in Tahiti-Polynesia and many restaurants offer a *plat du jour* designed for regular customers. This is often displayed on a blackboard near the entrance and is usually good value. Most restaurants stop serving lunch at 1400, dinner at 2200. The prices of alcoholic drinks dropped recently as taxation was eased to encourage tourism. Don't expect snappy service: what's the rush, anyway?

If it's all too expensive, groceries are a good alternative. There are lots of nice places to picnic and at f.35 a loaf, that crisp French white bread is incredibly cheap and good. Cheap red wines like Selection Faragui are imported from France in bulk and bottled locally in plastic bottles. Add a nice piece of French cheese to the above and you're ready for a budget travelers' banquet. There's also Martinique rum, and Hinano beer (f.119 in grocery stores) brewed locally by Heineken. Remember the deposit on Hinano beer bottles, which makes beer cheap to buy cold and carry out. Coconut patties are a local treat to watch for on grocery store checkout counters. *Casse croûtes,* big healthy sandwiches made with those long French baguettes, are f.200.

If you're going to the outer islands, take as many edibles with you as possible; food is always more expensive there. Keep in mind that virtually every food plant you see growing on the islands is cultivated by someone. Even fishing floats or seashells washed up on a beach, or fish in the lagoon near someone's home, may be considered private property.

Tahitian Food

If you can spare the cash attend a Tahitian *tamaaraa* (feast) and try some Polynesian dishes roasted in an *ahimaa* (underground oven). Basalt stones are preheated with a wood fire in a meter-deep pit, then covered with leaves. Each type of food is wrapped separately in banana leaves to retain its own flavor and lowered in. The oven is covered with more banana leaves, wet sacking, and sand, and left one to three hours to bake: suckling pig, mahimahi, taro, *umara* (sweet potato), *uru* (breadfruit), and *fafa*, a spinach-like cooked vegetable made from taro tops. Also sample the gamy flavor of *fei*, the red cooking banana that grows wild in Tahiti's uninhabited interior. *Miti hue* is a coconut-milk sauce fermented with the juice of river shrimp. Traditionally *maa Tahiti* is eaten with the fingers.

Poisson cru (ia ota), small pieces of raw bonito (skipjack) or yellowfin marinated with lime juice and soaked in coconut milk, is enjoyable, as is *fafaru* ("smelly fish"), prepared by marinating pieces of fish in seawater in an airtight coconut-shell container. Like the durian, although the smell is repugnant, the first bite can be addicting. Other typical Tahitian plates are chicken *fafa* and kid cooked in ginger.

Poe is a sweet pudding made of starch flour flavored with banana, vanilla, papaya, taro, or pumpkin, and topped with salted coconut-milk sauce. Many varieties of this treat are made throughout Polynesia. *Faraoa ipo* is Tuamotu coconut bread. The local coffee is flavored with vanilla bean, and served with sugar and coconut cream.

Taro is an elephant-eared plant cultivated in freshwater swamps. The sweet potato *(umara)* is a vegetable of South American origin—varying explanations of how it reached Oceania still provoke controversy. Papaya (pawpaw) is nourishing: a third of a cup contains as much vitamin C as 18 apples. To ripen a green papaya overnight, puncture it a few times with a knife. Don't overeat papaya—unless you *need* an effective laxative. Atoll dwellers especially rely on the coconut for food. The tree reaches maturity in eight years, then produces about 50 nuts a year for 60 years. Many islanders eat raw shellfish and fish, but know what you're doing before you join them—their stomachs may be stronger than yours. It's safer to eat well-cooked food, and to peel your own fruit.

Breadfruit

The breadfruit *(uru)* is the plant most often associated with Tahiti. The theme of a man turning himself into such a tree to save his family during famine often recurs in Polynesian legends. Ancient voyagers brought breadfruit shoots or seeds from Southeast Asia. When baked in an underground oven or roasted over flames, the now seedless Polynesian variety resembles bread. Joseph Banks, botanist on Capt. Cook's first voyage, wrote:

> If a man should in the course of his lifetime plant 10 trees, which if well done might take the labor of an hour or thereabouts, he would completely fulfill his duty to his own as well as future generations.

The French naturalist Sonnerat transplanted breadfruit to Reunion in the Indian Ocean as early as 1772, but it's Capt. William Bligh who shall always be remembered when the plant is mentioned. In 1787 Bligh set out to collect young shoots in Tahiti for transfer to the West Indies, where they were to be planted to feed black slaves. On the way back his crew mutinied in Tongan waters and cast off both breadfruit and Bligh. The indomitable captain managed to reach Dutch Timor in a rowboat and in 1792 returned to Tahiti with another ship to complete his task.

breadfruit (Artcarpus altilis)

The breadfruit *(Artocarpus altilis)*, a tall tree with large green leaves, provides shade as well as food. A well-watered tree can produce as many as 1,000 pale green breadfruits a year. Robert Lee Eskridge described it thus:

> Its outer rind or skin, very hard, is covered with a golf-ball-like surface of small irregular pits or tiny hollows. An inner rind about a half-inch thick surrounds the fruit itself, which when baked tastes not unlike a doughy potato. Perhaps fresh bread, rolled

up until it becomes a semi-firm mass, best describes the breadfruit when cooked.

The starchy, easily digested fruit is rich in vitamin B. When consumed with a protein such as fish or meat it serves as an energy food. The Polynesians learned to preserve breadfruit by pounding it into a paste which was kept in leaf-lined pits to ferment into *mahi*. Like the coconut, the breadfruit tree itself had many uses, including providing wood for outrigger canoes.

SHOPPING

Most local souvenir shops sell Marquesas-style wooden "tikis" carved from wood or stone. The original Tiki was a god of fertility, and really old tikis are still shrouded in superstition. Today they're mainly viewed as good-luck charms and often come decorated with mother-of-pearl. Other items carved from wood include mallets (to beat tapa cloth), *umete* bowls, and slit *toere* drums. Carefully woven pandanus hats and mats come from the Australs. Other curios to buy include vanilla for use in flavoring coffee,

hand-carved mother-of-pearl shell, bamboo fish-hooks, and Tahitian music cassettes.

As this is a French colony it's not surprising that many of the best buys are related to fashion. A tropical shirt, sundress, or T-shirt is a purchase of immediate use. The *pareu* is a typically Tahitian leisure garment consisting of a brightly colored hand-blocked or painted local fabric about two meters long and a meter wide. There are dozens of ways both men and women can wear a *pareu*. Local cosmetics like Monoi

PATTI COOK AND ASSOCIATES

Monoi Tiare Tahiti is a scented coconut oil used to replenish natural skin oils lost to the effects of the tropical sun and seas.

Tiare Tahiti, a fragrant coconut-oil skin moisturizer, and coconut-oil soap will put you in form. Jasmine shampoo, cologne, and perfume are also made locally from the tiare Tahiti flower. Imported perfumes from France are sold, too.

Black-pearl jewelry is nontraditional but widely available throughout Tahiti-Polynesia. The color, shape, weight, and size of the pearl are important. The darkest pearls are the most valuable. Prices vary considerably, so shop around before purchasing pearls. For more information on Polynesia's fabulous black pearls, see "Economy," above. Sharks'-tooth pendants are also available as jewelry.

Those who've been thrilled by hypnotic Tahitian music and dance will want to take some Polynesian music home with them on cassette (f.1800) or compact disc (f.3100), available at hotels and souvenir shops throughout the islands. The largest local company producing these CDs is Editions Manuiti or Tamure Records (B.P. 755, Papeete; tel. 42-82-39). Among the well-known local singers appearing on Manuiti are Charlie Manu, Guy Roche, Yves Roche, Coco Temaeva, Emma Terangi, Andy Tupaia, and Henriette Winkler. Small Tahitian groups like the Moorea Lagon Kaina Boys and Tamarii Punaruu and large folkloric ensembles such as Maeva Tahiti, Tiare Tahiti, and Temaeva (often recorded at major festivals) are also well represented. Manuiti's South Pacific Drums (PS 65066), a compilation of 39 of the best percussion recordings in their archives, is an excellent introduction to the traditional music of Polynesia.

If you buy any commercial travel videotapes keep in mind that three incompatible video systems are loose in the world: NTSC (used in North America), PAL (used in Britain, Germany, Japan, and Australia), and SECAM (used in France and the Commonwealth of Independent States). Don't get the wrong one.

Hustling and bargaining are not customs in Tahiti-Polynesia: it's expensive for everyone. Haggling may even by considered insulting, so just pay the price asked or keep looking. Many local food prices are fixed by the government. Avoid whopping mark-ups and taxes; instead purchase food and handicrafts from the producers themselves at markets or roadside stalls.

When making purchases, beware of objects made from turtle shell/leather or marine mammal ivory. These are prohibited entry into the U.S. and many other countries with endangered species acts (fine of US$20,000 and five years imprisonment). Also resist the temptation to purchase jewelry or other items made from seashells and corals, the collection of which damages the reefs. When you return home, Customs may wish to see receipts to judge whether you're within your tax exemption limits ($400 for Americans). Luckily, there's no sales tax in Tahiti!

VISAS

TAHITI - POLYNÉSIE FRANÇAISE
CARTE DÉBARQUEMENT - EMBARQUEMENT/Disembarkation - Embarkation card

IMPORTANT
Veuillez remplir ce document
avec soin.
Toutes les copies doivent
être lisibles.
Please print clearly.
All copies must be legible.

Nom/Surname (En caractères d'imprimerie/Block letters)
....

Nom de jeune fille/Maiden name
....

Prénom/Given name
....

Sexe/Sex :
(Cochez/Tick)
☐ Masculin/Male   ☐ Féminin/Female

Date de naissance
Date of birth
Quantième/Day   Mois/Month   Année/Year

Lieu de naissance
Place of birth

Nationalité
Nationality

Profession
Occupation

Domicile permanent
Permanent address   Rue/Street

Ville/City   Département/State   Pays/Country

Port d'embarquement .... Vol n° ....
Port of embarkation   Flight

Port de débarquement après la Polynésie Frse ....
Port of disembarkation after French Polynesia

Adresse ou hôtel(s) en Polynésie Frse ....
Address or hotel(s) in French Polynesia

Durée de séjour en Polynésie Frse .... jours   ☐ Transit (moins de 24 h)
Length of stay in French Polynesia .... days   (less than 24 h)

Je suis ☐ Visiteur   ☐ Résident temporaire de P.F.   ☐ Résident permanent de P.F.
I am   ☐ Visitor   ☐ Temporary resident of F.P.   ☐ Permanent resident of F.P

Passeport N° ....
Passport N°

N° 144196

Everyone needs a passport. French citizens are admitted freely for an unlimited stay, and citizens of the European Community (EC) countries, Austria, New Zealand, Norway, Sweden, and Switzerland get three months without a visa. Citizens of the United States, Canada, and Japan can obtain a one-month "visa" free upon arrival at Papeete (no different than any other passport stamp). Most others (Australians included) must apply to a French diplomatic mission for a three-month visa, but it's usually issued without delay. Extensions of stay up to three months are possible after you arrive, but these cost f.3000 so it's better to ask for enough time upon arrival. Visa regulations for Tahiti have a way of changing according to the political climate in France, but your airline will know the current requirements.

Tahiti-Polynesia requires a ticket to leave of everyone (even French!). If you arrive without one, you'll be refused entry or required to post a cash bond equivalent to the value of a ticket back to your home country. If you're on an open-ended holiday, you can easily get around this requirement by purchasing a refundable ticket back to the U.S. from Air New Zealand before leaving home. If you catch a boat headed to Fiji (for example), simply have the airline reissue the ticket so it's a ticket to leave your next destination—and on you go. You may also be required to prove that you have "sufficient funds."

Here are a few **French consulates general:**

Australia: St. Martin's Tower 31 Martin St., Sydney, NSW 2000 (tel. 612- 261-5779); 492 St. Kilda Rd., Melbourne, Victoria 3004 (tel. 613-266-2591)

Canada: French consulates general are found in Edmonton, Moncton, Montreal, Ottawa, Quebec, Toronto, and Vancouver.

Chile: Calle Condell 65, C.C. 38-D, Santiago de Chile (tel. 562-225-1030)

Fiji: Dominion House, Thomson St., Private Mail Bag, Suva (tel. 679-300991)

Hawaii: 2 Waterfront Plaza, 500 Ala Moana Blvd., Honolulu, HI 96813 (tel. 808-599-4458)

Japan: 1-1-44, 4 Chome, Minami Azabu, Minato-Ku, Tokyo 106 (tel. 813-473- 0171); Ohbayashi Bldg., 37 Kyobashi 3, Chome Higashi-Ku, Osaka (tel. 8106- 946-6181)

Hong Kong: Admiralty Center Tower 2, 26th Floor, 18 Harcourt Rd., G.P.O. Box 13, Hong Kong (tel. 852-5-294351)

New Zealand: 1 Willeston St., Box 1695, Wellington (tel. 644-720200)

Singapore: 5 Gallop Rd., Box 42, Singapore 1025 (tel. 65-466-4861)

U.S.A.: French consulates general exist in Boston, Chicago, Detroit, Houston, Los Angeles, Miami, New Orleans, New York, San Francisco, and Washington. Get the address of the one nearest you by dialing the toll-free number of UTA French Airlines or Air France.

Yacht Entry

The main port of entry for cruising yachts is Papeete. Upon application to the local gendarme, entry may also be allowed at Moorea, Huahine, Raiatea, Bora Bora, Rurutu, Tubuai, Raivavae, Rangiroa, Nuku Hiva, Hiva Oa, or Ua Pou. The gendarmes are usually friendly and courteous. Boats arriving from Tonga, Fiji, and the Samoas must be fumigated.

Anyone arriving by yacht without an onward ticket must post a bond equivalent to the airfare back to the country of origin at a local bank. In Taiohae the bond is US$1200 pp, in Papeete it's only US$600 (for Americans). This is refundable upon departure at any branch of the same bank, less a one percent fee. Make sure the receipt shows the original currency in which the deposit was made. To reclaim the bond you'll also need a letter from Immigration verifying that you've officially checked out. If any individual on the yacht doesn't have the bond money, the captain is responsible. Once the bond is posted a "temporary" three-month visa (US$30) is issued, which means you have three months to get to Papeete where an additional three months (another US$30) may be granted. Actually, the rules are not hard and fast, and everyone has a different experience.

Yachts staying longer than one year are charged full Customs duty on the vessel. After clearing Customs in Papeete, outbound yachts may spend the duration of their period of stay cruising the outer islands. Make sure every island where you *might* stop is listed on your clearance. The officials want all transient boats out of the country by 31 Oct., the onset of the hurricane season. Crew changes should be made at Papeete.

MONEY AND COMMUNICATIONS

The French Pacific franc or *Cour de Franc Pacifique* (CFP) is legal tender in both Tahiti-Polynesia and New Caledonia. The origin of this currency is interesting. During WW II the French franc (FF) had been devalued to less than a third its prewar value, while prices remained stable in the Pacific. When the French colonies reestablished contact with metropolitan France after wartime separation, a new currency was needed to avoid economic chaos. Thus the CFP was created in 1945 at the rate of 2.4 FF to one CFP. Over the next few years the French franc was further devalued three times and each time the CFP was revalued against it, lowering the French franc to 5.50 to one CFP by 1949. At the same time 100 old FF became one new FF; thus, 5.5 new FF equaled 100 old CFP, a relationship which has been maintained ever since. Until 1967 the Banque de l'Indochine was responsible for issuing and circulating the Pacific franc, a function now carried out by the French government.

The CFP is fixed at one French franc to 18.18 Pacific francs, so you can determine how many CFP you'll get for your dollar or pound by finding out how many FF you get, then multiplying by 18.18. Or to put it another way, 5.5 FF equals f.100, so divide the number of FF you get by 5.5 and multiply by 100. A rough way to convert CFP into U.S. dollars is simply to divide by 100, so f.1000 is US$10, etc. The exact rate is published weekly in the "World Value of the Dollar" column in the Monday issue of the *Wall Street Journal.* There are beautifully colored big banknotes of 500, 1000, 5000, and 10,000 francs, coins of 1, 2, 5, 10, 20, 50, and 100 francs.

Businesses open early in Tahiti-Polynesia and often close for a two-hour siesta at midday. Banking hours are variable, either 0800-1530 or 0800-1100/1400-1700 weekdays. A few open Sat. mornings (ask). Many banks levy a rip-off commission of f.350 on each transaction. Instead, patronize the **Banque Socredo** (B.P. 130, Papeete; tel. 41-51-23) which charges no commission and has branches everywhere. (A few readers have written in to report that the Westpac Bank gives good rates and has stopped charging commission.) Traveler's checks bring a slightly higher rate of exchange than cash but have your passport ready for identification (photocopy sometimes accepted). Also bring a few U.S. dollars in small bills to cover emergency expenses. You'll probably do better waiting to change money upon arrival rather than trying to purchase CFP from your home bank which may give you a poor rate, if they accomplish it at all.

If your American Express traveler's checks are stolen call Australia tel. 61-2-886-0688 collect to report the loss and find out about a refund. The American Express representative on Tahiti is Tahiti Tours (tel. 42-78-70) in Papeete, so you could also turn to them for help. They'll also cancel lost credit cards if they are stolen with the checks. Of course, they'll need to know the numbers!

Credit cards are accepted at the large hotels, but Pacific francs in cash are easier at restaurants, shops, etc. To avoid wasting time hassling at banks for cash advances it's best to bring enough traveler's checks cover all your out-of-pocket expenses and then some. If you do wish to use a credit card at a restaurant, ask first. Visa credit cards are universally accepted in the Society Islands but MasterCard is not. On the outer islands of the Tuamotus credit cards, traveler's checks, and foreign banknotes won't be accepted; it's essential to change enough money before leaving Papeete.

Tahiti used to be the most expensive corner of the South Pacific but in recent years things have changed. While prices increased sharply in Fiji in the wake of two destabilizing military coups, Tahiti-Polynesia has one of the lowest rates of inflation in the South Pacific (never over three percent between 1986 and 1990 compared to 10% in many neighboring countries). Facilities for budget travelers are now highly developed throughout the Society Islands, and with a little care you'll find these islands as affordable as neighboring English-speaking countries, with that special Franco-Polynesian flair thrown in for free. Bargaining is not common in Tahiti-Polynesia and no one will try to cheat you. There's **no tipping** and they *mean* it.

Post

The 34 regular post offices and 58 authorized agencies throughout Tahiti-Polynesia are open weekdays from 0700-1500. Main branches sell ready-made padded envelopes and boxes. Parcels with an aggregate length, width, and height of over 90 cm or weighing more than 20 kilograms cannot be mailed. Rolls (posters, calendars, etc.) longer than 90 cm are also not accepted. Letters cannot weigh over two kilograms. Registration *(recommandation)* and insurance *(envois avec valeur déclarée)* are possible. Always use airmail *(poste aérienne)* when posting a letter; surface mail takes months to arrive. Postcards can still take up to two weeks to reach the U.S.

To pick up poste restante (general delivery) mail you must show your passport and pay f.40 apiece. If you're going to an outer island and are worried about your letters being returned to sender after 15 days, pay f.600 for a *garde de courrier* which obliges the post office to hold all letters for at least a month. For a flat fee of f.800 you can have your mail forwarded by surface mail for one year, f.1600 by airmail. Ask for an *"Ordre de Réexpédition Temporaire."*

In this book all post office box numbers are rendered B.P. *(Boîte Postale)*. Always include the B.P. when writing to a local address as there are usually no street addresses, plus the name of the commune

EXCHANGE RATES

(as of mid-1992; subject to change)

One French Franc =	18.18	Pacific Francs
One U.S. Dollar =	101	Pacific Francs
One Canadian Dollar =	90	Pacific Francs
One Australian Dollar =	80	Pacific Francs
One New Zealand Dollar =	57	Pacific Francs
One Pound Sterling =	174	Pacific Francs
One German Mark =	60	Pacific Francs
One Dutch Guilder =	53	Pacific Francs
100 Japanese Yen =	77	Pacific Francs

or village and the island. The postal authorities recognize "French Polynesia" as the official name of this country and it's best to add "South Pacific Ocean" to that for good measure. Tahiti-Polynesia issues its own colorful postage stamps—available at local post offices. They're good investments and make excellent souvenirs. On Tahiti the postal information number is tel. 41-42-42.

Telephone

Local telephone calls are f.50 and the pay phones usually work! A flashing light means you're about to be cut off, so have another coin ready. All calls within a single island are considered local calls, except on Tahiti which is divided into two zones. Long-distance calls are placed at post offices, which also handle fax *(posteclair)* services. Calls made from hotel rooms are charged double. Collect calls over-

seas are possible. Dial 19 and say you want a *conversation payable a l'arrive.* To get the operator dial 12.

Anyone planning on making a lot of calls should pick up a telephone card *(télécarte),* sold at all post offices. They're valid for both local and overseas calls and are available in denominations of 30 units (f.1000), 60 units (f.2000), and 150 units (f.5000).

It's *much* cheaper to call Tahiti from the U.S. than the other way around, so if you want to talk to someone periodically leave your hotel telephone numbers (provided in this book) and travel dates with them so they can try to get hold of you. If you need to consult the local phone book ask for the *annuaire.* To call Tahiti-Polynesia direct from the U.S. dial 011-689 and the six-digit telephone number. International access codes do vary, so check in the front of your telephone book.

Throughout this book we've tried to supply the local telephone numbers you'll need. Any tourist-oriented business is sure to have someone handy who speaks English, so don't hesitate to call ahead. You'll get current information, be able to check prices and perhaps make a reservation, and often save yourself a lot of time and worry.

Electricity

The electric voltage is 220 volts AC, 60 cycles. If you're taking along an American 110-AC razor or other appliance you'll need a converter. Some hotels with their own generators operate on 110 volts, 60 cycles, however, so be sure to ask before plugging in. Most electrical outlets have two round holes, so an adaptor may also be necessary. Also keep this situation in mind if you buy any duty-free appliances.

Time

Tahiti-Polynesia operates on the same time as Hawaii, 10 hours behind Greenwich Mean Time or two hours behind California (except May to Sept. when it's three hours). The Marquesas are 30 minutes behind the rest of Tahiti-Polynesia. Tahiti-Polynesia is east of the International Dateline so the day is the same as that of the Cook Islands, Hawaii, and the U.S., but a day behind Fiji, New Zealand, and Australia.

In this book all clock times are rendered according to the 24-hour airline timetable system, i.e. 0100 is 1:00 a.m., 1300 is 1:00 p.m., 2330 is 11:30 p.m. Normal shopping hours in Papeete are weekdays 0730-1130/1400-1730, Sat. 0800-1100. The islands operate on coconut time: the nut will fall when it is ripe.

HEALTH

For a tropical location, Tahiti-Polynesia has very few pest or insect problems. Malaria is nonexistent. Yellow-fever vaccinations are required if you've been in an infected area (such as the Amazon basin) within the previous six days (infants under the age of one are excused). Cholera vaccinations are not really effective but may be required if there was an outbreak in your last destination. Tetanus-diphtheria, polio, and typhoid boosters are not required, but always a good idea if you're going to out-of-the-way places. Filariais (elephantiasis), leprosy, and dengue fever are the endemic diseases of Polynesia, but there's little chance of visitors contacting these. By mid-1990 there had been 15 AIDS deaths in Papeete and 80 carriers diagnosed.

Cuts and scratches infect easily and take a long time to heal. Prevent infection from coral cuts by washing with soap and fresh water, then rubbing vinegar or alcohol (whisky will do) into the wounds—painful but effective. Tahitians usually dab coral cuts with lime juice. For bites, burns, and cuts, an antiseptic spray such as Solarcaine speeds healing and helps prevent infection. Bites by nono flies itch for days and can become infected.

Prickly heat, an intensely irritating rash, is caused by wearing heavy, inappropriate clothing. When the glands are blocked and the sweat is unable to evaporate, the skin becomes soggy and small red blisters appear. Synthetic fabrics like nylon are especially bad in this regard. Take a cold shower, apply calamine lotion, dust with talcum powder, and take off those clothes! Until things improve avoid alcohol, tea, coffee, and any physical activity which makes you sweat. If you're sweating profusely, increase your intake of salt slightly to avoid fatigue, but not without concurrently drinking more water.

Frequently the feeling of thirst is false and only due to mucous membrane dryness. Gargling or taking two or three gulps of warm water should be enough. Other means to keep moisture in the body are to have a hot drink like tea or black coffee, or any kind of slightly salted or sour drink in small quantities. Salt in fresh lime juice is remarkably refreshing. For diarrhea take egg yolk mixed with nutmeg or have a rice and tea day. For constipation eat pineapple or any fruit you have peeled. The tap water is safe to drink in Papeete, but ask first elsewhere. The local bottled mineral water is called Eau Royale.

Most of the products in local pharmacies are imported from France, although some U.S. brands are available at twice U.S. prices. If you're not particular about the kind of medicine you take, go to any large Chinese general store and ask the owner to recommend a good Chinese patent medicine for what ails you. The price will be a third what the European medicines or herbs cost and they're often just as effective or better.

Don't go from winter weather into the steaming tropics without a rest before and after. Turn in early the day before you leave to allow for the two-hour time difference (from California). Airplane cabins have low humidity, so drink lots of juice or water instead of carbonated drinks. It's also best to forego coffee as it will only keep you awake. Alcohol helps dehydrate you. Avoid

Fewer than 200 specimens of the rare glory-of-the-sea cone (Conus gloriamaris) are known. Some species of cone shells have a deadly stinging dart which can reach anywhere on the shell's outer surface, so never pick one up.

overeating in flight. Don't scuba dive on your departure day as you're risking a severe case of the bends.

For a token donation of US$10 the International Association for Medical Assistance to Travelers will provide a membership card guaranteeing medical attention at controlled prices in Papeete. Here are a few IAMAT offices: 417 Center St., Lewiston, NY 14092, U.S.A.; 1287 St. Clair Ave. West, Toronto, ON M6E 1B8, Canada; Box 5049, Christchurch 5, New Zealand; 57 Voirets, 1212 Grand-Lancy-Geneva, Switzerland.

The sale of travel insurance is big business but the value of the policies themselves varies. If your national health insurance policy at home covers you while you're traveling abroad it's probably enough. If you do opt for the security of travel insurance, look for a policy that covers theft or loss of luggage and emergency medical evacuations. If you'll be involved in any "dangerous activities," such as scuba diving, read the fine print to make sure your policy is valid.

Sunburn

The Tahitian name for us white folks, *papaa,* means literally "sunburned skin." It was used in pre-European days to designate Tuamotu islanders, and since the discovery, all foreigners. Though you may think a tan will make you *look* healthier and more attractive, it's very damaging to the skin, which becomes dry, rigid, and prematurely old and wrinkled, especially on the face. And a burn from the sun greatly increases your risk of getting skin cancer. Begin with short exposures to the sun, perhaps half an hour, followed by an equal time in the shade. Drink plenty of liquids to keep your pores open. Avoid the sun from 1000 to 1400. Clouds and beach umbrellas will not protect you fully. Wear a T-shirt while snorkeling to protect your back. Beware of reflected sunlight. Sunbathing is the main cause of cataracts to the eyes, so wear sunglasses and a wide-brimmed hat.

Use a sunscreen lotion containing PABA rather than oil (don't forget your nose, lips, forehead, neck, hands, and feet). Sunscreens protect you from ultraviolet rays (a leading cause of cancer), while oils magnify the sun's effect. A 29- or 30-factor sunscreen such as Presun 29 or Sundown 30 will provide adequate protection.

Take care, however, as PABA can stain clothing and bedding. Apply the lotion *before* going to the beach to avoid being burned on the way, and reapply periodically to replace sunscreen washed away by perspiration. After sunbathing take a tepid shower rather than a hot one that would wash away your natural skin oils. Stay moist and use a vitamin E evening cream to preserve the youth of your skin. Calamine ointment soothes skin already burned, as does coconut oil. A local remedy for sunburn is Wing Wah's Soothing Lotion (Lotion Magic), available at Chinese general stores. Pharmacists recommend Solarcaine (more expensive) to soothe burned skin. A vinegar solution reduces peeling. Take aspirin if your skin itches. Vitamin A and calcium counteract overdoses of vitamin D received from the sun. The fairer your skin the more essential it is to take care.

Toxic Fish

Over 400 species of tropical reef fish, including wrasses, snappers, groupers, barracudas, jacks, moray eels, surgeonfish, and shellfish, are known to cause seafood poisoning, ciguatera. There's no way to tell if a fish will cause ciguatera: a species can be poisonous on one side of the island but not on the other.

Several years ago scientists on Tahiti determined that a micro-algae called *dinoflagellate* was the cause. Normally these algae are found only in the ocean depths, but when a reef is disturbed by natural or human causes they can multiply dramatically in a lagoon. The toxins have no effect on the fish which feed on them but become concentrated in large predatory fish and enter the food chain.

Tahiti-Polynesia's 700-800 cases of ciguatera a year are more than the rest of the South Pacific combined, clear evidence that the French nuclear-testing program is responsible. Ciguatera didn't exist on Hao atoll in the Tuamotus until military dredging for a 3,500-meter runway begin in 1965. By mid-1968, 45% of the population had been affected and only after 1975 did the toxicity begin to decline. Between 1960 and 1984 the entire population of Mangareva near the Moruroa test site had suffered from over four documented cases of seafood poisoning.

There's no treatment except to relieve the symptoms (tingling, prickling, itching, vomiting, joint and muscle pains), which usually subside in a few days. Induce vomiting and take castor oil. Symptoms can recur for up to year, and victims can be made allergic to all seafoods. Avoid biointoxication by cleaning fish as soon as they're caught, discarding the head and organs, and taking special care with oversized fish. Whether the fish is consumed cooked or raw has no bearing on this problem. Local residents often know from experience which species may be eaten.

INFORMATION

Tourism to Tahiti-Polynesia is organized by the Office de Promotion et d'Animation Touristique de Tahiti et ses Îles (OPATTI), or simply the Tahiti Tourist Promotion Board. They can provide free brochures and answer questions but are not a travel agency, so you must make your own hotel reservations at a pay phone. Ask for their current information sheets on the islands you intend to visit to check current prices. Below is a list of their offices around the world.

There are two French-owned morning papers, *La Dépêche de Tahiti* (B.P. 50, Papeete; tel. 42-43-43) and *Les Nouvelles de Tahiti* (B.P. 629, Papeete; tel. 43-44-45). *La Dépêche* is the larger with more international news, but both papers provide the daily exchange rate. In 1989 the previously locally owned *Les Nouvelles* was purchased by French publishing magnate Robert Hersant who also owns *La Dépêche*.

The free weekly *Tahiti Beach Press* (B.P. 887, Papeete; tel. 42-68-50), edited by Al Prince, was called the *Tahiti Sun Press* from 1980 till the end of 1990, when the paper was forced to drop all news coverage unrelated to tourism due to economic pressure from the big hotel chains and government tourism officials. The present "sanitized" newspaper is still well worth perusing; just don't expect to find Al's excellent articles on social or political conditions in Tahiti-Polynesia in it anymore. On the brighter side, in early 1992 the *Tahiti Sun Press* was relaunched as an uncensored monthly magazine (f.250). It's well worth picking up a copy at a newsstand or hotel boutique to get a feel for the local scene.

The French government attempts to control what happens in the territory through the state-owned TV and radio. Television was introduced to Tahiti in the mid-1960s and two government-operated stations broadcast in French and Tahitian. Nine private radio stations also operate.

For a recorded weather report (in French) call 42-27-27; for the time dial 41-84-00.

The best local guidebook is *Tahiti, Circle Island Tour Guide* by Bengt Danielsson (Singapore: Les Editions du Pacifique, 1986). Bengt and his wife, Marie-Thérèse, have also written a superb account of the French nuclear-testing program entitled *Poisoned Reign* (Australia: Penguin Books, 1986). Other books on Tahiti-Polynesia are described in the "Booklist," at the back of this volume.

TAHITI TOURIST BOARD OFFICES

Tahiti Tourist Board
B.P. 65, Papeete,
Tahiti-Polynesia
(tel. 42-96-26)

Tahiti Tourist Board
6151 W. Century Blvd.
Suite 1024
Los Angeles, CA 90045 U.S.A.
(tel. 213-649-2884)

Tahiti Tourist Board
620 St. Kilda Rd. Suite 301
Melbourne 3004, Victoria, Australia
(tel. 613-521-3877)

Tahiti Tourist Board
Box 5172 Wellesley St.
Auckland, New Zealand
(tel. 949-732-649)

Office du Tourisme de Tahiti
B.P. 443 Noumea
New Caledonia
(tel. 27-81-03)

Pacific Leisure
149 Rochor Road #05-06
Fu Lu Shou Complex
Singapore 0718
(tel. 338-1612)

Tahiti Tourist Board
Sankyo Bldg. (No.20) Room 802
3-11-5 Iidabashi, Chiyoda-Ku
Tokyo 102, Japan
(tel. 3-265-0468)

Oficina de Turismo de Tahiti
Casilla 16057
Santiago 9, Chile
(tel. 562-251-2826)

Office du Tourisme de Tahiti
28 Blvd. Saint Germain
75005 Paris, France
(tel. 4634-5059)

WHAT TO TAKE

Packing
Assemble everything you simply must take and cannot live without—then cut the pile in half. If you're still left with more than will fit into a medium-size suitcase or backpack, continue eliminating. Now put it all into your bag. If the total (pack and contents) weighs over 16 kilograms, you'll sacrifice much of your mobility. If you can keep it down to 10 kilograms, you're traveling *light*. Categorize, separate, and pack all your things into plastic bags or stuff sacks for convenience and protection from moisture. In addition to your pack or suitcase you'll want a day pack or flight bag. When checking in for flights, carry anything which can't be replaced in your hand luggage.

Your Bag
A soft, medium-size backpack with an internal frame is best. Big, external-frame packs are fine for mountain climbing, but don't fit into public lockers and are very inconvenient on public transport. The best packs have a zippered compartment in back where you can tuck in the straps and hip belt before turning your pack over to an airline or bus. Jansport's "Framesack," among others, is of this type. This type of pack has the flexibility of allowing you to simply walk when motorized transport is unavailable and with the straps zipped in it looks like a regular suitcase should you wish go upmarket for a while.

Look for a pack with double, two-way zipper compartments and pockets, which you can lock with miniature padlocks. It might not *stop* a thief, but it could be deterrent enough to make him look for another mark. A 60-cm length of lightweight chain and another padlock will allow you to fasten your pack to something. Though theft is not a major problem in Tahiti-Polynesia it's always smart to keep valuables locked in your bag, out of sight.

Camping Equipment And Clothing
A small nylon tent guarantees you a place to sleep every night. It *must* be mosquito- and waterproof. Get one with a tent fly, then waterproof both tent and fly with a can of waterproofing spray such as Thompson's Water Seal (available at any U.S. hardware or outdoors store). You'll seldom need a sleeping bag in the tropics. A youth hostel sleeping sheet is ideal—all YHA handbooks give instructions on how to make your own.

For clothes take loose-fitting cotton washables, light in color and weight. Synthetic fabrics are hot and sticky in the tropics. The dress is casual, with slacks and a sports shirt okay for men even at dinner parties. Local women wear long, colorful dresses in the evening, but shorts are okay in daytime. If you're in doubt, pack clothes which can be discarded and buy tropical garb here. Stick to clothes you can rinse in your room sink. The *pareu* (pronounced "par-RAY-o") is a bright two-meter piece of cloth both men and women wrap about themselves as an all-purpose garment. Any Tahitian can show you how to wear it.

Go native in a Tahitian pareu. Throw one corner over your right shoulder, then pass the other under your left arm and pull tight. Tie the ends and you're dressed.

DIANA LASICH HARPER

Neutral gray eyeglasses protect your eyes from the sun and give the least color distortion. Take comfortable shoes that have been broken in. Rubber thongs (zories) are very handy. Scuba divers' rubber booties are lightweight and perfect for both crossing rivers and reefwalking, though an old pair of sneakers may be just as good. Below we've provided a few checklists to help you assemble your gear. All the listed items weigh well over 16 kilograms, so eliminate what doesn't suit you:

pack with internal frame
day pack or airline bag
nylon tent and fly
tent patching tape
mosquito net
synthetic sleeping bag
YH sleeping sheet
sun hat
essential clothing only
bathing suit
hiking boots
rubber thongs
rubber booties
mask and snorkel

Accessories

Look in the ads in photographic magazines for the best deals on mail-order cameras and film, or buy at a discount shop in any large city. Run a roll of film through it to be sure it's in good working order. Register valuable cameras or electronic equipment with Customs before you leave home so there won't be any argument about where you bought the items when you return, or at least carry the original bill of sale.

The type of camera you choose could depend on the way you travel. If you'll be mostly staying in one place a heavy SLR with spare lenses and other equipment won't trouble you. If you'll be moving around a lot for a considerable length of time a 35mm compact camera may be better. The compacts are mostly useful for close-up shots; landscapes will seem spread out and far away. A wide-angle lens gives excellent depth of field, but hold the camera upright to avoid converging verticals. A polarizing filter prevents reflections from glass windows. Avoid overexposure at midday by reducing the exposure half a stop. Ask permission before photographing people.

Keep your camera in a plastic bag during rain and while traveling in motorized canoes, etc. Silica-gel crystals in the bag will protect film from humidity and mold growth. Protect camera and film from direct sunlight and load film in the shade. Never leave a camera or film in a hot place like a car floor or glove compartment. When packing protect your camera against vibration. Checked baggage is scanned by powerful airport X-ray monitors, so carry both camera and film aboard in a clear plastic bag and ask for a visual inspection. Otherwise use a lead-laminated pouch. On Tahiti camera film costs over double what you'd pay in the U.S., so bring along the 10 rolls you're allowed to import duty free. Whenever purchasing film in the islands take care to check the expiration date. Don't plan on having any slides developed locally: it can cost over US$50 to develop a roll of 36!

Bring some reading material, as English-language books are expensive or hard to find. A clip-on book light and extra batteries allows campers to read at night. A mask and snorkel are essential equipment—you'll be missing half of Polynesia's beauty without them. Serious scuba divers bring their own regulators and buoyancy-control devices.

camera and five rolls of film
compass
pocket flashlight
extra batteries
candle
pocket/alarm calculator
pocket watch
sunglasses
padlock and lightweight chain
collapsible umbrella
twine for a clothesline
powdered laundry soap
sink plug (one that fits all)
mini-towel
sewing kit
mini-scissors
nail clippers
fishing line for sewing gear
plastic cup
can and bottle opener
cork screw
pen knife
spoon

water-bottle
matches
tea bags
dried fruits
nuts
crackers
plastic bags
gifts

Toiletries And Medical Kit

Since everyone has his/her own medical requirements, and brand names vary from country to country, there's no point going into detail here. Note, however, that even the basics (such as aspirin) are unavailable on some outer islands, so be prepared. Bring medicated powder for prickly heat rash. Charcoal tablets are useful for diarrhea and poisoning (absorbs the irritants). Bring an adequate supply of any personal medications, plus your prescriptions (in generic terminology).

Women should know that high humidity causes curly hair to swell and bush, straight hair to droop. If it's curly have it cut short or keep it long in a ponytail or bun. A good cut is essential with straight hair. Water-based makeup is best as the heat and humidity cause oil glands to work overtime. See "Health" above for more ideas.

soap in plastic container
soft toothbrush
toothpaste
stick deodorant
shampoo
comb and brush
skin creams
makeup
tampons or napkins
white toilet paper
multiple vitamins and minerals
Cutter's insect repellent
PABA sunscreen
ChapStick
a motion sickness remedy
contraceptives
iodine
water purification pills
delousing powder
a diarrhea remedy
Tiger Balm
a cold remedy

Alka Seltzer
aspirin
antihistamine
antifungal
Calmitol ointment
antibiotic ointment
painkiller
antiseptic cream
disinfectant
simple dressings
Band-Aids

Money And Documents

All post offices have passport applications. Carry your valuables in a money belt worn around your waist or neck under your clothing; most camping goods stores have these. Leave unneeded credit cards and jewelry at home. Bring along a small supply of US$1 and US$5 bills to use if you don't manage to change money immediately upon arrival or if you run out of CFP and can't get to a bank. If you have a car at home, bring along the insurance receipt so you don't have to pay insurance every time you rent a car. Ask your agent about this.

Make several photocopies of the information page of your passport, personal identification, driver's license, scuba certification card, credit cards, airline tickets, receipts for purchase of traveler's checks, etc.—you should be able to get them all on one page. A brief medical history with your blood type, allergies, chronic or special health problems, eyeglass and medical prescriptions, etc. might also come in handy. Put these inside plastic bags to protect them from moisture. Carry the lists in different places, and leave one home.

passport
vaccination certificates
airline tickets
scuba certification card
driver's license
traveler's checks
some U.S. cash
photocopies of documents
money belt
address book
notebook
envelopes
extra ballpoint pens

GETTING THERE

Your plane ticket will be your biggest single expense, so spend some time considering the possibilities. Start by calling the airlines directly at their toll-free 800 numbers to get current information on fares. The ones to call are Air Caledonie International, Air France, Air New Zealand, Hawaiian Airlines, Japan Air Lines, LAN Chile, Minerve/Air Liberté, Qantas Airways, and UTA French Airlines, all with flights to Papeete. In North America, to get the airline's toll-free number call (800) 555-1212 (all 800 numbers are free). Call them all and say you want the *lowest possible fare*. Ask about restrictions. If you're not happy with the answers you get, call back later and try again. Many different agents take calls on these lines and some are more knowledgeable than others. The numbers are busy during business hours, so call at night or on the weekend. *Be persistent.*

Also try your local travel agent, though any agent worth his/her commission will want to sell you a package tour. Even if you decide to take advantage of the convenience of an agent, do call the airlines yourself beforehand so you'll know if you're getting the right deal. Often vacation packages cost less than regular roundtrip airfare. If they'll let you extend your stay to allow the time you want to yourself this could be a good deal, especially with the hotel thrown in for "free." But check the restrictions. Airline tickets are often refundable only in the place of purchase, so ask about this before you invest in a ticket you may not use.

Check the Sunday travel section of a newspaper like the *San Francisco Chronicle* or a major entertainment weekly. They often carry ads for "bucket shops," agencies which sell seats for less than airline offices will. Most airlines have more seats than they can market through normal channels, so they sell their unused long-haul capacity on this "gray" market at discounts of 40-50% off the official IATA tariffs. There are well-known centers around the world where globetrotters regularly pick up onward tickets (Amsterdam, Athens, Bangkok, Hong Kong, London, San Francisco, and Singapore are only a few). Rates are competitive so check a few agencies before deciding. Despite the shady appearance, most of the bucket shops are perfectly legitimate and your ticket will probably be issued by the airline itself. Don't hand over the full price until you see it, though. Most discounted tickets look and are exactly the same as regular full-fare tickets. They're usually nonrefundable.

UTA French Airlines (Union de Transports Aériens, 71 Stevenson St., Suite 1400, San Francisco, CA 94105-2938 U.S.A.) is *the* international carrier to the French colonies in the South Pacific. Their schedules are more convenient than those of some of the others, since they're built around Tahiti rather than mere stopovers on the way to somewhere else. Their in flight meals and service are excellent, but you pay for it. UTA has a policy of keeping their ticket prices high in France, North America,

PACIFIC AIR ROUTES

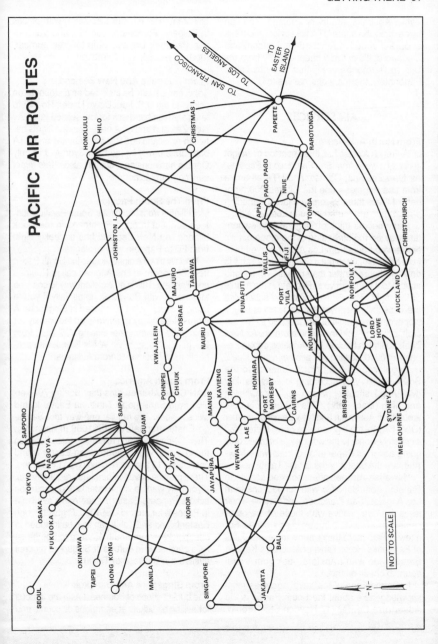

NOT TO SCALE

Tahiti, Australia, and New Zealand. You can buy exactly the same UTA tickets for much less at bucket shops in Amsterdam, London, and Singapore. It's actually cheaper to fly from the U.S. to Rarotonga or Fiji than to fly to Tahiti! Fortunately, there are alternatives to UTA.

AIR SERVICES

From North America

UTA French Airlines has three nonstop overnight services a week from San Francisco to Papeete. Air New Zealand, Qantas, and UTA all arrive from Los Angeles—use the toll-free 800 numbers of these three to compare fares. Canadian passengers are routed through Los Angeles.

Many people think of Tahiti as somewhere far away on the other side of the globe but it's only seven hours from Los Angeles, five hours from Honolulu. Or to put it another way, Tahiti is only two hours farther than Hawaii, yet a world apart. Most flights arrive at Papeete in the middle of the night. The Air New Zealand schedules are especially inconvenient as Tahiti is only a stopover and flight times are planned so the aircraft arrive in Auckland in the morning. Air New Zealand flights back to Los Angeles depart Papeete at 0240, costing you another night's sleep.

Regular fares from North America to the South Pacific vary according to seasons: low (May-Aug.), shoulder (March, April, Sept.-Nov.), and high (Dec.-Feb.). This schedule is built around the Australian and New Zealand summer (Dec.-Feb.)—the high season down there—but it certainly works to the advantage of those only going as far as Papeete as climate-wise May-Aug. are the best months to visit Tahiti!

Hawaiian Airlines offers nonstop service to Papeete from Honolulu with connections from Los Angeles, San Francisco, and Seattle. Their fares are competitive with those of the other carriers and Hawaii is thrown in as a bonus. For a few dollars more they'll throw in seven nights at Papeete's Hotel Tahiti or Moorea's Kaveka Beach Club with transfers—ask your travel agent to check on this.

In Canada one of the travel agencies most knowledgeable about the South Pacific is the **Adventure Center** (17 Hayden St., Toronto,

ON M4Y 2P2; tel. 416-922-7584) with offices in Calgary, Edmonton, Toronto, and Vancouver. Call their Canada-wide toll-free number, (800) 661-7265, for information.

From Australia And New Zealand

Tahiti can usually be included as a stopover on tickets to the U.S. from Down Under. Roundtrip fares are high but check for low-season rates. Air New Zealand and UTA have nonstop flights between Auckland and Papeete. Qantas and UTA both have direct flights from Sydney, but only Qantas has nonstops. Qantas also offers direct service from Melbourne.

From The South Pacific

Most flights from the insular South Pacific countries connect through Rarotonga in the Cook Islands. Air New Zealand has a weekly flight from Fiji to Papeete via Rarotonga.

Virtually all UTA flights across the South Pacific from Singapore to Los Angeles call at Noumea and Papeete. This is an excellent way to combine Melanesia with Polynesia, especially if you're using a cheap ticket purchased in Singapore. A more off-beat way to arrive is on the weekly Air Caledonie International Boeing 737 flight from Noumea to Papeete via Wallis Island, with connections in Noumea to/from Australia.

From South America

LAN Chile Airlines runs their Boeing 707 service from Santiago to Tahiti via Easter Island twice a week. The regular one-way fare Santiago-Easter-Papeete is US$1068 in economy. Their 30-day roundtrip excursion fares between these points with a stopover on Easter Island cost US$1113 and up, depending on the season. There may be advance purchase requirements. If you only want to visit Easter Island, excursion tickets Papeete-Easter-Papeete are available in Papeete for around US$1000. Flights through Easter Island and Tahiti can also be included in cheap tickets from South America to Southeast Asia purchased in Europe or Singapore (but not available in Santiago or Tahiti).

From Singapore And Bangkok

The bucket shops of Southeast Asia are famous for selling air tickets at enormous discounts and the Pacific budget travelers' standby are cheap UTA or Air New Zealand tickets from Singapore to Los Angeles or Santiago with stops in places like Jakarta, Bali, Sydney, Noumea, Auckland, Fiji, Rarotonga, and Papeete. To get the cheapest fare you must shop around. These are open tickets and you can fly any flight but the planes are often full, so book and reconfirm your next leg well ahead.

One recommended agency is **German Asian Travels Ltd.** (126 Telok Ayer St. #02-01, Singapore 0106; tel. 221-5539; fax 221-4220). They offer two routings on UTA: Singapore-Sydney-Noumea-Auckland-Papeete-Los Angeles for US$1100 or Singapore-Sydney-Noumea-Auckland-Papeete-Easter Island-Santiago for US$1550. On Qantas they'll sell you Singapore-Melbourne-Papeete-Los Angeles for US$900, or an Air New Zealand ticket Singapore-Auckland-Fiji-Rarotonga-Papeete-Los Angeles at US$1050. A round-the-world ticket Singapore-Bali-Noumea-Auckland-Papeete-San Francisco-Paris-Singapore from German Asian will be about US$2000.

Similar tickets are available from **MAS Travel Center Ltd.** (19 Tanglin Rd., #06-01 Tanglin Shopping Center, Singapore 1024; tel. 737-8877) and **K. Travel Service** (21/33 Soi Ngam Duphli, near Malaysia Hotel, Bangkok 10120, Thailand; tel. 287-1468). All three of the above companies have been operating for many years and we've heard no complaints about them. North Americans and Europeans can avail themselves of these bargains by flying direct to Singapore on the cheapest one-way ticket and working their way back from there.

Circle Pacific Fares

If you'd like to include Tahiti in a larger Pacific trip look into a "Circle Pacific" fare. For example,

Qantas links up with Northwest Airlines to offer a choice of any four of 30 possible stopovers around the Pacific for US$1970 RT from Seattle, San Francisco, or Los Angeles, C$2599 RT from Vancouver, or around A$2200 RT from any one of seven Australian cities. These tickets are valid six months and the same fare applies all year. You must book the first leg and pay for the ticket at least 21 days in advance and the cancellation penalty is 25%. Additional stopovers are US$50 extra each to a maximum of six stops in total. These tickets are readily available at travel agencies in North America and Australia. Air New Zealand also offers such fares.

Charter Flights

Nouvelles Frontières Inc. (87 boulevard de Grenelle, 75738 Paris Cedex 15, France; tel. 4273-1064) handles charter flights to Papeete on **Minerve/Air Liberté,** the largest independent French charter company. A 13-to-80-day RT excursion ticket on their weekly Paris-Los Angeles-Papeete flight costs 9549 French francs low season (mid-Jan. to March and Oct. to mid-Dec.), 12,750 FF high season. From Los Angeles to Papeete the fare is about US$750 RT. Small reductions are available for students under 31 and youths under 26. Once ticketed there's a $50 penalty to change your flight dates, and in Papeete changes of date must be made 15 days in advance. Refunds (minus a $75 penalty) are only possible if the agency manages to resell your ticket, but you're forbidden to sell your own ticket to a third party. Minerve reserves the right to alter flight times up to 48 hours without compensation, but if you miss your flight you lose your money. Still, if you're sure when you'll be traveling, these prices are a couple of hundred dollars lower than anything offered by the scheduled airlines.

A few Nouvelles Frontières offices selling these tickets include: 12 East 33rd St., 11th Floor, New York, NY 10016 U.S.A., tel. (212) 779-0600; 800 boulevard de Maisonneuve Est, Montreal, PQ H2L 4M7, Canada, tel. (514) 288-4800; and 11 Blenheim St., London W1, England, tel. (071) 629-7772. Nouvelles Frontières also has offices throughout Europe. Their toll-free "Numero Vert" within France is tel. 0548-4848.

From Europe

Air New Zealand flights connect for London in Los Angeles, while UTA and Air France passengers change in Paris. UTA flies around the world several times a week on a routing Paris-San Francisco-Papeete-Auckland-Noumea-Bali-Jakarta-Singapore-Bahrein-Paris.

The British specialist in South Pacific itineraries is **Trailfinders** (42-50 Earls Court Rd., Kensington, London W8 6EJ; tel. 071-938-3366), in business since 1970. They offer a variety of round-the-world tickets through Tahiti: London-Los Angeles-Tahiti-Rarotonga-Fiji-Auckland-London (1020 pounds sterling), London-Los Angeles-Tahiti-Rarotonga-Auckland-Singapore-London (1130 pounds), London-Bangkok-Cairns-Brisbane-Sydney-Tahiti-Los Angeles-London (1031 pounds), and London-South America-Easter Island-Tahiti-Rarotonga-Fiji-Auckland-Australia-Bali-Hong Kong-New Delhi-London (2160 pounds). All these and more are described in their free quarterly magazine *Trailfinder*. They also book discount rooms in luxury hotels on Tahiti and Moorea.

In Amsterdam **Malibu Travel** (Damrak 30, 1012 LJ Amsterdam) has low round-the-world fares which include Tahiti and Easter Island. Their ticket Amsterdam-Singapore-Perth-Sydney-Tahiti-Los Angeles is 2695 Dutch guilders. Alternatively Amsterdam-Singapore-Jakarta-Sydney-Noumea-Auckland-Tahiti-Easter Island-Santiago or vice versa is 4550 guilders. The **World Ticket Center** (Nieuwe Zijds Voorburgwal 159, 1012 RK Amsterdam; tel. 020-626-1011) offers Amsterdam-Singapore-Jakarta-Sydney-Noumea-Auckland-Tahiti-Los Angeles-Amsterdam for 3800 guilders. Another good place to try is **Reisbureau Amber** (Da Costastraat 77, 1053 ZG Amsterdam; tel. 31-20-685-1155)—also the best spot in Amsterdam to look

for books on the Pacific. The author of this travel guide often buys his tickets to the South Pacific from Amber!

In Switzerland try **Globetrotter Travel Service** (Rennweg 35, 8001 Zürich; tel. 01-211-7780) with offices in Zürich, Bern, Basel, Luzern, St. Gallen, Winterthur, and Baden. Their newsletter *Ticket-Info* lists hundreds of cheap flights, including many through Tahiti. Just for example, Frankfurt-Los Angeles-Tahiti-Fiji-Rarotonga-Tahiti-Los Angeles-Frankfurt costs US$1860 from Globetrotter. Similarly, Brussels-Frankfurt-Asuncion-Santiago-Easter Island-Tahiti-Auckland-Noumea-Sydney-Jakarta-Singapore-Karachi-Frankfurt is US$3020. Highly recommended.

From Japan

Air France and Japan Air Lines have a joint weekly nonstop flights from Tokyo to Papeete. Traveling from Japan to Tahiti on UTA involves changing planes in Noumea.

Student Fares

If you're a student or recent graduate you can benefit from lower student fares by booking through a student travel office. There are two rival organizations of this kind, both completely reliable. In the U.S. **Council Travel Services** (919 Irving St., Suite 102, San Francisco, CA 94122 U.S.A.; tel. 415-661-6124), a division of the Council on International Educational Exchange (CIEE), has 35 offices in college towns right across the country. Though they specialize mostly in flights to Europe they will arrange student fares to Papeete on Air New Zealand and Qantas, plus student circle-Pacific fares. There are no restrictions on these tickets but you do have to prove that you're really a student and buy an International Student Identity Card (ISIC) for $14. A similar organization in Canada is **Travel Cuts** (171 College St., Toronto, Ont. M5T 1P7; tel. 416-977-3703) with offices in all large Canadian cities. Call either of the above numbers for the student travel office closest to you.

The other such company is the **Student Travel Network** (82 Shattuck Square, #4, Berkeley, CA 94704 U.S.A.; tel. 415-841-1037), the American branch of **Student Travel Australia** (220 Faraday St., Carlton, Melbourne, Victoria 3053, Australia; tel. 61-03-347-6911). Due to the Australian connection they're usually more knowledgeable about tickets to the South Pacific and they aren't as picky about checking student identification. They offer a RT student fare on Air New Zealand from California to Tahiti, Cook Islands, and Fiji of US$909 low season, US$989 shoulder, US$1119 high. Both STN and STA have branch offices in many U.S. and Australian cities—call for the nearest. In Auckland, New Zealand, call 64-9-39-9723; in London, England, it's 44-71-938-4711.

PROBLEMS

If your flight is canceled due to mechanical problems with the aircraft, the airline will cover your hotel bill and meals. If they reschedule the flight on short notice for reasons of their own or you're bumped off an overbooked flight, they should also pay. They may not feel obligated to pay, however, if the delay is due to weather conditions, a strike by another company, national emergencies, etc., although the best airlines still pick up the tab in these cases. But don't expect much from small commuter companies.

To compensate for "no shows," most airlines overbook their flights. To avoid being "bumped," check in early and go to the departure area well before flight time. Overbooked airlines often offer meals, rooms, and even cash to volunteers willing to relinquish their seats. In some airports flights are not called over the public address system, so keep your eyes open. Whenever you break your journey for more than 72 hours, always reconfirm your onward reservations. Failure to do so could result in the cancellation of your complete remaining itinerary. When planning your trip allow a minimum two-hour stopover between connecting flights, although with airport delays on the increase even this might not be enough. Whenever traveling always have a paperback or two, some toiletries, and a change of underwear in your hand luggage.

Baggage
Most airlines allow two pieces of checked baggage plus a carry-on. Surfboards and bicycles are carried for about US$50 extra. If you'll be changing aircraft at a gateway city don't check your baggage straight through or it could be left behind. Collect it at the transfer point and check in again. Stow anything which could conceivably be considered a weapon (scissors, pen knife, toy gun, mace, etc.) in your checked luggage.

Tag your bag with name, address, and phone number inside and out. Get into the habit of removing used baggage tags, unless you want your luggage to travel in the opposite direction. As you're checking in, look to see if the three-letter city code on your baggage tag and the one on your boarding pass are the same. If your baggage is damaged or doesn't come out on arrival at your destination, future claims for compensation will be compromised unless you inform the airline officials *immediately* and have them fill out a written report.

Airlines usually reimburse out-of-pocket expenses if your baggage is lost or delayed over 24 hours—the amount varies from US$25-50. Your chances of getting the cash are better if you're polite but firm. Keep receipts for any money you're forced to spend to replace missing articles. Claims for lost luggage can take weeks to process. Keep in touch with the airline to show your concern; also, hang onto your baggage tag until the matter is resolved. If you feel you did not receive the attention you deserved, write the airline an objective letter outlining the case. Get the names of the employees you're dealing with so you can mention them in the letter.

ORGANIZED TOURS

Inclusive Tours
Ted Cook Tours (Box 1398, Newport Beach, CA 92663 U.S.A.; tel. 714-645-8300), founded in 1965, was the first American travel company to specialize exclusively in the South Pacific (no connection with James or Thomas). Ted's "Islands in the Sun" packages to Tahiti and Moorea begin as low as US$899 for six nights, airfare and double-occupancy accommodation included, though these budget trips are usually fully booked and most of the packages end up costing around US$2000 pp. If you're intending to stay at luxury hotels anyway, however, it does work out much cheaper than paying as you go. The main problem with all packaged

tours is that you can't change your dates or itinerary at the last minute without paying heavy penalties and you end up stuck on the beaten tourist track. The Ted Cook Tours Tahiti brochure does include innovative packages built around shareboat yacht charters, *Wind Song* cruises (see below), and freighter travel to the Marquesas Islands. You must reserve through a travel agent as direct bookings are not accepted.

Another California-based company, **Manuia Tours and Travel** (55 New Montgomery, Suite Mezz A, San Francisco, CA 94105 U.S.A.; tel. 415-495-4500), also offers packaged holidays to Tahiti-Polynesia and it's fully owned and operated by Tahitians!

In New Zealand **ASPAC Vacations Ltd.** (Box 4330, Auckland; tel. 09-623-0259) offers the same sort of packages as Ted Cook Tours, with "weekend escapes" to Tahiti beginning as low as NZ$899, airfare and accommodation included. Similarly, ASPAC arranges bareboat yacht charters and *Wing Song* cruises. Australians can obtain the same from *Jetabout Holidays* (141 Walker St., North Sydney, NSW 2060, Australia; tel. 02-957-0768). European travel agents should book through Jetabout's U.K. office (Jetabout Holidays, Sovereign House, 359-367 King St., Hammersmith, London W6 9NJ, England; tel. 081-748-8676). All bookings with ASPAC and Jetabout must be through a travel agent.

Club Méditerranée (40 West 57th St., New York, NY 10019 U.S.A.; tel. 212-977-2100) offers one-week packages to their Moorea resort for US$1950-2440 from Los Angeles or San Francisco. Bora Bora packages are about US$300 more to cover the cost of air transfers from Tahiti. The price includes room, food, watersports, airfare, and transfers. Rental bicycles are charged extra. Due to all the activities, Club Med's a good choice for single travelers; families with small children should look elsewhere. Book a couple of months in advance, especially if you want to travel in July, Aug., or December. For more information on *le Club*, see the Moorea chapter in this book.

Tours For Sportspeople

Although scuba diving can be arranged directly at island dive shops, divers with limited time may want to consider a tour package that includes airfare, accommodations, and scuba diving. One company offering these is **Sea Safaris** (3770 Highland Ave., Suite 102, Manhattan Beach, CA 90266 U.S.A.; tel. 213-546-2464). Another is **Poseidon Venture Tours** (359 San Miguel Dr., Newport Beach, CA 92660 U.S.A.; tel. 714-644-5344), which has a seven-night package to Rangiroa and Manihi for US$2600, including airfare, double-occupancy accommodations, and three days of diving.

New Zealanders requiring information about scuba-diving facilities in Tahiti-Polynesia should call up Ed Meili of **The Diving Network** (Box 38-023, Howick, Auckland, New Zealand; tel. 09-535-8443). Ed has firsthand knowledge of diving facilities on Raiatea and Rangiroa and can provide valuable tips.

The expert on scuba diving around Tahiti-Polynesia is marine biologist and divemaster Richard Johnson, director of **Paradise Dive Travel** (B.P. 6008, Faaa, Tahiti; tel. 42-80-42; fax 689-41-08-54). Dick sells "prepaid diving vouchers" for customized scuba diving at Tahiti, Moorea, Huahine, Raiatea, Bora Bora, Rangiroa, and Manihi at discounts of five to 20%. Write or fax for his free leaflet, "Why Dive Tahiti?" that outlines the advantages and disadvantages of each island in refreshingly straightforward language. Dick's U.S. representative is **Tahiti Vacations** (call 800-553-3477 and ask about the "Dive Tahiti" program).

The only American company offering bicycle tours to Polynesia is **Off The Deep End Travels** (Box 7511, Jackson, WY 83001 U.S.A.; tel. 307-733-8707). Their 10-day bike and sail trip to the Society Islands is offered about five times a year. Interisland travel is by chartered yacht and participants get to cycle around Tahaa, Huahine, Bora Bora, and Raiatea. The US$1950 price includes guides, accommodations, and most meals, but airfare (US$799 RT California to Papeete, plus US$190 RT Papeete to Raiatea) and bicycle rentals (US$120) are extra. If fewer than 12 people sign up for this tour, a supplemental charge is added.

Cruises Out Of Papeete

Windstar Sail Cruises (300 Elliot Ave. W, Seattle, WA 98119 U.S.A.) offers cruises around the

Society Islands year-round in their gigantic, four-masted *Wind Song*. Participants join the boat at Papeete. The pp price for one of 74 double, classless cabins for a seven-day cruise varies according to season: US$2195 (low), US$2395 (base), US$2595 (peak), plus US$95 port charges. Single occupancy is 50% more and airfare to Tahiti is extra. Although this 134-meter-long, 62-meter-high Norwegian-registered ship could hardly be classed as a yacht, it is a step up from the impersonal pretension of a love boat. One of three identical high-tech vessels, which also ply the Mediterranean and Caribbean, the *Wind Song's* sails are fully computer-controlled, saving on both fuel and crew! Though the ship can heel up to six degrees, ballast tanks and stabilizers ensure a smooth ride. The Windstar fleet, commissioned at Le Havre, France, from 1986-88, deserves credit for experimenting with an alternative energy (the wind!).

In 1992 Club Méditerranée copied the *Wind Song* concept by inaugurating Society Island cruises on their 188-meter, five-masted cruise ship, the *Club Med 2*. Combination packages with stays at their Moorea and Bora Bora resorts are offered.

From October to February one of the five *Princess* ships of Princess Cruises shuttles between Honolulu and Papeete on a 11-night luxury cruise with stops at Lahaina, Kona, Hilo, Bora Bora, and Moorea. Double-occupancy cabins begin at US$2485, airfare from all west coast North American cities included,when booked through **Saga Holidays Ltd.** (120 Boylston St., Boston, MA 02116 U.S.A.; tel. 800-343-0273).

For information on cruises to the Marquesas Islands aboard the freighter *Aranui*, see "Getting Around" below.

Yacht Tours

Bareboat and shareboat yacht charters in the Leeward Islands are offered by **The Moorings Ltd.** (19345 US 19 North, Ste. 402, Clearwater, FL 34624 U.S.A.; tel. 813-530-5424). Bareboat prices begin at US$311 a day for a small yacht accommodating five and go up to US$569 daily for a large 10-person sailing boat. Prices are 10% higher during the March to Oct. high

season. "Sail-away gourmet" provisioning is US$29 pp a day (plus US$85 a day for a cook, if required). If you're new to sailing, a skipper can be hired at US$95 a day. The charterer is responsible for the skipper/cook's provisions. Security insurance is US$14 a day and local tax three percent. All charters are from noon to noon. For singles and couples who don't wish to charter an entire yacht, The Moorings has six-night "Cabin 'N Cruise" shareboat charters costing US$1499 pp from Nov. to Feb., US$100 more the rest of the year. Captain and cook are provided and the price includes double occupancy accommodation and most meals, but airfare is extra.

Ocean Voyages Inc. (1709 Bridgeway, Sausalito CA 94965-1994 U.S.A.; tel. 415-332-4681) arranges yacht charters to the remote islands of the Tuamotus and Marquesas. There are also two annual trips from Tahiti to Pitcairn Island (US$6250 for 57 days all inclusive). Ask Ocean Voyages about shareboat yacht cruises on fixed one- and two-week itineraries, usually between Huahine and Bora Bora. Individuals are welcome, and there are about 10 departures a year from April to November. Scuba diving is possible at extra cost on some boats (ask). Trips should be booked and paid for at least 60 days in advance.

Cruising Connection (Box 31496, San Francisco, CA 94131 U.S.A.; tel. 415-337-8330) is an independent yacht charter brokerage arranging bareboat charters throughout the region. A European company arranging bareboat charters in Polynesia is **Yachting Partners International** (28/29 Richmond Place, Brighton, BN2 2NA, East Sussex, England; tel. 0273-571722).

In Australia try **Charter World** (579 Hampton St., Hampton 3188, Australia; tel. 03-521-0033) which arranges bareboat yacht charters with The Moorings and ATM Yachting on Raiatea. Prices per night for the whole bareboat (not pp) are A$485 for a six-berth Beneteau 38, A$570 for an eight-berth Beneteau 43, A$655 for a 10-berth Beneteau 432, and A$795 for a 12-berth Beneteau 51. If you have a small group, yachting works out cheaper and much more exciting than a hotel-based holiday, though a knowledge of sailing is required

BY SAILING YACHT

Papeete is one of the prime yachting centers of the South Pacific. If you don't have your own boat and can't afford a charter, signing on as crew is an alternative. After a month at sea some of the original crew may have flown home or onward, opening a place for you at Tahiti. Cruising yachts are recognizable by their foreign flags, wind-vane steering gear, sturdy appearance, and laundry hung out to dry. Ask around. It's also quite possible to arrive this way. The **Seven Seas Cruising Association** (521 South Andrews Ave., Suite 10, Fort Lauderdale, FL 33301 U.S.A.; tel. 305-463-2431) is in touch with yachties all around the Pacific.

Most yachts sail from California to Tahiti via the Marquesas or Hawaii, then on to Rarotonga, Vava'u, Suva, and New Zealand. In the other direction, you'll sail on the westerlies from New Zealand to a point south of the Australs, then north on the trades to Tahiti. Some 300 yachts leave the U.S. West Coast for Tahiti every year, almost always crewed by couples or men only. Most stay in the South Seas about a year before returning to North America. Cruising yachts average about 150 km a day. When calculating time, allow a month to get from the West Coast to Hawaii, then another month from Hawaii to Papeete. Be aware of the hurricane season Nov. to March as few yachts will be cruising at this time.

If you've never crewed before it's better to try for a short passage the first time. Once at sea there's no way they'll turn around to accommodate a seasick crew member. Good captains evaluate crew on personality and attitude more than experience, so don't lie. Be honest and open when interviewing with a skipper—a deception will soon become apparent.

To crew on a yacht you must be willing to wash and iron clothes, cook, steer, keep watch at night, and help with engine work. Other jobs might include changing and resetting sails, cleaning the boat, scraping the bottom, pulling up the anchor, climbing the main mast to watch for reefs, etc. Expense-sharing crew members pay US$50 or more a week per person. Crew members are very much under the control of the captain who's entitled to hold their passports and onward plane tickets. If there's any chance you'll want to do something like this, read up on sailing before you leave home.

DIANA LASICH HARPER

GETTING AROUND

BY AIR

The domestic carrier, **Air Tahiti** (B.P. 314, Papeete; tel. 42-24-44), is the largest private company in Tahiti-Polynesia. It's owned by its 500 employees (15%), the territorial government (19%), local banks (24%), UTA (7.5%), and small local shareholders (34.5%). Air Tahiti flies to 35 airstrips in every corner of Tahiti-Polynesia with important hubs at Papeete (Windward Islands), Bora Bora (Leeward Island), Rangiroa (western Tuamotus), Hao (eastern Tuamotus), and Nuku Hiva (Marquesas).

Air Tahiti doesn't allow stopovers on its tickets, so if you're flying RT from Tahiti to Bora Bora and want to stop at Raiatea on the way out and Huahine on the way back, you'll have to purchase four separate tickets (total US$285). No student discounts are available but persons under 25 and over 60 can get discounts of up to 50% on certain flights by paying f.1000 for a discount card *(carte de réduction)*.

A slightly better deal than point-to-point fares are the Air Tahiti "Air Passes." These are valid 28 days but only one stopover can be made on each island included in the package. For example, you can go Papeete-Moorea-Huahine-Raiatea-Bora Bora-Papeete for f.29,000. Otherwise pay f.43,500 for Papeete-Moorea-Huahine-Raiatea-Bora Bora-Rangiroa-Manihi-Papeete. This compares with an individual ticket price of f.32,150 to do the first circuit, f.64,800 for the second, which makes an air pass good value if you want to get to Rangiroa and Manihi as well as Bora Bora but hardly worth considering if you're only going as far as Bora Bora. The passes may be used on Air Moorea flights to Moorea but are not valid for the Austral or Marquesas islands. Tahiti Tourist Board offices around the world act as Air Tahiti agents, so inquire at any of them about Air Passes. The passes are non-refundable once travel has begun.

Air Tahiti tickets are refundable at the place of purchase, but you must cancel your reservations at least two hours before flight time to avoid a f.1000 penalty. Do this in person and have your flight coupon amended. "No shows" are charged f.2000 to make a new reservation. It's not necessary to reconfirm confirmed reservations for flights between Tahiti, Moorea, Huahine, Raiatea, Bora Bora, Rangiroa, and Manihi, but elsewhere it's essential to reconfirm. Beware of planes leaving 20 minutes early.

The main Air Tahiti office in Papeete is upstairs in Fare Tony, the commercial center off boulevard Pomare just west of rue Georges Lagarde. They're closed on weekends. Check carefully to make sure all the flights listed in their published timetable are actually operating! Any travel agency in Papeete can also book Air Tahi-

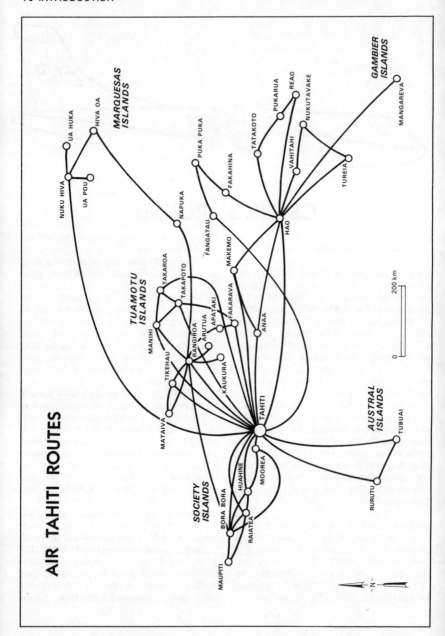

AIR TAHITI ROUTES

ti flights for the same price and the service tends to be better than at the Air Tahiti office itself.

If you buy your ticket locally, the baggage allowance on domestic flights is 10 kilograms. If your flight tickets were purchased prior to your arrival in Tahiti-Polynesia, however, the allowance is 20 kilograms. Exceptions are flights to Ua Huka and Ua Pou where the small size of the aircraft makes the 10-kilogram limit mandatory for everyone. Fresh fruit and vegetables cannot be carried from Tahiti to the Austral, Tuamotu, Gambier, or Marquesas islands.

Air Tahiti uses four 46-seat ATR 42 aircraft and one 20-seat Dornier 228. Two 66-seat ATR 72s will join the fleet in 1994. The Italian-made ATRs are economical in fuel consumption and maintenance requirements and perform well under island conditions. Smoking aboard the aircraft is prohibited on flights under one hour. On Bora Bora, Maupiti, and Nuku Hiva passengers are transferred from the airport to town by boat. This ride is included in the airfare at Bora Bora, but costs extra at Maupiti (f.400) and Nuku Hiva (f.800).

An Air Tahiti subsidiary, **Air Moorea** (B.P. 6019, Papeete; tel. 42-44-29), has hourly flights between Tahiti and Moorea (f.2750 OW) during daylight hours only. Reservations are not necessary on this commuter service. Just show up 15 minutes before the flight you wish to take. The Air Moorea terminal is in a separate building at the east end of Faaa Airport. You can also charter an Air Moorea plane. It's a big part of the Moorea experience to go over by ferry but you could consider returning to Tahiti by plane.

Air Tahiti Services

Air Tahiti flies from Papeete to Hauhine (f.8400), Raiatea (f.9750), and Bora Bora (f.11,550) several times a day. Three times a week there's a direct connection from Moorea to Huahine (f.9050), as well as a flight from Raiatea to Maupiti (f.5350) four times a week. The four weekly transversal flights between Bora Bora and Rangiroa (f.19,000) eliminate the need to backtrack to Papeete (no flight operates westbound from Rangiroa *to* Bora Bora, however).

Flights between Papeete and Rangiroa (f.12,950) operate daily, continuing on from Rangiroa to Manihi (f.8400) three times a week. Air Tahiti has numerous flights to the East Tuamotu atolls and Mangareva, but these are usually closed to tourists due to French military activity in the area. Check with Air Tahiti or the Tahiti Tourist Board for the current situation. Many flights between outer islands of the Tuamotus operate in one direction only.

Flights bound for the Marquesas are the longest, most expensive, and most heavily booked of Air Tahiti's services. Try to get confirmed reservations before arriving in Tahiti-Polynesia if you'll be heading this way. A weekly Dornier 228 flight links Rangiroa to Atuona (f.24,150). More commonly used is the ATR 42 service from Papeete to Nuku Hiva (f.37,800), operating twice a week. Once a week this flight continues to Hiva Oa. At Nuku Hiva the Papeete flights connect for Ua Pou (f.4700), Atuona (f.8400), and Ua Huka (f.4950). If you know you'll be going on to Hiva Oa, Ua Huka, or Ua Pou, get a through ticket there from Papeete; the fare is the same as a ticket only as far as Nuku Hiva.

The Austral Group is better connected to Papeete, with flights to Rurutu (f.17,350) and Tubuai (f.19,450) three times a week. These operate Papeete-Rurutu-Tubuai-Papeete twice a week and Papeete-Tubuai-Rurutu-Papeete weekly, with the leg Tubuai-Rurutu costing f.7900.

During July and August, the peak holiday season, extra flights are scheduled. Air Tahiti is fairly reliable. Still, you should never schedule a flight back to Papeete on the same day that your international flight leaves Tahiti. It's always best to allow a couple of days leeway in case there's a problem with the air service. Maybe save your travels to Moorea or around Tahiti till the end.

BY SEA

The best way to really get the feel of Tahiti-Polynesia is to take a field trip by ship. And there's a certain romance and adventure to taking an interisland freighter. You can go anywhere by copra boat, including islands without airstrips and popular resorts like Moorea, Bora Bora, and Rangiroa. Ships leave Papeete several times a day for the different island groups. You'll meet local people and fellow travelers, and receive a gentle introduction to the island of your choice. Problems about overweight baggage, tight reservations, and airport transport are eliminated, and travel by ferry or passenger-carrying freighter is four times cheaper than the plane. Sea sickness, cockroaches, diesel fumes, and the heavy scent of copra are all part of the experience.

Below you'll find specific information on the main interisland boats. The tourist office in Papeete also has lists. Prices and schedules have been fairly stable over the past few years and new services are being added all the time. Lots of visitors travel this way to Moorea and Bora Bora, so don't feel intimidated if you've never done it before.

For the cheapest ride and the most local color, travel deck class. There's usually an awning in case of rain and you'll be surrounded by Tahitians, but don't count on getting a lot of sleep if you go this way—probably no problem for one night, right? Otherwise take a cabin, which you'll share with three or four other passengers, still a lot cheaper than an airplane seat. Food is usually not included (ask), but may be sold on board. On a long trip you're better off taking all your own food than buying a meal plan.

For any boat trip farther than Moorea check the schedule and pick up tickets the day before at the company office listed below. If you're headed for a remote island outside the Societies or want cabin class, visit the office as far in advance as possible. Except on the *Aranui* it's not possible (nor recommended) to book your passage before arriving on Tahiti. If you really want to go there'll be something leaving around the date you want. On an outer island be wary when someone, even one of the crew, tells you the departure time of a ship: they're as apt to leave early as late.

Boat trips are always smoother westbound than eastbound because you go with the prevailing winds. Take this into consideration if you plan to come back by air or vice versa. *Bon voyage.*

Ferry To Moorea

Two large car ferries named *Tamarii Moorea* (B.P. 9012, Papeete; tel. 43-76-50) shuttle five times a day between Papeete and Vaiare on Moorea (f.700 OW, child under 13 f.350, bicycle f.200). Departure times are posted at the ferry landing on the Papeete waterfront (punctual). Reservations are not required: buy your ticket just before you board. Stroll around the open upper deck and enjoy the scenic one-hour crossing. Coffee is available at the snack bar below. A fast motor vessel, the *Aremiti,* tel. 42-88-88, also makes four trips a day between Tahiti and Moorea for f.800 pp. *Le truck* meets all ferries on the Moorea side and will take you anywhere on that island for f.200, just don't be too slow getting on or it could be full. The ferry crossing can be rather rough on a stormy day so if you're prone to seasickness, try to cross in good weather.

Ships To The Leeward Islands

You have lots of choices if you're headed for the Leeward Islands. Two ships, *Taporo IV* and *Temehani II,* depart Papeete every Mon. afternoon around 1700. *Taporo IV* calls at Huahine at 0200 and Raiatea at 0530, reaching Bora Bora at 1100 Tuesday. It departs for Papeete once again Tues. at 1300, calling at Raiatea at 1500 and Huahine at 1800, reaching Papeete early Wed. morning (you can stay on board till dawn). *Temehani* follows a similar route, but turns around at Raiatea.

Wednesday at 1700 *Taporo IV* makes the shorter trip to Huahine, Raiatea, and Tahaa only, while *Temehani* goes on to Bora Bora. *Taporo IV* undertakes a third weekly voyage from Papeete Fri. at 1700 to all four Leeward Islands, returning to Papeete on Sunday. Although they do make an effort to stick to their timetables these times are approximate—ask at the company offices. Beware of voyages marked "carburant" on the schedules: they don't take passengers.

Temehani is slightly larger than *Taporo IV* and has a good covered sleeping area for deck passengers. They'll open the hold for you if there's not too much cargo. You won't get much sleep, however, due to noise and commotion during the early-morning stops. No mattresses or bedding are provided for deck passengers. *Taporo IV* has a huge inside dormitory with 50 beds.

Fares on the *Taporo IV* to Huahine, Raiatea, and Bora Bora are f.1600 deck, f.2240 dorm. *Temehani* charges the same deck fare, but also has small four-bed cabins which are about twice the deck fare. If you're only traveling between the islands of Huahine, Raiatea, and Bora Bora the interisland deck fare is f.1200 each. A bicycle is about f.600 extra, but if you say nothing and load/unload it yourself you may not be charged. (Don't tell anyone you read that here!) No meals are included, although *Taporo IV* has a snack bar. Take food with you.

The **Bureau Temehani** (B.P. 9015, Papeete; tel. 42-98-83) is near the interisland wharf at Motu Uta and *Taporo IV* has an office in the next room. The main *Taporo IV* ticket agency is the **Compagnie Française Maritime de Tahiti** (B.P. 368, Papeete; tel. 42-63-93) in Fare Ute.

This company also runs the *Taporo V* from Papeete to Maiao monthly. (The CFMT itself has a place in local history, having been founded around 1890 by Sir James Donald who had the contract to supply limes to the British Pacific fleet. At the turn of the century Donald's schooner, the *Tiare Taporo,* was the fastest in Polynesia. The CFMT is still the Lloyd's of London agent.)

Cabin or dormitory space on the ships is recommended—try to reserve at least a week ahead. Deck passage is usually available right up to departure day (except holidays), but buy your ticket in advance as there can be problems for non-Tahitians trying to pay once the ship is underway. In the Leeward Is. buy a ticket from the agent on the wharf as soon as the boat arrives. In Papeete board two hours prior to

LEEWARD ISLAND FERRY SCHEDULES

MV *Taporo IV* (160 passengers)
MV *Raromatai Ferry* (550 passengers, 50 cars)

		Northbound				Ports of		Southbound				
A	C	E	G	I		Call		B	D	F	H	J
1700	1700	1700	1900	1900	dep	Papeete	arr.	0500	0330	0330	0530	0430
0200	0200	0200	0430	0430	arr.	Huahine	dep.	1900	1500	1600	1930	1900
0300	0300	0300	0500	0500	dep.	Huahine	arr.	1800	1400	1500	1900	1830
0530	0500	0500	0700	0700	arr.	Raiatea	dep.	1600	1200	1300	1700	1630
0700	0700	0700	0730	0730	dep.	Raiatea	arr.	1500	1100	1200	1615	1600
	0900	0900	0830		arr.	Tahaa	dep.		1000	1100		1415
		1000	0845		dep.	Tahaa	arr.			1000		1400
1100		1200	1045	0930	arr.	Bora Bora	dep.	1300		0800	1400	1200

A—*Taporo IV* departs Papeete Monday
B—*Taporo IV* departs Bora Bora Tuesday.
C—*Taporo IV* departs Papeete Wednesday.
D—*Taporo IV* departs Tahaa Thursday.
E—*Taporo IV* departs Papeete Friday.
F—*Taporo IV* departs Bora Bora Sunday.
G—*Raromatai Ferry* departs Papeete Tuesday.
H—*Raromatai Ferry* departs Bora Bora Wednesday.
I—*Raromatai Ferry* departs Papeete Friday.
J—*Raromatai Ferry* departs Bora Bora Sunday.
Schedules can be modified during holidays or otherwise.

departure to be sure of a reasonable place on deck to sleep (mark your place with a beach mat). If you've got some time to kill before your ship leaves Papeete, have a look around the coconut-oil mill beside the wharf.

The **Compagnie Maritime des Îles Sous-Le-Vent,** (85 rue des Remparts Prolongee, Fare Ute, Papeete; tel. 43-90-42; open weekdays 0730-1145/1330-1630), handles the car-carrying, 550-passenger *Raromatai Ferry.* This ship departs from the landing behind the tourist office downtown for Huahine, Raiatea, Tahaa, and Bora Bora Tues. and Fri. at 1900. Tickets for walk-on passengers are usually available just prior to departure. Prices from Papeete to Bora Bora are f.3800 for a seat in the salon, f.6000 in a four-berth cabin, f.500 for a bicycle. A double "cruise cabin" is f.17,000 for two people.

The *Raromatai* salon is a spacious sitting room with aircraft-style Pullman seats, but French TV shows blast at you nonstop and the over-powerful air conditioning means you freeze at night unless you have a sleeping bag. The *Raromatai* rolls a lot in rough weather. Between the Leeward Is. the *Raromatai* is a good deal (f.1000 salon interisland) for these daylight crossings with an excellent open promenade deck on top, but on the overnight run between Papeete and Huahine *Taporo IV* and *Temehani* are better value.

Ships To The Austral Islands

The *Tuhaa Pae II* leaves twice a month for the Austral Is.: f.22,750 cabin for the 10-day RT (no meals included). Food is f.2300 pp a day extra. Their office (**Service de Navigacion des Australes,** B.P. 1890, Papeete; tel. 42-93-67) is at the interisland wharf on the west side of the copra sheds. Some of the cabins are below the waterline and very hot. The rear deck has a diesely romantic feel, for a day or two. For sanitary reasons the seats have been removed from the ship's toilets (squat). The *Tuhaa Pae II* calls at Rimatara, Rurutu, Tubuai, Raivavae, and very occasionally Rapa Iti. Maria Atoll is visited annually. Another ship, the *Manava III,* occasionally goes to Tubuai and Raivavae only.

Ships To The Tuamotus And Gambiers

Many smaller copra boats such as the *Auura Nui II, Cobia II, Kauaroa Nui, Manava II, Manava III, Maina Nui, Matariva, Rairoa Nui, Rauhatu, Saint-Corentin, Saint-Xavier Marie-Stella,* and *Vaihere* service the Tuamotu and Gambier groups. Ask around the large workshops west of the interisland wharf. Some of the ships serving the forbidden military zone in the Tuamotus won't accept tourists as passengers.

The *Manava II,* tel. 43-76-17, runs to the northern Tuamotus (Rangiroa, Tikehau, Mataiva, Ahe, Manihi, Takaroa, Takapoto, Aratika, Kauehi, Fakarava, Toau, Apataki, Arutua, and Kaukura) once or twice a month. There are no cabins: the deck passage to Rangiroa is f.3000. Due to the vessel's routing it can take only 22 hours to go from Papeete to Rangiroa but 72 hours to return. The *Manava III,* tel. 43-32-65, departs Papeete for Rangiroa every Monday.

The *Ruahatu,* tel. 43-86-82, runs to the southern Tuamotu and Gambier islands monthly. The deck fare to Rikitea is f.5500 OW for the nine-day trip, plus f.1700 a day for food. Roundtrip on the *Ruahatu* is f.60,000 deck, food included. The *Vaihere,* tel. 43-76-58, plies to the southern Tuamotus (Anaa, Faaite, Katiu, Hikueru, Marokau, Hao, Amanu, and Anaa) twice a month. Deck passage to Anaa or Faaite is f.2000 (no cabins) with f.1700 a day extra for food.

The *Kauaroa Nui* (office opposite the Bureau Temehani at the interisland wharf) has three departures a month for the middle Tuamotus (Fakarava, Faaite, Raraka, Katiu, and Makemo), leaving Thurs. afternoons. Roundtrip fares are f.8000 deck, f.14,000 in a basic double cabin, f.20,000 in an a/c single cabin, no meals included. For information on travel restrictions within the Tuamotu Is. turn to that chapter of this book.

The motor vessel *Dory* leaves every Mon. at 1600 from the Moorea ferry wharf for Tikehau (Tues. 1100), Rangiroa (Tues. 1500), Ahe, Manihi, Arutua, and Apataki, arriving back in Papeete Fri. at 1100 (f.6000 RT). The OW fare to Ahe is about US$30 and there are no cabins. The *Dory* delivers frozen bread, chicken, and ice cream to the islands, picking up fish.

a pirogue Tahiti

Ships To The Marquesas

The *Taporo V* departs Papeete Thurs. at 1400 every two weeks for Tahuata, Hiva Oa, Nuku Hiva, and Ua Pou. Three to eight hours are spent at each port. The RT fare is f.30,000 deck, f.45,000 cabin, or f.16,000 deck and f.22,000 cabin OW to Hiva Oa. Food is included but it's marginal, so take extras like grapefruit and nuts. Bring your own bowl. Meals are served at 0600, 1100, and 1800. No pillows or towels are supplied in the cabins. The shower is open three hours a day. The agent is **Compagnie Française Maritime** (B.P. 368, Papeete; tel. 42-63-93) at Fare Ute. If you can avoid taking the meals you should be able to cut the fare in half.

The *Tamarii Tuamotu II* departs every five weeks to the Marquesas, f.5500 OW deck (no cabins), plus f.1750 a day for basic meals. This ship runs from Papeete direct to the Marquesas, but visits several of the Tuamotu atolls on the way back. It calls at every inhabited bay in the Marquesas (this alone takes 12 days). Check at their city office (Vonken et Cie., B.P. 2606, Papeete; tel. 42-95-07), corner of rue des Remparts and Ave. du Prince Hinoi.

The *Aranui,* a luxury passenger-carrying freighter, cruises 16 times a year between Papeete and the Marquesas. The ship calls at most of the inhabited Marquesas islands, plus a couple of the Tuamotus. The routing might be Papeete-Takapoto-Ua Pou-Nuku Hiva-Hiva Oa-Fatu Hiva-Hiva Oa-Ua Huka-Nuku Hiva-Ua Pou-Rangiroa-Papeete. There's a vigorous daily program with fairly strenuous hikes (included in the tour price). The only docks in the Marquesas are at Taiohae, Hakahau, and Atuona; elsewhere everyone must get in and out of whale boats and wade ashore, a problem for elderly passengers. Still, the *Aranui* is fine for the adventuresome visitor who wants to see a lot in a short time. The food's good aboard the *Aranui* and the largely French roster of passengers is congenial. Aside from three classes of cabins there's a large covered area where the deck passengers sleep.

This modern 105-meter freighter had its inaugural sailing in 1990, replacing a smaller German-built boat that had served the Marquesas since 1981. It's clean and pleasant compared to the other schooners, but more expensive, far more than *Taporo V.* A hundred passengers are accommodated in 32 a/c cabins or given mattresses on the bridge deck. Deck passage for a 15-day, eight-island cruise to the Tuamotus and Marquesas costs US$1390 RT; the cheapest cabin is US$2730 RT (double occupancy), all meals included. An additional US$45 port tax is charged. There are cheaper one-way deck fares on the *Aranui* for local residents, but these are not available to tourists. Their office (**Compag-**

nie Polynésienne de Transport Maritime, B.P. 220, Papeete; tel. 42-62-40, fax 43-48-89) is at the interisland wharf adjacent to Bureau Temehani. In the U.S. advance bookings should be made through the CPTM office at 595 Market St., Ste. 2880, San Francisco, CA 94105 U.S.A. (tel. 415-0677). Schedules are regular and unlike *Tamarii Tuamotu II*, no permit from the harbormaster is required for travel on the *Aranui*.

LOCAL TRANSPORT

By Road

Polynesia's entertaining *le truck* provides an unscheduled passenger service on Tahiti and some outer islands. Passengers sit on long wooden benches in back and there's no problem with luggage. Fares are fairly low and often posted on the side of the vehicle. You pay through the window on the right side of the cab. Drivers are generally friendly and will stop to pick you up anywhere if you wave—they're all privately owned so no way they'd miss a fare! On Tahiti the larger *trucks* leave Papeete for the outlying districts periodically throughout the day until 1700; they continue running to Faaa Airport and the Maeva Beach Hotel until around 2200. On Huahine and Raiatea service is usually limited to a trip into the main town in the morning and a return to the villages in the afternoon. On Moorea and Bora Bora they meet the boats from Papeete.

Car rentals are available at most of the airports served by Air Tahiti, but they ain't cheap. On the big islands of Tahiti and Raiatea there's often a mileage charge, whereas all rentals on Moorea and Bora Bora come with unlimited mileage. Public liability insurance is included by law, but gas and collision damage waver (CDW) insurance are extra. If you can get a small group together consider renting a minibus for a do-it-yourself island tour. Unless you have a major credit card you'll have to put down a cash deposit on the car. Your home driver's license will be accepted, although visitors under the age of 25 are usually refused service unless they show a major credit card. Those under 21 cannot rent a car and you must have had your driver's license for at least a year. Rental

scooters are not available on Tahiti but you can usually get them elsewhere. A strictly enforced local regulation requires you to wear a helmet *(casque)* at all times (f.5000 fine).

Two traffic signs to know: a white line across a red background indicates a one-way street, while a slanting blue line on a white background means no parking. At unmarked intersections in Papeete the driver on the right has priority. As in France and the U.S., driving is on the right-hand side of the road. The speed limit is 40 kph in Papeete, 60 kph around the island. Drive with extreme care in congested areas—traffic accidents are frequent.

Taxis are a rip-off in Papeete, but may be usable elsewhere. Always verify the fare before getting in. The hitching is still fairly good in Polynesia, although local residents along the north side of Moorea are getting tired of it. Hitching around Tahiti is only a matter of time.

By Ocean Kayak

Ocean kayaking is experiencing a boom in Hawaii, but Polynesia is still virgin territory. Virtually every island has a sheltered lagoon readymade for the excitement of kayak touring, but this effortless new transportation mode hasn't yet arrived. So you can be a real independent 20th-century explorer! Most airlines accept folding kayaks as checked baggage at no charge.

Companies like **Long Beach Water Sports** (730 E. 4th St., Long Beach, CA 90802 U.S.A.; tel. 310-432-0187) sell inflatable one- or two-person sea kayaks for around US$1,800, fully equipped. If you're new to the game, LBWS runs four-hour sea kayaking classes (US$55) every Sat. morning and all-day advanced classes (US$80) every couple of months—a must for L.A. residents. They also rent kayaks by the day or week. Write for a free copy of their newsletter *Paddle Strokes*.

Since 1977 **Baidarka Boats** (Box 6001, Sitka, AK 99835 U.S.A.; tel. 907-747-8996) has been a leading supplier of mail-order folding kayaks by Klepper and Nautiraid. **Aire** (Box 3412, Boise, ID 83703 USA; tel. 208-344-7506) makes the "Sea Tiger" self-bailing touring kayak which weighs only 16 kilograms. Write these companies for their free catalogs.

For a better introduction to ocean kayaking than is possible here, check at your local public library for *Sea Kayaking, A Manual for Long-Distance Touring* by John Dowd (Seattle: University of Washington Press, 1981) or *Derek C. Hutchinson's Guide to Sea Kayaking* (Seattle: Basic Search Press, 1985).

By Canoe
Never attempt to take a dugout canoe through even light surf: you'll be swamped. Don't try to pull or lift a canoe by its outrigger: it will break. Drag the canoe by holding the solid main body. A bailer is *essential* equipment. If you get off the beaten track, more than likely a local friend will offer to take you out in his canoe.

By Bicycle
Cycling in Polynesia? Sure, why not? You'll be able to go where and when you please, stop easily and often to meet people and take photos, save money on taxi fares—really *see* the islands. It's great fun, but it's best to have bicycle-touring experience beforehand. Most roads are flat along the coast but be careful on coral roads, especially inclines: if you slip and fall you could hurt yourself badly.

A sturdy, single-speed mountain bike with wide wheels, safety chain, and good brakes might be best. Thick tires and a plastic liner between tube and tire will reduce punctures. Know how to fix your own bike. Take along a good repair kit (pump, puncture kit, freewheel tool, spare spokes, cables, chain links, assorted nuts and bolts, etc.) and a repair manual; bicycle shops are poor to nonexistent in the islands. Don't try riding with a backpack: sturdy, waterproof panniers (bike bags) are required. You'll also want a good lock, and refuse to lend your bike to *anyone*.

Many international airlines will carry a bicycle free as checked luggage. Take off the pedals and panniers, turn the handlebars sideways, and clean off the dirt before checking in (or use a special bike-carrying bag). Air Tahiti won't usually accept bikes on their small planes. Boats sometimes charge a token amount to carry a bike; other times it's free. Bicycling on the island of Tahiti is risky due to wild devil-may-care motorists, but most of the outer islands (Moorea included) have excellent uncrowded roads. It's best to use *le truck* on Tahiti, though a bike will come in real handy on the other islands where *le truck* is rare. The distances are just made for cycling!

INTERNATIONAL AIRPORT

Faaa Airport (PPT) is 5½ km southwest of Papeete. A taxi into town is f.1000 (f.1200 on Sun.), double that after 2200. *Le truck* up on the main highway will take you to the same place for only f.100 (f.150 at night) and they start running around 0530. There's a self-serve tourist information counter at the airport. The airport information numbers are tel. 42-60-61 and 42-95-71. The Westpac Bank (f.350 commission) opens weekdays 0745-1530, and one hour before and after the arrival and departure of all international flights. If you don't change here you can use cash U.S. dollars to pay for your *truck* ride into town.

The airport luggage storage counter is open 0700-1700 and two hours prior to international departures (you hope). They charge f.140 per piece per day (f.300 for surfboards, etc.). A bookstore in the terminal and duty-free shops in the departure lounge can help you spend those leftover Pacific francs. The Fare Hei just outside

LOUISE FOOTE

the terminal sells shell and flower leis for presentation to arriving or departing passengers.

Many flights to Tahiti arrive in the middle of the night, but if you go up the stairs to the terrace, turn left, and stretch out on the clean floor the security guard will wake you gently at dawn. All passengers arriving from Samoa or Fiji must have their baggage fumigated upon arrival, a process which takes about two hours (don't laugh if you're told this is to prevent the introduction of the "rhinoceros" into Polynesia—they mean the rhinoceros *beetle*). Fresh fruits, vegetables, and flowers are prohibited entry. There's no airport tax.

One nice touch is the welcoming committee the Tahiti Tourist Board sends out to meet every incoming international flight. As *pareu*-clad musicians strum their guitars or ukuleles, a smiling *vahine* puts a white tiare Tahiti blossom behind your ear. There's no catch; it's only their way of saying *maeva*.

SOCIETY ISLANDS
The Windward Islands
Tahiti, Moorea, Tetiaroa

King Pomare II of Tahiti
(reigned 1803-1821)

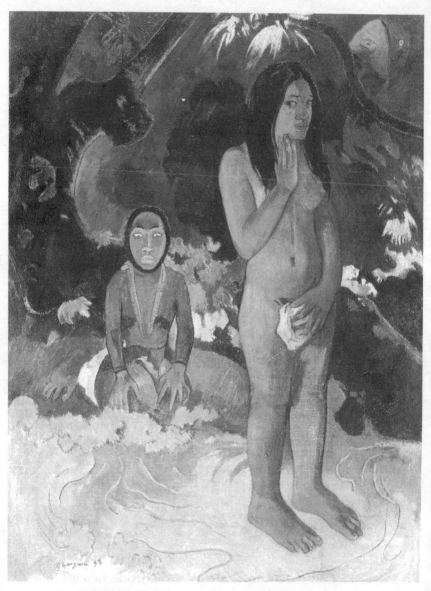

Parau na te Varua ino (Words of the Devil); *Paul Gauguin; National Gallery of Art, Washington; gift of the W. Averell Harriman Foundation in memory of Marie N. Harriman*

TAHITI

Tahiti, largest of the Societies, is an island of legend and song lying in the eye of Polynesia. Though only one of 118, this lush island of around 135,000 inhabitants is paradise itself to most people. Here you'll find an exciting city, big hotels, restaurants, nightclubs, things to see and do, valleys, mountains, reefs, trails, and history, plus transportation to everywhere. Since the days of Wallis, Bougainville, Cook, and Bligh, Tahiti has been the eastern gateway to the South Pacific.

In 1891 Paul Gauguin (goh-GANN) arrived at Papeete after a 63-day sea voyage from France. He immediately felt that Papeete "was Europe—the Europe which I had thought to shake off . . . it was the Tahiti of former times which I loved. That of the present filled me with horror." So Gauguin left the town and rented a native-style bamboo hut in Mataiea on the south coast, where he found happiness in the company of a 14-year-old Tahitian *vahine,* whose "face flooded the interior of our hut and the landscape round about with joy and light." Somerset

Maugham's *The Moon and Sixpence* is a fictional tale of Gauguin's life on the island.

Legends created by the early explorers, amplified in Jean-Jacques Rousseau's "noble savage" and taken up by the travel industry, make it difficult to write objectively about Tahiti. Though the Lafayette Nightclub is gone from Arue and Quinn's Tahitian Hut no longer graces Papeete's waterfront, Tahiti remains a delightful, enchanting place. In the late afternoon, as Tahitian crews practice canoe racing in the lagoon and Moorea gains a pink hue, the romance surfaces. If you steer clear of the traffic jams and congestion in commercial Papeete and avoid the tourist ghettos west of the city, you can get a taste of the magic Gauguin encountered. In fact, it's only on the outer islands of Polynesia, away from the tourists and military complexes, that the full flavor lingers.

The Land
The island of Tahiti accounts for almost a quarter of the land area of Tahiti-Polynesia. Like

TAHITI AND MOOREA

OROHENA (2241m)

POINT VENUS   PAPEETE

TAHITI, NORTH COAST

TOHIVEA (1212m)

MOOREA, EAST COAST

Hawaii's Maui, Tahiti was formed by two ancient volcanos joined at the isthmus of Taravao. The rounded, verdant summits of Orohena (2,241 meters) and Aorai (2,066 meters) rise in the center of Tahiti Nui and deep valleys radiate in all directions from these central peaks. Steep slopes drop abruptly from the high plateaus to coastal plains. The northeast coast is rugged and rocky without a barrier reef and thus exposed to intense, pounding surf; villages lie on a narrow strip between mountains and ocean. The south coast is broad and gentle with large gardens and coconut groves; a barrier reef shields it from the sea's fury.

Tahiti Iti (also called Taiarapu) is a peninsula with no road around it. Mount Rooniu (1,323 meters) is its heart. The populations of big *(nui)* and small *(iti)* Tahiti are concentrated in Papeete and along the coast; the interior of both Tahitis is almost uninhabited. Contrary to the popular stereotype, mostly brown/black beaches of volcanic sand fringe this turtle-shaped island. To find the white/golden sands of the travel brochures you must cross over to Moorea.

Orientation

Almost everyone arrives at Faaa International Airport five km west of Papeete, the capital and main tourist center of Tahiti-Polynesia. East of Papeete are Arue and Mahina with a smattering of hotels and things to see, while south of Faaa lie the commuter communities Punaauia, Paea, and Papara. On the narrow neck of hourglass-shaped Tahiti is Taravao, a refueling stop on your 117-km way around Tahiti Nui. Tahiti Iti is a backwater, with dead-end roads on both sides. Boulevard Pomare curves around Papeete's harbor to the tourist office near the market—that's where to begin. Moorea is clearly visible to the northwest and the mornings are softly, radiantly calm.

Papeete as it looked around the turn of the century

PAPEETE

Papeete (pa-pay-EH-tay) means "Water Basket." The most likely explanation for this name is that islanders originally used calabashes enclosed in baskets to fetch water at a spring behind the present Territorial Assembly. In the 1820s whalers began frequenting its port, which offered better shelter than Matavai Bay. It became the seat of government when young Queen Pomare settled here in 1827. The French governors who "protected" the island from 1842 also used Papeete as their headquarters.

Today Papeete is the political, cultural, economic, and communications hub of Tahiti-Polynesia. Some 69,000 persons live in this cosmopolitan city and its satellite towns, Faaa, Pirae, and Arue—over half the people on the island. "Greater Papeete" extends for 32 km from Paea to Mahina. In addition, some 4,000 French soldiers are stationed here, mostly hardened foreign legionnaires and policemen. The French Navy maintains facilities in the harbor area to support its nuclear-testing program in the Tuamotus. If you don't see any ships it means there's about to be another test and they're down there patrolling the site.

Since the opening of Faaa International Airport in 1961, Papeete has blossomed with new hotels, expensive restaurants, bars with wild dancing, radio towers, skyscrapers, and electric rock bands pulsing their jet-age beat. Where a nail or red feather may once have satisfied a Tahitian, VCRs and Renaults are now in demand. Over 70,000 registered vehicles jam Tahiti's 200 km of roads. Noisy automobiles, motorcycles and mopeds clog Papeete's downtown and roar along the boulevards buffeting pedestrians with pollution and noise. Crossing the street you can literally take your life in your hands.

Yet along the waterfront the yachts of many countries rock luxuriously in their Mediterranean moorings (anchor out and stern lines ashore). Many of the boats are permanent homes for expatriate French working in the city. "Bonitiers" moored opposite the Vaima Center fish for *auhopu* (bonito). One should not really "tour" Papeete, just wander about without any set goal. Visit the highly specialized French boutiques, Chinese stores trying to sell everything, and Tahitians clustered in the market. Avoid the capital on weekends when life washes out into the countryside; on Sunday afternoons it's a ghost town. Explore Papeete, but make it your starting point—not a final destination.

Orientation

Thanks to airline schedules you'll probably arrive at the crack of dawn. Change a traveler's check at the airport bank or use a US$1 bill to take a *truck* to Papeete market. The helpful tourist office on the waterfront nearby opens early, as does the Banque Socredo branch nearby. You'll probably want a hotel in town for the first couple of nights to attend to "business": reconfirm your flights, check out the boats or planes, then kick back.

A trip around the island will fill a day if you're waiting for connections, and Papeete itself can be fun. Fare Ute, north of French naval headquarters, was reclaimed with material dredged from the harbor in 1963. West across a bridge, past more military muscle, is Motu Uta where you may catch your boat. For a day at the beach take a *truck* to Point Venus (see below).

SIGHTS

Papeete

Begin your visit at teeming **Papeete market,** a sensual delight. You'll see Tahitians selling fish, fruit, root crops, and breadfruit, Chinese gardeners with their tomatoes, lettuce, and other vegetables, and Frenchmen or Chinese offering meat and bakery products. The colorful throng is especially picturesque from 1600-1700 when the fishmongers spring to life. The biggest mar-

DIANA LASICH HARPER

ket of the week begins around 0500 Sun. morning and is over by 0730. You can catch a *truck* to anywhere from here.

The streets to the north of the market are lined with two-story Chinese stores built after the great fire of 1884. The US$14-million **Town Hall** on rue Paul Gauguin was inaugurated in 1990 on the site of a smaller colonial building demolished to make way. The architect designed the three-story building to resemble the palace of Queen Pomare that once stood on Place Tarahoi near the present post office. **Notre Dame Catholic Cathedral** (1875) is on rue du Général de Gaulle 1 1/2 blocks southwest of the market. Notice the Polynesian faces and the melange of Tahitian and Roman dress on the striking series of paintings of the crucifixion inside.

Farther down on rue de Gaulle is Place Tarahoi. The **Territorial Assembly** on the left occupies the site of the former royal palace demolished in 1966. The adjacent residence of the French high commissioner is private, but the assembly and its lovely gardens are worth a brief visit. In front of the entrance gate is a monument to **Pouvanaa a Oopa** (1895-1977), a Tahitian WW I hero who struggled all his life for the independence of his country. The plaque on the monument says nothing about Pouvanaa's fight for independence and against the bomb!

Beside the post office across the busy avenue from Place Tarahoi is **Bougainville Park**. A monument to Bougainville himself, who sailed around the world in 1766-69, is flanked by two old naval guns. One, stamped "Fried Krupp 1899," is from the German raider *Seeadler* which ended up on the Maupihaa reef in 1917; the other is off the French gunboat *Zélée* sunk in Papeete harbor by German cruisers in 1914.

Much of the bureaucracy works along Ave. Bruat just west, a gracious tree-lined French provincial avenue. You may observe French justice in action at the **courthouse** (weekdays 0800-1100/1400-1600). The public gallery is up the stairway and straight ahead. Farther up Ave. Bruat, beyond the War Memorial, are the colonial-style French army barracks, **Quartier Broche**.

Back on the waterfront just before the Protestant church is the **Tahiti Perles Center** (B.P. 850, Papeete; tel. 43-85-58). A black-pearl museum (weekdays 0800-1730, Sat. 0900-1200;

1. the beach near Club Med, Moorea (Don Pitcher); 2. a peak on Moorea (Tahiti Tourist Board)

1. Mouaroa or "Shark's Tooth," Moorea (Paul Bohler); **2.** Papeete, Tahiti (Tahiti Tourist Board)

admission free) and aquarium are the main attractions, but look around the showroom where the famous Gambier black pearls are sold. A 20-minute video presentation shown on request explains how cultured black pearls are "farmed" in the Gambier Islands.

Next to the pearl museum is Paofai, the headquarters of the Evangelical Church in Tahiti-Polynesia, with a church (rebuilt 1980), public cafeteria, girl's hostel, and health clinic. The British consulate occupied the hostel site from 1837 to 1958 and George Pritchard had his office here. Continue west along the bay past the outrigger racing canoes to the "neo-Polynesian" **OTAC Cultural Center** (1973) which houses a library, snack bar, notice boards, and auditoriums set among pleasant grounds. The municipal swimming pool is beyond.

Back east of the downtown is the Catholic **Archbishop's Palace** (1869), a lonely remnant of the Papeete that Gauguin saw. To get there take the road behind the Catholic Cathedral, keep straight, and ask for the *archevêché catholique*. Without doubt, this is the finest extant piece of colonial architecture in a territory where historic buildings are fast disappearing. The park grounds planted in citrus and the modern open-air church nearby also merit a look.

Bain Loti

If you'd like to make a short trip out of the city, go to the corner of rue Paul Gauguin and rue Albert Leboucher near the market and take a "Mamao-Titioro" *truck* to the **Bain Loti**, three km up the Fautaua Valley from the Mormon Temple. A bust of writer Pierre Loti marks the spot where he had the love affair described in *The Marriage of Loti,* but the area has been spoiled by tasteless construction. Since the valley is part of a water catchment you're not permitted to walk farther up, the most beautiful part.

Back on Ave. Georges Clemenceau near the Mormon Temple is the impressive **Kanti Chinese Temple,** built in 1986. On the fourth floor at **Mamao Hospital** (1967) nearby you can peep at newborn babies through the windows!

East Of Papeete

Point Venus and the tomb of Pomare V at Arue (pronounced a-roo-AY) can be easily done as a half-day sidetrip from Papeete by *truck* (12 km each way). Begin by taking a "Mahina" *truck* from the market to the **Hyatt Regency Hotel** (PK 8.1) on One Tree Hill. There's a superb view of Point Venus, Tahiti, and Moorea from the "Governor's Bench" on the knoll just beyond the hotel entrance. In Matavai Bay below the Hyatt Regency, Capt. Samuel Wallis anchored in 1767 after having "discovered" Tahiti.

Go into the hotel itself to see the Polynesian artifacts and historical displays tastefully arrayed in showcases around the lobby. Outside the gift shop downstairs is a free cold water fountain. The Mahana Bar by the pool nearby offers two drinks for the price of one during happy hour 1700-1800. This hotel was built in 1968

Matavai Bay, Tahiti, as it appeared in the early 19th century

Capt. James Cook (1728-1779) as painted at the Cape of Good Hope by John Webber, 1776

on a spectacular series of terraces down the hillside to conform to a local regulation that no building should be more than two-thirds the height of a coconut tree.

Catch another *truck* or walk on to **Point Venus** (PK 10). Captain Cook camped on this point between the river and the lagoon during his visit to observe the transit of the planet Venus across the Sun on 3 June 1769. Captain Bligh also occupied Point Venus for two months in 1788 while collecting breadfruit shoots for transportation to the West Indies. Bligh moved his ship over to Arue, where the Yacht Club now is, at Christmas 1788. On 5 March 1797, the first members of the London Missionary Society landed here, as a monument recalls. From Tahiti, Protestantism spread throughout Polynesia and as far as Vanuatu.

Today there's a beautiful park on the point with a 25-meter-high lighthouse (1867) among the palms and ironwood trees. A great trunk of wood inscribed "Wallis 1767," "Bougainville 1768," and "Cook 1769" was placed there for the bicentenary of the observation of the transit of Venus in 1969, even though Bougainville never came near Point Venus. The view of Tahiti across Matavai Bay is superb, and twin-humped Orohena, highest peak on the island, is in view (you can't see it from Papeete itself). Topless sunbathing is common on the wide, dark sands along the bay. Weekdays, Point Venus is a peaceful place, the perfect choice if you'd like to get away from the rat race in Papeete and spend some time at the beach (weekends it gets crowded).

To get in a little **hiking**, take the road inland by the bridge just east of the Point Venus turnoff. You can drive a car 3 1/2 km along the Tuauru River past several ugly garbage dumps, then bushwhack up the valley through a forest of wild orchids. There are many river crossings along the way, so wear rubber booties or immersible tennis shoes. In his *Journal of Researches* Charles Darwin described a hike he made up this way in Nov., 1835.

As you're returning to Papeete stop to visit the **tomb of King Pomare V** at PK 4.7 Arue, five km outside the city. The mausoleum was built in 1879 for Queen Pomare IV, but her remains were subsequently removed to make room for her son, Pomare V, who died of drink in 1891. Paul Gauguin witnessed the funeral. A century earlier on 13 Feb. 1791 his grandfather, Pomare II, then nine, was made first king of Tahiti on the great *marae* (Polynesian temple) which once stood on this spot. Pomare II, the first Christian convert, built a 215-meter-long version of King Solomon's Temple here. Nothing remains of either temple.

AROUND THE ISLAND

A 117-km Route de Ceinture (Belt Road) runs right around Tahiti Nui, the larger part of this hourglass-shaped island. Construction began in the 1820s as a form of punishment. For orientation you'll see red-and-white kilometer stones, called PK *(point kilométrique)*, along the inland side of the road. These are numbered in each direction from Papeete cathedral, meeting at Taravao. Go clockwise to get over the most difficult stretch first; also, you'll be riding on the inside lane of traffic and less likely to go off a cliff in case of an accident (an average of 55 people a year are killed and 700 injured in accidents on the island). If you want an excellent second resource, pick up Bengt Danielsson's *Tahiti, Circle Island Tour Guide* at a Papeete bookstore before you set out. Southern Tahiti is much quieter than the northwest, whereas from Paea to Mahina it's even hard to slow down as tailgating motorists roar behind you.

TAHITI

SOUTH PACIFIC OCEAN

TAHITI NUI

TAHITI ITI
(TAIARAPU PENINSULA)

PARI COAST

VAIAARAVA
VALLEY

VAITEPIHA
VALLEY

VAIPOIRI
GROTTO

MT. ROONIU
(1,332 m)

TAUTIRA

PUEU

VAUFAUFA
VIEWPOINT

PUUNUI RESORT

TEAHUPOO

VAIRAO

VAIAO

TOAHOTU

PORT PHAETON

TARAVAO

AFAAHITI

FARE NANA'O

FAAONE

HITIAA

MAHAENA

TIAREI

ARAHOHO BLOWHOLE

PAPENOO

POINT VENUS

MATAVAI BAY

HYATT REGENCY

MAHINA

OROFARA
LEPER COLONY

PAPENOO
VALLEY

FAARUMAI
FALLS

VAIHARURU
FALLS

TRAIL CLOSED

PITO HITI
(2,110 m)

MT. OROHENA
(2,241 m)

RELAIS
DE LA MAROTO

LAKE VAIHIRIA

ARUE

PIRAE

BAIN LOTI

FARE APE

RAU APE

FARE
HAMUTA

FARE
RAU APE

OFARE
ATA

MT. AORAI
(2,066 m)

PLATEAU OF
LE DIADEME
(1,321 m)

FAUTAUA
VALLEY

FAUTAUA FALLS

PUNARUU
VALLEY

PLATEAU OF
ORANGES

MT. TETUFERA
(1,799 m)

MT. IVIRAIRAI
(1,696 m)

FAAA

PAPEETE

AIRPORT

BEACHCOMBER HOTEL

SOFITEL MAEVA
BEACH HOTEL

MARINA TAINA

LAGOONARIUM

MUSEUM OF TAHITI

PUNAAUIA

OROFERO
VALLEY

PAEA

MARAE OF
ARAHURAHU

MARAA
FERN GROTTO

MARAA

MAHAIATEA

MARAE OF
MAHAIATEA

ATIMAONO

PAPARA

MATAIEA

GAUGUIN
MUSEUM

PAPEARI

0   10 km

N

the "buffoon" of the leper colony, Tahiti

The Northeast Coast

The coast is very rugged all along the northeast side of the island. The **leper colony** at Orofara (PK 13.2) was founded in 1914. Previously the colony was on Reao atoll in the Tuamotus, but this proved too remote to service. Some 50 patients are housed at Orofara today.

Surfers ride the waves at Chinaman's Bay, Papenoo (PK 16). The bridge over the broad **Papenoo River** (PK 17.1) allows a view up the largest valley on Tahiti.

At the **Arahoho Blowhole** (PK 22) jets of water shoot up through holes in the lava rock beside the highway at high tide. Just a little beyond it a road to the right leads to the three **Faarumai Waterfalls**. Vaimahuta Falls are accessible on foot in five minutes along the easy path to the right across the bridge. The trail to the left leads to two more waterfalls, but it's more difficult—even impassible if the river is high. The farthest falls have a pool deep enough for swimming. Bring insect repellent. Beware of theft if you park a rental car at these falls.

At **Mahaena** (PK 32.5) is the battleground where 441 well-armed French troops defeated a dug-in Tahitian force twice their size on 17 April 1844 in the last fixed confrontation in the French-Tahitian War. The Tahitians carried on a guerrilla campaign another two years until the French captured their main mountain stronghold.

The French ships *La Boudeuse* and *L'Étoile* carrying explorer Louis-Antoine de Bougainville anchored by the southernmost of two islets off **Hitiaa** (PK 37.6) on 6 April 1768. Unaware that an Englishman had visited Tahiti a year before, Bougainville christened the island "New Cythera" after the Greek isle where love goddess Aphrodite rose from the sea. A plaque near the bridge recalls the event. The clever Tahitians recognized a member of Bougainville's crew as a woman disguised as a man. An embarrassed Jeanne Baret entered history as the first woman to sail around the world.

From the bridge over the Faatautia River at PK 41.8 **Vaiharuru Falls** are visible in the distance. The American filmmaker John Huston intended to make a movie of Herman Melville's *Typee* here in 1957. When Huston's other Melville film, *Moby Dick,* became a box office flop the idea was dropped.

Tahiti Iti

At Taravao (PK 53), on the strategic isthmus joining the two Tahitis where the PKs meet, is an **old fort** built by the French in 1844 to cut off the Tahitians who had retreated to Tahiti Iti after the battle mentioned above. Germans were in-

Capt. Louis-Antoine de Bougainville

terned here during WW II and the fort is still in use today.

The small assortment of grocery stores, banks, gasoline stations, and restaurants at Taravao make it a good place to break your trip around the island, but accommodations in this area are inadequate. If you have your own transportation, three roads are explorable on rugged Tahiti Iti. If you're hitching or traveling by *truck*, choose the Tautira route.

A paved nine-km road runs straight up the Taravao Plateau from just before the hospital in Taravao. If you have a car and only time to take one of Tahiti Iti's three roads, this one should be your choice. At the 600-meter level on top is the **Vaiufaufa Viewpoint** with a breathtaking view of both Tahitis. No one lives up here; in good weather it would be possible to pitch a tent on the grassy hill above the reservoir at the end of the road (or sleep in your car if it's raining). The herds of cows grazing peacefully among the grassy meadows give this upland an almost Swiss air. A paved side-road near the viewpoint cuts down to join the Tautira road.

An excellent 18-km highway runs east from Taravao to **Tautira**, where Spaniards from Peru attempted to establish a Catholic mission in 1774; it lasted for only one year. Scottish author Robert Louis Stevenson stayed at Tautira for two months in 1888 and called it "the most beautiful spot, and its people the most amiable, I have ever found." The road peters out a few km beyond Tautira. Obstructions by landowners and high cliffs make it impractical to try hiking right around the Pari Coast to Teahupoo. Intrepid sea kayakers have been known to paddle the 30 km around, although a wild four-km stretch is not protected by reefs.

The unoccupied beach at the mouth of the **Vaitepiha River** near Tautira is a perfect campsite. A dirt road runs two km up the right bank of the river, where you could find more secluded places to camp. Hike beyond the end of the road for a look at this majestic, unoccupied valley and a swim in the river. In the dry season, rugged backpackers could hike south across the peninsula to the Vaiarava Valley and Teahupoo in two days (guide necessary). The ruins of at least three old *maraes* are at the junction of the Vaitia and Vaitepiha rivers a cou-

ple of hours inland, and it's reported that tikis are hidden in there.

The third road on Tahiti Iti runs 18 km along the south coast to Teahupoo. At the bottom of the hill below Puunui Resort is a **marina** with an artificial white-sand beach (admission f.300) where outrigger canoes can be rented for f.500 an hour. Boat excursions to Vaipoiri Grotto can sometimes be arranged here. The marina restaurant offers a lunchtime salad bar on weekends. American pulp Western writer Zane Grey had his fishing camp near here in the '30s. Just east of the marina is a natural white-sand beach. **Restaurant Anne de Bretagne** (tel. 57-18-08) faces this beach (crêpes from f.250 all day on weekends, fish and chips for f.900). It's one of the best of its kind in Polynesia, and if you're there for dinner you'll see fisherman spearing by torchlight on the opposite reef. Tahiti's best surfing is possible out there in the pass, but you'll need a boat.

The **Teahupoo** road ends abruptly at a river crossed by a narrow footbridge. There's an excellent mountain view from this bridge, but walk east along the beach to capture one of the only remaining glimpses of outer-island Polynesian life-style remaining on Tahiti. After a couple of km the going becomes difficult due to yelping dogs, seawalls built into the lagoon, fences, fallen trees, and *tapu* signs. Beyond is the one-time domain of "nature men" who tried to escape civilization by living alone with nature over half a century ago.

Three hours on foot from the end of the road is **Vaipoiri Grotto**, a large water-filled cave best reached by boat. Try hiring a motorized canoe or hitch a ride with someone at the end of the road. Beyond this the high cliffs of Te Pari terminate all foot traffic along the shore; the only way to pass is by boat. All the land east of Teahupoo is well fenced off, so finding a campsite would involve getting someone's permission.

Gauguin Museum
Port Phaeton on the southwest side of the Taravao Isthmus is an excellent harbor. Timeless oral traditions tell that the first Polynesians to reach Tahiti settled at Papeari (PK 52—measured now from the west). In pre-contact times the chiefly family of this district was among the most prestigious on the island.

Teha'amana, who lived with Gauguin at Mataiea from 1892-93, was Gauguin's great love and is mentioned often in Noa Noa.

The **Gauguin Museum** (B.P. 7029, Taravao; tel. 57-10-58; open daily 0900-1700, f.450) is at PK 51.2 in Papeari District. The museum, opened in 1965, tells the painter's tormented life story and shows the present location of his works throughout the world. Strangely, Gauguin's Tahitian mistresses get little attention in the museum. A couple of his minor woodcarvings and prints are exhibited.

Ex-Paris stockbroker Paul Gauguin arrived at Papeete in 1891 at age 43 in search of the roots of "primitive" art. He lived at Mataiea with his 14-year-old mistress Teha'amana for a year and a half, joyfully painting. In 1893 he returned to France with 66 paintings and about a dozen woodcarvings which were to establish his reputation. Unfortunately, his exhibition flopped and Gauguin returned to Tahiti a second time, infected with V.D. and poor, settling at Punaauia. After a failed suicide he recovered somewhat and in 1901 a Paris art dealer named Vollard signed a contract with Gauguin assuring him a

monthly payment of 350 francs and a purchase price of 250 francs per picture. His financial problems alleviated, the painter left for Hiva Oa, Marquesas Islands, to find an environment uncontaminated by Western influences. During the last two years of his life at Atuona, Gauguin's eccentricities put him on the wrong side of the ecclesiastical and official hierarchies. He died in 1903 at age 53, a near outcast among his countrymen in the islands, yet today a Papeete street and school are named after him!

The two-meterish, two-ton stone tiki on the museum grounds is said to be imbued with a sacred *tapu* spell. Tahitians believe this tiki, carved on the island of Raivavae hundreds of years ago, still lives. The three Tahitians who moved the statue here from Papeete in 1965 all died mysterious deaths within a few weeks. A curse is still said to befall all who touch the tiki.

A **botanical garden** rich in exotic species is part of the Gauguin Museum complex (f.250 extra admission). This 137-hectare garden was created in 1919-21 by the American botanist Harrison Smith (1872-1947) who introduced over 200 new species to the island, among them the sweet grapefruit (pomelo), mangosteen, rambutan, and durian. Two Galapagos tortoises have lived in an enclosure in the gardens since 1930. The park along the beach behind the museum snack bar is free to everyone.

Lake Vaihiria

From PK 47.6 a rough track leads 12 km up to **Lake Vaihiria**, Tahiti's only lake. The route follows the Vaihiria River, which has been harnessed for hydroelectricity. Two km up the road you'll encounter a white hydro substation and the first of a series of "Piste Privée" signs advising motorists that the road is closed to nonresidents, though open to pedestrians. This regulation is not always enforced; in dry weather a rental car could continue another five km to a dam and the lower power station, provided the chain across the road isn't locked.

A km beyond is an archaeological site with restored *marae*. Three km beyond this (11 km from the main road) is a second dam and an upper (larger) power station. Beyond this point only a 4WD jeep could proceed, passing prominent "Danger" signs, another km up a steep concrete track to Lake Vaihiria itself.

Sheer cliffs and spectacular waterfalls squeeze in around the spring-fed lake, and the shore would make a fine campsite (overrun by mosquitos). Native floppy-eared eels known as *puhi taria* up to 1.8 meters long live in these cold waters. With its luxuriant vegetation, this rain-drenched 473-meter-high spot is one of the most evocative on the island. The track proceeds up and through a 200-meter tunnel and over to the Papenoo Valley, a four-hour trip by 4WD jeep or two days on foot. One must wade through the rivers about 20 times.

The **Relais de la Maroto** (B.P. 5664, Pirae; tel. 41-48-60 or 43-65-87) in the upper Papenoo Valley provides comfortable accommodation at f.5000 pp, f.4000 extra for breakfast and dinner. Other than 4WD jeep and foot, the only access is by chartered helicopter (f.42,000 RT). The Relais provides a good base for exploring the many archeological remains in this area.

The South Coast

Tahiti-Polynesia's only golf course, the **International Golf Course Olivier Breaud** (B.P. 12008, Papara; tel. 57-40-32) at PK 41, Atimaono, stretches up to the mountainside on the site of "Terre Eugenie," a cotton and sugar plantation established by Scotsman William Stewart at the time of the U.S. Civil War (1863). Many of today's Tahitian Chinese are descended from Chinese laborers imported to do the work. A novel by A. T'Serstevens, *The Great Plantation,* was set here. The present 6,355-meter, 18-hole course (run by the Tahiti Tourist Board) was laid out in 1970 with a par 72 for men, par 73 for women. If you'd like to do a round, the greens fees are f.2000 and clubs rent for another f.2500 (open daily 0800-1700). The Tahiti Open in June or July attracts professionals from around the Pacific.

The **Marae of Mahaiatea** (PK 39.2) at Papara was once the most hallowed temple on Tahiti. Captain Cook's botanist Joseph Banks wrote: "It is almost beyond belief that Indians could raise so large a structure without the assistance of iron tools." Less than a century later planter William Stewart raided the *marae* for building materials and storms did the rest. Today it's only a rough heap of stones, but still worth visiting for its aura and setting. The unmarked turnoff is a hundred meters west of Chez Mahaiatea Restaurant, then straight down to the beach.

Surfers take the waves at Papara Beach (PK 38), one of the best sites on Tahiti. By the church at **Papara** (PK 36) is the grave of Dorence Atwater (1845-1910), U.S. consul to Tahiti from 1871 to 1888. Atwater's claim to fame dates back to the American Civil War when he recorded the names of 13,000 dead Union prisoners at Andersonville Prison, Georgia, from lists the Confederates had been withholding. Himself a

Tahiti's Mahaiatea Marae as illustrated in James Wilson's A Missionary Voyage (London, 1799): this 11-step pyramid was once the largest pagan temple on the island.

Union prisoner, Atwater escaped with his list in March 1865. When you consider the concern the U.S. government still shows about troops allegedly missing in Vietnam, the importance of Atwater's contribution is clear. Atwater's tombstone provides details.

At PK 31 stop for some "Eau de Roche, Pape Mato"—fill your water bottle with the fresh mineral water! **Maraa Fern Grotto** (PK 28.5) is also by the road just across the Paea border. An optical illusion, the grotto at first appears small but is quite deep. Some Tahitians believe *varua ino* (evil spirits) lurk in the shadowy depths. Others say that if you follow an underground river back from the grotto you'll emerge at a wonderful valley in the spirit world. Paul Gauguin wrote of a swim he took across the small pond in the cave; you're also welcome to jump in the ice-cold black water.

The Southwest Coast

The **Marae Arahurahu** at PK 22.5, Paea, is up the road from Magasin Laut—take care, the sign faces Papeete, not visible if you're traveling clockwise. This temple, lying in a tranquil verdant spot under high cliffs, is perhaps Tahiti's only remaining pagan mystery. The ancient open altars built from thousands of cut stones were completely restored in 1954 (open daily, free). Historical pageants recreating pagan rites are performed here during the July festivities.

For some hiking, Paea's **Orofero Valley** is recommended; camping might be possible up beyond the end of the road (six km). From the main highway take the first road inland south of the large Catholic church by the Vaiatu River at PK 20. You can drive a car three km up. When you get to the *tapu* sign, park, cross the river, and continue up the other side on foot. A jeep track runs another three km up the valley (half-hour walk) through half a dozen river crossings (wear rubber booties or zories). At the end of the road a tall waterfall is to the left and the trail continues ahead. Orofero is one of the few Tahitian valleys free of trash!

At PK 20 by the mouth of the Vaiatu River **handicrafts** are sold in a pavilion beside the tiny post office. Three long rectangular compounds comprise **Marae Taata,** just off the road inland from PK 19.

The West Coast

On Fishermen's Point, Punaauia, is the **Museum of Tahiti and the Islands** (B.P. 6272, Faaa; tel. 58-34-76; open Tues.-Sun. 0930-1700; admission f.300). Located in a large, modern complex on the lagoon about a km down a narrow road from PK 15.1, this worthwhile museum has four halls devoted to the natural environment, the origins of the Polynesians, Polynesian culture, and the history of Polynesia. What isn't covered is the history of France's nuclear-testing program in Polynesia and how the Polynesians feel about it. Outside is a huge double-hulled canoe and Capt. Cook's anchor from Tautira. Most of the captions are in French, Tahitian, and English (photography allowed).

When the waves are right you can sit on the seawall behind the museum and watch the Tahitian surfers bob and ride, with the outline of Moorea behind. On your way back to the main highway from the museum, look up to the top of the hill at an **old fort** used by the French to subjugate the Tahitians in the 1840s. The crown-shaped pinnacles of **Le Diadème** (1,321 meters) are also visible from this road.

If you want to see pollution on a massive scale follow the route up the once-beautiful **Punaruu Valley** behind the Punaauia industrial zone (PK 14.8). You can drive a normal car five km up a valley incredibly trashed out with garbage dumps all the way. At the end of the valley is a water catchment and, although the way leads on to the fantastic **Plateau of Oranges,** entry is forbidden. Tahitian enterprises dump their refuse in valleys all around the island, but this has got to be the ugliest!

Gauguin had his studio at PK 12.6 Punaauia from 1896 to 1901, but nothing remains of it; his *Two Tahitian Women* was painted here. The **Lagoonarium** (B.P. 2381, Papeete; tel. 43-62-90) below the lagoon behind Captain Bligh Restaurant at PK 11.4, Punaauia, provides a vision of the underwater marinelife of Polynesia safely behind glass. The big tank full of black-tip sharks is a feature. Entry is f.500 pp, open daily, half price for restaurant customers, and f.300 for children under 12. The shark feeding takes place around noon.

Punaauia and Paea are Tahiti's "Gold Coast," with old colonial homes along the lagoonside

This photo, taken by Bengt Danielsson in the 1950s and published in his book Gauguin in the South Seas, *shows Emile Marae a Tai, son of Gauguin and his vahine, Pau'ura a Tai. The resemblence is striking.*

and *nouveau riche* villas dotting the hillside above. At PK 8 is the turnoff for the RDO bypass to Papeete, Tahiti's only superhighway!

On the old airport road just north are Tahiti's biggest hotels: the **Sofitel Maeva Beach** (PK 7.5) and **Beachcomber** (PK 7), both worth a stop—though their beaches are polluted. From the point where the Beachcomber is today, the souls of deceased Tahitians once leapt onto their journey to the spirit world. A sunset behind Moorea's jagged peaks across the Sea of the Moon from either of these hotels is a spectacular finale to a circle-island tour. If you're there by 1730 you'll also coincide with happy hour at the bar.

If you've been living rough on your way around the island and could use a wash, patronize the public toilets at Faaa International Airport (PK 5.5). The runway here was created in 1959-61, using material dredged from the lagoon or trucked in from the Punaruu Valley. The municipality of Faaa has declared itself a nuclear-free zone; a monument at a Faaa intersection recalls Tahitian resistance to French colonialism. As you reenter Papeete, **Uranie Cemetery** (PK 1.5) is on your right.

The west coast of Tahiti can also be visited as a day-trip from Papeete; start by taking a *truck* to Paea and work your way back. *Trucks* back to Papeete from the vicinity of the Maeva Beach Hotel run late into the night, but the last one from the Museum of Tahiti is around 1630.

MOUNTAIN CLIMBING

Tahiti's finest climb is to the **summit of Aorai** (2,066 meters), third-highest peak on the island. A beaten 10-km track all the way to the top makes a guide optional. Food, water, flashlight, and long pants *are* required, plus a sleeping bag and sweater if you plan to spend the night up there. Some maps show "chalets" and "refuges" along the trail, but don't count on it. They're often blown away by hurricanes, though at last report the ones at Fare Mato and Fare Ata were usable. There are places to pitch a tent at Hamuta (900 meters), Fare Mato (1,400 meters), Fare Ata (1,800 meters), and on the summit itself, but try to limit what you carry as this climb is tough.

Le Belvédère (closed Wed.; tel. 42-73-44), an expensive restaurant near the trailhead at Far Rau Ape (600 meters), offers a free *truck* from Papeete at 1100 and 1700 for those willing to spend f.3900 on a meal, the easiest way to get there. Taxis want f.3000 and up for the eight-km trip to the restaurant. Few people live up there, so hitching would be a matter of finding some tourists headed for the restaurant. Weekends are best for this.

You'll get this unobstructed view of Le Diadème from the Mt. Aorai Trail.

DAVID STANLEY

Just above the restaurant is the French Army's Centre d'Instruction de Montagne, where you must sign the register. From Fare Rau Ape to the summit takes seven hours: 1½ hours to Hamuta, another two to Fare Mato (good view of Le Diadème, not visible from Papeete), then 2½ to Fare Ata, where most hikers spend the first night in order to cover the last 40 minutes to the summit the following morning.

The view from Aorai is magnificent, with Papeete and many of the empty interior valleys in full view. To the north is Tetiaroa atoll, while Moorea's jagged outline fills the west. Even on a cloudy day the massive green hulk of neighboring **Orohena** (2,241 meters) often towers above the clouds like Mt. Olympus. A bonus is the chance to see some of the original native vegetation of Tahiti, which survives better at high altitudes and in isolated gullies. In good weather Aorai is exhausting but superb; in the rain it's a disaster.

When the author of this book climbed Aorai in 1984 the trip could be done by anyone in reasonable physical shape. By mid-1988 the trail had deteriorated with sheer slopes and slippery, crumbly ridges to be negotiated. In past we've asked readers to write in with current information on Aorai and we're grateful to Charlie Appleton of Nottingham, England, for sending us this report:

The trail has been restored and is now (July 1991) well maintained. The chalets at Fare Mato and Fare Ata were in excellent order, the former being brand new and sitting on a recently reconstructed platform. They'll sleep 12-15 without difficulty, though only the hut at Fare Ata has drinking water. Just above Fare Mato cables have been fixed along the section of trail with the steepest drops on both sides, allowing some fairly inexperienced hikers I met to traverse it with confidence. Very few people do the climb and if you go in the middle of the week you can expect to have the mountain to yourself. It might be worth mentioning that the compelling reason for spending the night on top (apart from sunset and sunrise) is that those who make the roundtrip in a day are likely to find that by the time they near the summit the mountain will have donned its midday hat of clouds, limiting their views.

Orohena is seldom climbed since the way is very dangerous and difficult. For the record the route up Orohena begins at the town hall *(mairie)* of Mahina opposite the military laboratories. You can drive about six km to the 500-meter level, where the road dead-ends at "Private Property" signs and warnings about dogs.

Guides

These and other hikes on Tahiti are led on weekends and holidays by **Pierre Florentin** (B.P. 5323, Pirae; tel. 43-72-01), a professional mountain guide with years of experience. Pierre charges a fixed rate of about f.20,000 a day for groups of up to 10 persons maximum—well worth considering if there are a few of you. The trips offered include climbs up Orohena (three days, f.45,000) and Aorai (two days), the hike across Tahiti Iti (two days), and day-trips to Fautaua Falls, Mt. Marau, a lava tube, etc. Transport to the trailheads, backpacks, tents, and sleeping bags are available at an additional charge (when required) and participants must bring their own food. Pierre's services are highly recommended to small groups of serious hikers/ climbers concerned about both safety and success.

Another professional guide, **Angélien Zena** (B.P. 7426, Taravao; tel. 57-22-67), specializes in hikes around the Pari Coast at the east end of Tahiti Iti. Angélien's three-day trip costs f.110,000 for up to 10 persons, meals and transport from/to Taravao included. Time off is allowed for swimming and fishing. A boat from Vairao to Vaipoiri Grotto is used on the two-day hikes, and day-trips can also be arranged. Even if there are only a few of you it's worth calling both Pierre and Angélien to learn if they have any trips scheduled that you might join. Also call the president of the Tahitian Alpine Club, Marc Allain (tel. 48-10-59).

The **Fédération des Associations de Protection de l'Environment "Te Ora Naho"** (B.P. 9304, Papeete) sponsors organized weekend hikes on Tahiti and Moorea several times a month. For information call Pierre Wrobel (tel. 43-04-64) or François Collin (tel. 41-09-19) during the day weekdays, or Fabien Lebec (tel. 42-53-12) between 1800 and 1900.

PRACTICALITIES

ACCOMMODATIONS

Almost all of the places to stay are in the congested Mahina to Punaauia strip engulfing Papeete and Faaa International Airport. Representatives of the various hotels often meet incoming flights and most provide free transport to their establishments. If they're not there, call them up and ask. The hotels are listed below clockwise in each category, beginning in Punaauia.

Cheaper Hotels Around Papeete

The **Heitare Inn** (B.P. 6830, Papeete; tel. 43-33-52 or 42-77-53) at PK 4, Faaa, provides the closest budget accommodations to the airport. It's just across the highway from the French military base and is buffeted by traffic noise and fumes from 0500 on. There are 11 rooms at f.4000 s, f.5000 d with shared bath, f.4500 s, f.5500 d with a/c, and f.6000 d with private bath. Communal cooking facilities are provided.

The **Hotel Shogun** (Bruno Gato, B.P. 2880, Papeete; tel. 43-13-93), 10 rue de Commandant Destremeau, Papeete, has a comfortable, quiet dormitory with three bunk beds for f.2000 pp. The 10 a/c rooms are f.5000 s or d facing the noisy road, f.5500 s or d on the back side. Monthly rates are available. Check in at the Boutique Keiko below the hotel. If they're closed when you arrive call 48-08-75 and someone will come to let you in.

The **Hotel Mahina Tea** (B.P. 17, Papeete; tel. 42-00-97), up rue Sainte-Amélie from Ave. Bruat, is about the only regular budget hotel in the city. The 16 rooms with private bath are f.4000 s or d (f.3500 with a single bed), discounted if you stay three or more nights. There are also six small studios with cooking facilities at f.90,000 a month double. Dishes are not provided, electricity is extra, and the hot water is irregular. The Mahina Tea could be cleaner and friendlier. And quieter—at night, the rooster noise here can be annoying.

To meet interesting people stay at **Hostel Teamo** (Kay and Gerald, B.P. 2407, Papeete; tel. 42-00-35), 8 rue du Pont Neuf, Quartier Mission, a characterful century-old house in an attractive neighborhood just a short walk east of downtown near the Archbishop's Palace. To get there from the market walk straight inland on rue Cardella. It's a little hard to find the first time, but very convenient once you know it. Shared

VICINITY OF PAPEETE

TAHITI ISLAND

-N-

0 2 km

MILITARY LABS
HITI MAHANA BEACH CLUB
MAHINA
SHERIFF DE MAHINA
TUAURU VALLEY
OROHENA TRAIL (CLOSED)
POINT VENUS
MAHINA TOWN HALL
MAHINA BAY
MATAVAI BAY
HYATT REGENCY
TOMB OF POMARE V
AORAI TRAIL
FARE RAU APE (600 m)
NUCLEAR TESTING SUPPORT BASE
ROYAL TAHITIEN HOTEL
YACHT CLUB
ARUE
RACETRACK
PIRAE VALLEY
ORSTOM
PIRAE
FAUTAUA VALLEY
HAMUTA VALLEY
TITIORO
BAIN LOTI
TAUNOA PASSAGE
CENTRE D'EXPERIMENTATION DU PACIFIQUE
MORMON TEMPLE
PAPEETE
HAMUTA
ARCHBISHOPS PALACE
HOSPITAL
SAINTE AMELIE VALLEY
PIC ROUGE (298 m)
MT. PAPAIONA (696 m)
PAOFAI
TIPAERUI VALLEY
MOTU UTA
PAPEETE PASSAGE
NUUTANIA PRISON
PAMATAI
HOTEL TAHITI
WATERFRONT
FAAA
COCO'S HOSTEL
OUTUMAORO
FAA CHANNEL
TERMINAL
HOTEL BEACHCOMBER
SOFITEL MAEVA BEACH HOTEL

sailboarders at Hiti Mahana Beach Club, Tahiti

dormitory-style accommodations with satisfactory cooking facilities are f.1300 pp, private rooms f.2300 d with shared bath, f.3300 d with private bath. Teamo is run by the retired Tahitian couple who live in the house at #3 across the street, so check there if no one's around. If you arrive in the middle of the night there's a couch on the veranda where you can stretch out. The place is clean, has a nice veranda with French TV, English is spoken, but beware of mosquitos. They'll hold luggage for f.100 a day. Checkout time is 1100, but you can stay until 1830 for an additional f.500 pp fee. The owner, Mr. Tiger, does seven-hour tours around the island with 10 stops for f.1800 pp if enough people sign up. He also provides free airport transfers upon request. Recommended.

Nearby on rue du Frère Alain is the **Tahiti Budget Lodge** (B.P. 237, Papeete; tel. 42-66-82), a quiet wooden house with 14 rooms at f.1500 pp for a shared triple, f.3500 d with shared bath, f.4500 d with private bath. There's also camping space for four tents. Cooking facilities are provided but use of the washing machine is extra.

Youth Hostels

The **Papeete Youth Hostel** (Centre d'Accueil Territorial, B.P. 1709, Papeete; tel. 42-68-02) on boulevard Pomare opposite the Cultural Center offers accommodations in 12 three-bed dorms without shower to those with a current Youth Hostel Association or student card only. There always used to be a line of people waiting to get in here; to reduce demand they tripled their prices to f.3000 pp for one night, f.2500 pp for subsequent nights—a lot to pay for a mere youth hostel! Now you should have no problem getting a bed. You can check in weekdays 0800-1200/1400-1800, Sat. 0800-1200/1500-1800, Sun. 1000-1200. The rooms are accessible all day (midnight curfew), but there are no cooking facilities or hot water. The management does not allow visitors or alcohol in the rooms, nor is it permitted to store luggage for friends not staying there. Only consider this place as a last resort.

In July and Aug. women can stay at the **Foyer de Jeunes Filles de Paofai** (B.P. 1719, Papeete; tel. 42-87-80) near the Protestant church on boulevard Pomare. Bed and breakfast at this Evangelical Church-operated girls' residence is f.1500 a day, f.15,000 a month.

Camping

The nicest (and as yet only) regular campsite on Tahiti is **Hiti Mahana Beach Club** (Pat and Coco Pautu, B.P. 11580, Mahina; tel. 48-16-13) near Point Venus, 12 km east of Papeete. It's f.700 pp to camp under the fruit trees on the spacious fenced grounds; if you don't have your own tent, you can rent one for f.600 a day extra.

Otherwise pay f.1500 pp to sleep on a mattress in the dormitory of the white colonial mansion adjacent to the club. Rooms here run f.3500 s, f.4500 d, and there's a communal kitchen, toilet, showers, and dining/lounge area. Sheets are available for f.200, towels f.100. A special "Blue Room" with king-size bed is f.4500 s, f.6000 d. If you stay a week the eighth night is free.

Cooking facilities and a shared fridge come with the above. Campers have simpler facilities of their own and there's a lighted area for reading in the evening. Only cold showers are available at Hiti Mahana, except in the Blue Room which has hot water. Other facilities include a beach barbecue with firewood provided, washing machine, and luggage storage. Princess the Horse grazes nearby. She loves old bread, but don't get behind her: she's not always friendly!

The best thing about Hiti Mahana is its location right on a black-sand beach. Sporting equipment is for rent and the resort has a tiny off-shore island of its own within swimming distance, where you could sunbathe nude or surf off the *motu's* east end. There's good snorkeling and plenty of fish. Sailboarders churn the waters. Cold beer and rum punch are on tap daily and happy hour runs from 1600 to 1900. Video films are shown on rainy days at 2030. The resort snack bar is only open weekends, but back on the main road are a few restaurants such as **Snack Tamarii Mahina**

(steak and *frites* for f.700). On Sun. the resort offers excursions to Faarumai Falls in the back of a pickup truck (f.300 pp). Hiti Mahana is also the perfect place to get an early start on a circle-island tour (clockwise).

To get to Hiti Mahana at PK 10.5 Mahina take the "Mahina" *truck* (f.140, no service after 1715) from near Papeete market. You pass the Point Venus turnoff, cross a bridge, then turn left at a school and follow the road straight to the beach (one km). The Hiti Mahana *truck* is often at the airport in search of arriving clients, even in the middle of the night, so ask. The office is closed 1200-1400. Resort owner Pat Pautu is a world of information, if you catch her. Picnickers pay f.300 for day use of the beach and facilities at Hiti Mahana (no charge to residents). Highly recommended.

Expensive Hotels Around Papeete

The French-owned **Sofitel Maeva Beach** (B.P. 6008, Faaa; tel. 42-80-42) at PK 7.5, Punaauia, is the oldest of the three big international hotels on Tahiti (the others are the Beachcomber and Hyatt Regency). The 224 a/c rooms in this pyramidal high-rise cost f.17,900 s or d garden view, f.20,700 s or d lagoon view, f.24,000 s or d panoramic view (children under 12 free). Breakfast and dinner are f.4000 pp extra. Decorated with Melanesian artifacts, the seven-story Maeva Beach faces

the black volcanic sands of Tahiti

TINI COLOMBEL

a man-made white beach. With pollution on the increase in the adjacent lagoon most swimmers stick to the hotel pool, however. The Tahitian dancing and feasting here are attractions.

The **Hotel Te Puna Bel Air** (B.P. 6634, Faaa; tel. 42-09-00) at PK 7.2, Punaauia, also known as the Belair Hotel, is one of the few large hotels owned and operated by a Tahitian family. The way in is rather confusing: around the corner and down a side road to an unmarked entrance. Rates are f.8000 s, f.9000 d, f.11,500 t for the 28 garden bungalows and 48 standard rooms. The beach is poor and watch out for eels if you decide to swim in their lovely pond. Scuba divers should contact Tahiti Plongée (B.P. 2192, Papeete) prior to arrival for concessional divers' rates at the Te Puna Bel Air.

The **Tahiti Country Club** (B.P. 13019, Punaauia; tel. 42-60-40), the former Ibis "Belle-Fleur" and Climat Punaauia, is up on the hillside above the Te Puna Bel Air. The 40 a/c rooms with fridge in a neat two-story building are officially f.10,000 s, f.12,000 d (children under 12 free), plus f.3600 pp extra for breakfast and dinner (if desired). Prices have almost doubled here during the last few years, though you may be able to wangle a reduction if you deal direct and not through a travel agency, which adds on its commission. Swimming pool, volleyball, and tennis courts are on the premises (free). The hike up to this hotel from the main road is also quite a workout!

The **Tahiti Beachcomber Parkroyal** (B.P. 6014, Faaa; tel. 42-51-10), PK 7 Faaa, the former TraveLodge (1974), was purchased by the Japanese corporation EIE in Sept. 1989 for US$35 million. It's the first hotel west of the airport and the most expensive. The 181 rooms in the main building begin at f.22,000 s, f.26,000 d, f.29,000 t; for one of the 17 overwater bungalows add 50% again. Children and teens sharing the room with their parents are free. A breakfast and dinner meal plan is f.5100 pp extra. Tahitian dancing and craft demonstrations are regular features. The hotel pool is reserved for guests and the beach is artificial, but the attendants in the water-sports kiosk on the beach will gladly ferry you out to the nudist pontoons anchored in mid-lagoon for f.500 RT. Every afternoon at 1630 there's a 1½-hour sunset cruise

along the coast from the Beachcomber (f.900 including one drink).

The traditional **Hotel Tahiti** (B.P. 416, Papeete; tel. 42-95-50) at PK 2.6 between Papeete and the airport is the most charming of the higher-priced hotels, with a gracious South Seas atmosphere. There are 92 units beginning at f.6000 s, f.7000 d, f.8500 t, or lagoon-front bungalows at f.9500 s or d—good value for Tahiti. Some of the rooms near the highway are prone to traffic noise, however, and seem in a state of prolonged decay. This colonial-style hotel opened in 1960 with a pool (empty), bar, restaurant, etc., plus a lovely lagoon-side setting on the grounds of what was the residence of Princess Pomare, daughter of the last king of Tahiti. The present manager, American expat Syd Pollock, is a colorful island character who has been running hotels around the islands for years. We recommend this place as your best choice in the middle to upper price range.

The 146-room **Hotel Matavai** (B.P. 32, Papeete; tel. 42-67-67) has little going for it at f.10,000 s, f.14,000 d, f.18,000 t. You can almost tell this four-floor concrete edifice was once a Holiday Inn—strippers in an upstairs lounge are its biggest attraction today.

If you want to be right in the center of town consider high-rise **Prince Hinoi** (B.P. 4545, Papeete; tel. 42-32-77), Ave. du Prince Hinoi at boulevard Pomare, formerly known as the Hotel Ibis Papeete. It's often used by business travelers. The 72 small a/c rooms are f.8500 s, f.9000 d, f.10,700 t, plus f.2650 for breakfast and dinner (if desired).

The **Hotel Le Mandarin** (B.P. 302, Papeete; tel. 42-16-33), 51 rue Colette, is a clean, modern hotel with an Oriental flair. The 37 rooms are somewhat overpriced at f.11,500 s, f.12,500 d, f.14,500 t (children under 12 free). The Mandarin's attractive Cantonese restaurant is closed Sunday.

The elegant old **Hotel Royal Papeete** (B.P. 919, Papeete; tel. 42-01-29), downtown on boulevard Pomare opposite the Moorea ferry landing, would be nice if it weren't for the noisy power plant adjacent. Papeete's nightlife also throbs in and around this hotel (perhaps an attraction!). The 85 "soundproofed" rooms begin at f.8000 s, f.9500 d, f.11,000 t. Ask for one on the quieter south side of the building. This is another good choice for business people. The management is friendly and helpful.

Hotel Pacific (B.P. 111, Papeete; tel. 43-72-82), formerly Hotel Kon Tiki, is the cheapest high-rise hotel in the city center. The 44 spacious rooms begin at f.7000 s, f.8300 d, f.10,300 t. Be aware, though, that the Pacific is on the opposite side of the same power plant which buffets the Royal Papeete and it's just as noisy here. This hotel is popular with military personnel and French secret agents in transit. Immerse yourself in the intrigue (and get an eyeful of Papeete) by having a drink in the bar (closed Mon.) on the seventh floor.

The **Royal Tahitien Hotel** (B.P. 5001, Papeete; tel. 42-81-13) at PK 3.5, Pirae, is a peaceful two-story building with 40 rooms facing beautifully kept grounds on a black-sand beach. The windsurfing offshore is good. For f.15,000 s or d, f.18,000 t you may just find here the Tahiti you imagined. Breakfast and dinner served on the terrace overlooking the lagoon are f.3850 pp extra.

The **Hyatt Regency Tahiti** (B.P. 1015, Papeete; tel. 48-11-22) at PK 8, Mahina, takes the award for charging the highest prices on the island. The 200 rooms begin at f.22,000 s or d, f.26,000 t (children under 12 free). Their breakfast and dinner meal plan is f.4600 pp extra. Formerly known as the Tahara'a Hotel, the Hyatt was built by Pan American Airways two decades ago and purchased for US$30 million in Sept. 1989 by the Japanese group Electronic and Industrial Enterprises which also has big investments in Fiji. Chances are you'll be on a package tour if you stay here and the isolation won't matter much. Built on a hillside overlooking Matavai Bay, this is one of the only hotels in the world where you take an elevator down to your room. The views from the balconies are superb. A black-sand beach is at the foot of the hill.

Accommodations Around The Island

The only reasonably inexpensive place to stay on the far side of the island is **Fare Nana'o** (B.P. 7193, Taravao; tel. 57-18-14), operated by sculptor Jean-Claude Michel and his wife Monique. It's on the lagoon side in a colorful compound overflowing with vegetation and fragments of sculpture, very near the PK 52 marker a km north of the old French fort at Taravao (no sign). The seven thatched bungalows vary in price, from f.4000 d for the treehouse (you climb up a pole), f.4500 d for an overwater *fare* on stilts (you must wade through the lagoon), f.5000 d for one of the three units with cooking facilities, or f.6000 d for the only room with private bath. A third person is f.500 at all these and the weekly discount is 10 percent. Although unique and wonderful, Fare Nana'o is not for everyone: the walls are constructed of tree trunks and branches left partially open, there's no hot water, flashlights are required to reach the shared toilet and shower at night, and you may be visited in the night by crabs, spiders, lizards, and a marauding cat. This Robinson Crusoe-style place has had TV exposure in Los Angeles, so advance reservations are essential, especially on weekends. Recommended.

The six-unit **Te Anuanua Hotel** (B.P. 1553, Papeete; tel. 57-12-54) just west of the church in Pueu at PK 10, Tahiti Iti, doesn't have a beach but the garden bungalows are fairly reasonable at f.6000 s, f.7000 d or t. Lagoon-front bungalows are f.2000 more. Check the rooms before checking in as some lack window screens, fans, or functioning plumbing. They'll loan you a bicycle, sailboard, and snorkeling gear free, though. A nice seafood restaurant faces the lagoon and locally made Tahitian handicrafts are sold at the hotel, making the Te Anuanua worth a stop as you travel around the island. Every Sun. at noon there's a buffet of authentic Tahitian food (f.3500 pp).

A more distant choice would be the **Puunui Resort** (B.P. 7016, Taravao; tel. 57-19-20), four km up a steep paved road off the Teahupoo road, seven km from Taravao. You'll have to rent a car if you stay here. At f.11,000 for one of the 54 four-bed bungalows or f.17,200 for each of the 23 six-bed villas, the Puunui is slightly overpriced unless you're in a small group. A breakfast and dinner meal plan is f.3500 pp extra, though the units have kitchenettes. They do offer horseback riding at f.1800 an hour (tel. 57-19-20 for reservations 48 hours in advance), so it may be worth dropping by for a ride and the view. Roundtrip airport transfers are f.4000 pp.

FOOD

Papeete Restaurants

Papeete's most famous restaurant is **Acajou** (closed Sun., tel. 42-87-58), corner of rue Georges Lagarde and boulevard Pomare near the Vaima Center. This is *the* place for a cup of coffee on the sidewalk or a gourmet meal in the elegant dining room. House specialties include onion soup, slices of mahimahi *au gratin,* and filet mignon with mustard sauce. The plates are individually prepared so allow some time. A cheaper branch of Acajou (open for breakfast and lunch only) is at 7 rue Cardella by the market, half a block from the tourist office.

For a taste of the Mediterranean, **La Pizzeria** (closed Sun. and holidays; tel. 42-98-30) on boulevard Pomare near the Tahiti Pearl Center prepares real pizza in a brick oven. The price is surprisingly reasonable for the waterfront location—it's all spelled out in a big tabloid menu.

Pizzeria Lou Pescadou (open Mon. to Sat. 1130-1400/1830-2230, closed Sun.; tel. 43-74-26) on rue Anne-Marie Javouhey behind the cathedral is friendly, unpretentious, breezy, and inexpensive. Their pizza pescatore makes a good lunch and a big pitcher of ice water comes in the price. Owner Mario Vitulli may be from Marseille but you won't complain about his spaghetti—a huge meal for about f.800. Drinks are on the house if you have to stand and wait for a table. The service is excellent and Lou Pescadou is very popular among local French, a high recommendation.

La Baie d'Along (Le Restaurant La Saigonnaise, closed Sun., tel. 42-05-35) on Ave. du Prince Hinoi has moderately expensive Vietnamese food. Saigonese soup makes a good lunch.

Many Chinese restaurants in Papeete specialize in chicken and Hinano beer, but none are special bargains. The most popular is the **Waikiki Restaurant** (open daily 1100-1300/1800-2100, closed Sun. lunch; tel. 42-95-27) on rue Leboucher near the market. At **Te Hoa Restaurant** (closed Sun., tel. 43-99-27), 30 rue du Maréchal-Foch behind the market, the furnishings aren't as neat but the portions are bigger and the prices slightly lower than at Waikiki.

Self-service Cafeterias

The **Foyer de Jeunes Filles de Paofai** (tel. 42-87-80) opposite the Protestant Church has a good modern cafeteria (closed Sat. and Sun.) with a fixed menu including a small salad, main plate, bread, and dessert for f.990 lunch or dinner. Alcohol is not available here. **Snack Paofai Self Service** (open Mon.-Sat. 1000-1300 only; tel. 42-65-75) near Clinique Paofai is another inexpensive cafeteria.

Self-Service Le Brasilia (tel. 42-46-24) upstairs in the Vaima Center offers excellent *plats du jour* for f.1100 or less on their breezy terrace with a view of Tahiti. Only lunch is available Mon.-Sat. 1100-1400; the bar/cafe is open the same days from 0900 to 1700. This place can be hard to find: if you stand in front of the Catholic cathedral and look directly above the Air New Zealand office across the street you'll see the sign, "Restaurant Bar Brasilia Club", on the roof.

Snack Bars

The snack bar at the **Cultural Center** is good for breakfast or lunch *(plat du jour)* 0800-1600 weekdays. An airy restaurant and snack bar are above the Municipal Swimming Pool.

The *plat du jour* at **Big Burger** (closed Sunday; tel. 43-01-98) beside Aline is often big value (f.1200), and it's not fast food as the name implies.

Snack Roger (tel. 42-80-38), 3 rue Jaussen next to the cathedral, offers good plate lunches, *plats du jour,* cheap salads, real espresso coffee, and ice cream. It's a good place to catch your breath, so locate it early in your visit!

To sample the local cuisine repair to **Cafe Snack Ella,** 23 rue Cardella right beside the market. Try *maa tinito,* a melange of red beans, pork, macaroni, and vegetables on rice (f.600). A large Hinano beer is f.450. Check out their Tahitian toilet (two treads and one squat) through the door below the blackboard in back.

If you're catching an interisland ship, it's good to know about the **Restaurant Motu Uta** near the wharf where the *Temehani* and *Taporo* dock. Lunch is good—especially with big bottles of cold beer. Indulge before you embark (if they're open).

Food Trailers

Take a stroll along the waterfront near the Moorea ferry landing in the early evening. After 1730 the

PAPEETE

scene changes completely with dozens of gaily lit vans known as *les roulettes* or *les brochettes* forming a colorful night market selling everything from couscous and pizza to steak with real *pommes frites* (f.800). Sailors promenade with their *vahines* as the city lights wink gently across the harbor, adding a touch of romance and glamour. The food and atmosphere are excellent but be prepared for regular restaurant prices. Even if you're not dining, it's a scene not to miss.

PAPEETE

1. offices of Tuamotu boats
2. Bureau Tuhaa Pae
3. coconut oil mill
4. Bureau Temehani/Aranui
5. *Raromatai Ferry* office
6. Bureau Taporo
7. New Town Hall
8. Hotel Pacific
9. Moorea ferries
10. Royal Papeete Hotel
11. Hotel Prince Hinoi
12. Municipal Swimming Pool
13. youth hostel
14. Cultural Center
15. Intermarket supermarket
16. Foyer de Jeunes Filles
17. Protestant Church
18. Tahiti Perles Center
19. public toilets
20. Hotel Shogun
21. courthouse
22. army barracks
23. Hotel Mahina Tea
24. High Commissioner's office
25. Territorial Assembly
26. post office
27. Vaima Center
28. Lou Pescadou Restaurant
29. Catholic Cathedral
30. market
31. tourist office
32. Archipels Bookstore
33. Pacificar
34. Teamo Hostel
35. Archbishop's Palace
36. Mamao Hospital
37. Chinese Temple
38. Mormon Temple
39. Union Sacrée Truck Terminal

No alcohol is available from *les roulettes* but on boulevard Pomare across the park from the Moorea ferry landing is a row of sidewalk cafes frequented by French servicemen, happy hookers, gays, and assorted groupies. Some even have a happy hour. This is a good place to sit and take in the local color of every shade and hue.

Supermarkets
Intermarket (open Mon.-Sat. 0715-1230/1445-1845) is a large supermarket on rue du Commandant Destremeau. Get whole barbecued chickens and chow mein in the small deli section.

At PK 8 Punuuai just south of the junction of the autoroute to Papeete is the **Centre Moana Nui,** Tahiti's first enclosed shopping mall, with a large adjoining supermarket, the **Euromarche.** The restaurant on the mall is rather poor; a barbecued chicken from the deli in the supermarket is a better deal.

Restaurants Around The Island
A good place for lunch on your way around the island might be **Snack Guilloux** (closed Mon.; tel. 57-12-91), a hundred meters down the road to Tautira from the Westpac Bank in Taravao. It's a regular restaurant, not a snack bar as the name implies.

The pretentious **Gauguin Museum Restaurant** (tel. 57-13-80) is half a kilometer west of the museum. Circle-island tour groups lunch here and you can join them for a steep f.3500 for the meal.

ENTERTAINMENT

Ask for the monthly program of activities at the Departement Fetes et Manifestations upstairs in the **Cultural Center** at "Te Fare Tauhiti Nui" (tel. 42-88-50) on the waterfront. Recitals by well-known classical musicians take place here Fri. and Sat. at 2000 (admission f.2000).

Five Papeete cinemas show B-grade films dubbed in French (admission f.650). The Concorde is in the Vaima Center; Hollywood I and II are on rue Lagarde beside the Vaima Center; Liberty Cinema is on rue Maréchal Foch near the market; and the Mamao Palace is near Mamao Hospital.

The food trucks along the Papeete waterfront near the Moorea ferry wharf are about the best places in the city to eat.

DAVID STANLEY

Nightlife

Papeete after dark is not just for the tourists! Lots of little bars crowding the streets around rue des Écoles are full of locals. The places with live music or a show generally impose a f.1000 cover charge which includes one drink. Nothing much gets going before 2200 and by 0100 everything is very informal for the last hour before closing. Luckily Papeete is still a pretty safe place and you probably won't get mugged even at these odd hours.

The **Piano Bar** (tel. 42-88-24), on rue des Écoles, is the most notorious of Papeete's *mahu* (transvestite) discos; **Lido Nightclub** (tel. 42-95-84) next door offers striptease (both f.1000 cover). Young French servicemen are in their element in these places.

Café des Sports (tel. 42-51-33), on the corner across the street from the Piano Bar, has beer on tap and usually no cover. More locals than tourists patronize this pleasant, inexpensive establishment, which has music on weekends.

A slightly rougher local drinking place is the **Bar Kikiriri** (no cover; tel. 43-58-64) on rue Colette. The **Champagne Club Bar Américain** (tel. 43-71-70) beside Liberty Cinema on rue du Maréchal Foch is another place where you can get a beer without paying a cover.

French soldiers and sailors out of uniform patronize the bars along boulevard Pomare opposite the Moorea ferry landing, such as **La Cave** (tel. 42-01-29) at the Royal Papeete Hotel (entry though the lobby) which has live Tahitian music for dancing on the weekends (closed Sun.-Tues.; cover charge).

The **Tiki d'Or Bar Américain** (no cover; tel. 42-07-37) on the back street near the Vaima Center gets lively around happy hour. You'll locate it by the ukuleles and impromptu singing.

Le Jonque (no cover; tel. 42-47-34), a floating bar on the waterfront opposite the end of Ave. Bruat, is a quiet, safe place to drink. The **Pitate Bar** (cover charge; tel. 42-83-04), on the corner of Ave. Bruat beside the UTA office, is loud and dark, but there's often Tahitian-style music you can dance to. Check out the Pitate on Sunday afternoon. **Club 106** (closed Sun. and Mon.; cover charge; tel. 42-72-92) nearby on boulevard Pomare is the disco for the "in" set.

Polynesian Shows

A Tahitian dance show takes place in the Bougainville Restaurant downstairs at the **Maeva Beach Hotel** (tel. 42-80-42) Mon., Wed., Fri., and Sat. at 2000. If you're not interested in having dinner, a drink at the Bar Moorea by the pool will put you in position to see the action (no cover charge). The first and third Sunday of each month this hotel puts on a full Tahitian feast at 1200, complete with earth oven *(ahima'a)* and show (f.4000).

Every evening the **Beachcomber Hotel** (tel. 42-51-10) presents one of the best Tahitian dance shows on the island; attend for the price of a drink at the bar near the pool (no cover charge). The dancers' starting time tends to vary (officially 2030), so arrive early and be prepared to wait. For something special take in the barbecue (on Wed.) and the Tahitian feast (on Sun.)—f.3700 each.

Le Tamure Hut at the Royal Papeete Hotel (tel. 42-01-29) on the waterfront opposite the Moorea ferry landing is one of the few downtown Papeete clubs designed for visitors. Through entertainment and decor they've attempted to recapture the nightlife milieu of a decade or more ago, before Quinn's Tahitian Hut closed in 1973. You can dance to '50s and '60s music here! The Tahitian floor show featuring superstar Yvon Arai is Thurs.-Sat. at 1930 (f.4200 pp including dinner and the show). Daily except Sun. from 1600 to 0200 the Hut operates as a bar. If you don't mind

LOUISE FOOTE

spending a little money, Le Tamure is a good choice for a night out.

SPORTS AND RECREATION

Tahiti Plongée (B.P. 2192, Papeete; tel. 43-62-51 or 41-00-62) offers scuba diving several times daily from its base at the Hotel Te Puna Bel Air, Punaauia. The charge is f.3500 per dive all-inclusive, or f.15,000 for a five-dive card, f.25,000 for 10 dives. Ocean dive at 0800 daily and at 1400 on Saturday; lagoon diving is at 1000 daily and 1400 weekdays. To dive with this company you must join the **Club Corail-Sub** (f.5000) which includes a medical examination and an insurance policy. Credit cards are not accepted.

Divemaster Henri Pouliquen was one of the first to teach scuba diving to children. The youngest person Henri has taken down was aged two years, nine months—the oldest was a woman of 78 on her first dive. Since 1979 Tahiti Plongée has arranged over 10,000 dives with children, certainly a unique accomplishment. Most diving is on the Punaauia reef. Other fa-

a Tahitian dancer at a Papeete hotel

vorite scuba locales include a scuttled Pan Am Catalina PBY seaplane near the airport, its upper wing 12 meters down, and a schooner wreck 10 meters down about 45 meters from the breakwater at the entrance to the harbor.

Tahiti Aquatique (B.P. 6008, Faaa; tel. 42-80-42) at the Maeva Beach Hotel also offers professional scuba-diving services. Ask for Dick Johnson at the office by the hotel wharf. Their prices are higher than those of Tahiti Plongée (f.5000 for scuba diving), but you don't have to pay a club membership fee. For f.700 pp RT they'll shuttle you out to their offshore sunbathing pontoon anchored above a fine snorkeling locale (no lifeguard or shade). Rental of mask, snorkel, and fins is f.800 extra. Underwater photography equipment and PADI certification courses are available. A full day of sailing with Tahiti Aquatique is f.5000.

Scuba diving can also be arranged with Pascal Le Cointre at the **Yacht Club of Tahiti** (B.P. 1456, Papeete; tel. 42-23-55) at PK 4, Arue. Outings are offered at 0900 and 1400 daily except Sun. (f.4500 a dive, or f.20,000 for five dives, f.35,000 for 10 dives). Night diving is f.6000.

If you only want to rent tanks go to **Marine Corail** (tel. 42-98-63) at Fare Ute. They can be a little slow understanding what you want—persist.

The **municipal swimming pool** (tel. 42-89-24) is open to the public Tues.-Fri. 1130-1700, Sat. and Sun. 0730-1700 (f.250). The pool on the roof of the **Vaima Center** next to Self-Service Le Brasilia has more class (open weekdays 0900-1700; f.300). In the evening after 1800 **football** is practiced in the sports field near the municipal swimming pool.

SHOPPING

Papeete's largest shopping complex is the **Vaima Center,** where numerous shops sell black pearls, designer clothes, cheap souvenirs, books, etc. It's certainly worth a look, then branch out into the surrounding streets. **Anuraro Pearls,** 7 rue Jeanne d'Arc next to the Vaima Center, is a good place to examine the famous Gambier black pearls. **Galerie Winkler,** 17 rue Jeanne d'Arc beside American Express, sells contemporary paintings of Polynesia.

Don't overlook the local fashions. **Tahiti Art** on boulevard Pomare just west of the Vaima Center has expensive block-printed fabrics: a men's short-sleeved shirt is f.5000. **Marie Ah You** on the waterfront between the Vaima Center and the tourist office sells very chic island clothing—also with prices to match.

For reproductions of authentic Marquesan woodcarvings have a look in **Manuia Curios** on the east side of the cathedral. Also try **Manuia Junior,** corner of rues Albert Leboucher and des Écoles opposite the Café des Sports.

If you're a surfer **Shop Tahiti Surf and Skate,** 10 rue Édouard Ahnne near the market, sells boards (f.65,000 and up) plus all attendant gear. **Caroline,** 41 rue Colette, and **Waikiki Beach,** 9 rue Jeanne d'Arc, also have surfing gear.

The **T-Shirt Center** on Ave. Georges Clemenceau between the Chinese Temple and Cours de l'Union Sacrée on the way to Baín

a Marquesan woodcarving

AUCKLAND INSTITUTE AND MUSEUM

Loti has the cheapest and best selection of Tahitian T-shirts.

SERVICES

To change money patronize the **Banque Socredo,** with over a dozen branches on Tahiti and no f.350 commission. The only place to get a cash advance on a MasterCard is UAP Assurances Chichong, 16 rue Jaussen, opposite Restaurant Bougainville back behind the cathedral.

The main **post office** is on boulevard Pomare across from the yacht anchorage. Aerograms and large mailing envelopes/boxes are sold at the counters up the escalators (closes at 1500). Pick up poste restante (general delivery) mail at window 15 downstairs (f.40 per piece). The Philatelic Bureau at the post office sells the stamps and first-day covers of all the French Pacific territories. Some are quite beautiful and inexpensive. The post office is also the place to place a long-distance telephone call.

If you have an **American Express** card or traveler's checks you can have your mail sent c/o Tahiti Tours, B.P. 627, Papeete. Their office (tel. 42-78-70) is at 15 rue Jeanne d'Arc next to the Vaima Center. They charge f.500 to forward mail.

For those uninitiated into the French administrative system, the **police station** (in emergencies tel. 17) opposite the War Memorial on Ave. Bruat deals with Papeete matters, while the **gendarmerie** (tel. 42-02-02) at the head of Ave. Bruat is concerned with the rest of the island. The locally recruited Papeete police wear blue uniforms, while the paramilitary French-import gendarmes are dressed in khaki.

Visa extensions are handled by the **Police de l'Air et des Frontières** (open weekdays 0800-1200/1400-1700; tel. 42-67-99) at the airport (up the stairs beside the snack bar). Extensions cost f.3000 and you must show your money, ticket to leave Tahiti-Polynesia, and provide two photos. North Americans are limited to three months total; it's far better to ask for a three-month stay on arrival—making this formality unnecessary. Be patient and courteous with these officials if you want good service.

The **honorary consul of Germany** is Claude-Eliane Weinmann (B.P. 452, Papeete; tel. 42-99-94), rue Tihoni Te Faatau off Ave. du Prince Hinoi in Afareru on the far east side of the city. The **honorary consul of Australia** is Brian Banston (B.P. 1695, Papeete; tel. 43-88-38) at the Qantas office in the Vaima Center. The **honorary British consul** is Robert Withers (B.P. 1064, Papeete, tel. 42-84-57) at Avis Rent-a-Car, 35 rue Charles Viénot. Other countries with **honorary consuls** at Papeete are Austria, Belgium, Britain, Chile, Denmark, Finland, Holland, Italy, Monaco, South Korea, and Sweden. There's no U.S. diplomatic post in Tahiti-Polynesia. All visa applications and requests for replacement of lost passports must be sent to Suva, Fiji, where it can take up to five weeks to get through the paperwork. Canada, Japan, and New Zealand are also *not* represented.

Yachts pay US$9 a day to moor Mediterranean-style (stern-to, bow anchor out) along the quay on boulevard Pomare. For half the price you can anchor farther west along the boulevard. A one-time entry fee and optional daily electricity hookup are charged. Public toilets and showers are on the waterfront near the end of Ave. Bruat. The port captain, customs, and immigration are all in a building near the tourist office near the market. The **Yacht Club of Tahiti** (B.P. 1456, Papeete; tel. 42-78-03) at PK 4, Arue, charges visiting boats f.4500 a month to use one of their anchor buoys.

L'Office Territorial d'Action Culturelle (OTAC), B.P. 1709, Papeete; tel. 42-88-50) at the Cultural Center (Te Fare Tauhiti Nui) offers Tahitian courses for those spending longer periods in Papeete. The charge is f.10,000 a month for an hour and a half of lessons twice a week.

There's no coin laundry in Papeete but **Central Pressing,** 72 rue Albert Leboucher (the street behind the Royal Papeete Hotel), offers a special service to visitors: for f.600 they'll wash, dry, and fold one kilogram of laundry.

HEALTH

If you need a doctor, the **Clinique Paofai** (B.P. 545, Papeete; tel. 43-02-02) accepts outpatients weekdays and Sat. mornings, emergencies anytime. The facilities and attention are excellent, but be prepared for fees of around f.5000. The **Clinique Cardella** (tel. 42-81-90) on rue Anne-Marie Javouhey is also open day and night.

Dr. Vincent Joncker and Dr. J.-M.P. Rosenstein in the building above the pharmacy opposite the Catholic cathedral operate a clinic, **S.O.S. Medecins** (tel. 42-34-56), open daily. They charge US$45 for a consultation if you were referred by IAMAT (the International Association for Medical Assistance to Travelers).

Get cholera and yellow fever **vaccinations** from the Service d'Hygiène (open weekdays 0800-0900; tel. 45-41-53) on rue des Remparts.

INFORMATION

The **Tahiti Tourist Promotion Board** (OPATTI) at Fare Manihini (B.P. 65, Papeete; tel. 42-96-26), a neo-Polynesian building on the waterfront not far from the market, can answer basic questions and supply maps. Ask about special events here, but check their information carefully. They have detailed accommodation lists for all the outer islands. They're open weekdays 0730-1700, Sat. 0800-1100/1300-1600.

The **Institute Territorial de la Statistique** (B.P. 395, Papeete; tel. 43-71-96), 2nd floor, Bloc Donald (behind Voyagence Tahiti, opposite the Vaima Center), puts out a quarterly *Statistical Bulletin* (f.525).

La Boutique Klima (B.P. 31, Papeete; tel. 42-00-63) behind the cathedral sells old topographical maps, nautical charts, and many interesting books on Polynesia.

Newer topographical maps (f.1200) of some islands are available from the **Service de l'Aménagement** (B.P. 866, Papeete; tel. 42-46-50), 4th floor, Administrative Building, 11 rue du Commandant Destremeau.

For the best selection of French nautical charts, visit O.C.I. (Ouverages Cartes et Instruments) in the white Marine Nationale building next to the UTA office on the waterfront.

A small **public library** (open Mon.-Thurs. 0800-1600, Fri. 0800-1500; tel. 42-88-50) is located in the Cultural Center. To take books out you must buy an annual card for f.2000. You can sometimes watch videos on the Pacific in the library "discothèque."

Papeete's largest French bookstore is **Hachette Pacifique** (B.P. 334, Papeete; tel. 42-56-10), 14 Ave. Bruat. You'll find a much better selection of English books at **Librairie Archipels**, 68 rue des Remparts (B.P. 1689, Papeete; tel. 42-47-30). Archipels is about the only place you can find books and guides to the Pacific. Tahiti's newest bookstore is **Librairie Le Petit Prince** (tel. 43-26-24) in the Centre Commercial Moana Nui, Punaauia. There's a **newsstand** with magazines in English in front of the Vaima Center by the taxi stand on boulevard Pomare.

Airline Offices

Reconfirm your international flight at your airline's Papeete office, most of which are in the Vaima Center: **Air France** (tel. 42-20-00), **Air New Zealand** (tel. 43-01-70), **Hawaiian Airlines** (tel. 43-15-00), **LAN Chile** (tel. 42-64-55), and **Qantas** (tel. 43-06-65). **Minerve Corail Polynesie/Air Liberté** (tel. 43-42-01) is at 90 rue des Remparts; **UTA French Airlines** (tel. 43-63-33), which also represents Air Caledonie International, is on boulevard Pomare near Ave. Bruat.

GETTING AROUND

Le Truck

You can go almost anywhere on Tahiti by *le truck,* converted cargo vehicles with long benches and loudspeakers in back. *Trucks* marked "Outumaoro" run from Papeete to Faaa International Airport and the Maeva Beach Hotel every few minutes during the day, with sporadic service after dark until 2000 daily, then again in the morning from 0500 on. On Sundays long-distance *trucks* run only in the very early morning and evening; weekdays the last trip to Mahina, Paea, and points beyond is around 1700.

Trucks don't run right around the island. Although a couple go as far as Tautira and Teahupoo on Tahiti Iti, you could have difficulty getting a *truck* back to Papeete from those remote villages in the afternoon. To go around the island by *truck,* start early and travel clockwise. Get out at Taravao and walk down to the Gauguin Museum (three km). With lots of traffic along the south coast, it'll be easy to find a ride back this way, though the last Papeete-bound *truck* leaves around 1300. Luckily, so far, hitching is usually no problem.

The eastbound *trucks* park on the north side of Papeete market and face the waterfront, westbound *trucks* are on the south side and face inland. Other trucks terminate at Tipaerui near the Municipal Swimming Pool on the west side of town or on Cours de l'Union Sacrée on the east. The terminals are in the process of being changed, so its always a good idea to ask.

Destinations and fares are posted on the side of the vehicle: f.120 to Punaauia, f.140 to Mahina, f.150 to Paea, f.170 to Papara, f.220 to Mataiea or Papeari, f.320 to Teahupoo. After dark all *truck* fares increase. Outside Papeete you don't have to be at a stop: *trucks* stop anywhere if you wave. Luggage rides for free.

Others

Taxis in Papeete are a bit of a rip-off. Don't get in unless there's a meter that works or a rate card you can check. Fares are 25% more on Sundays and holidays; from 2200 to 0600 they double. They also charge extra for luggage at these times. The three taxi stands are at the Vaima Center (tel. 42-33-60), the market (tel. 43-19-62), and at the airport (tel. 43-30-07). If you feel cheated by a taxi driver take down the license number and complain to the tourist office.

Hitching *(autostop)* on Tahiti is fairly easy and relatively safe. It's great adventure because the local people are quite receptive to visitors. Your chances are better if it's obvious you're not French. Treat yourself to a circle-island tour by thumb!

Car Rentals

To rent a car you must be 21 (or 25 with Avis and Budget) and have held a driver's license for at least a year. Check the car as carefully as they check you. Comment on dents, scratches, flat tires, etc. All the car rental agencies include third-party public liability insurance in the basic price, but collision damage waiver (CDW) varies from f.500 to f.1200 extra per day. Some agencies charge the client for damage to the tires, insurance or no insurance. Tahiti insurance isn't valid if you take the car across to Moorea. Of course the car comes full of gas and you're supposed to return it that way. You'll see Mobil and Total gas stations all around Tahiti, but an outer island may only have one.

There's no way you can whiz around Tahiti in a rental car for less than US$50. If you choose a per-km rate (instead of unlimited mileage) it's better value to take several days to go around the island. You'll need two days minimum anyway if you want to explore Tahiti Iti. A trip around the island in two days, one of the roads on Tahiti Iti included, would be just under US$75 (based on the cheapest per-km rental from the cheapest agency without insurance). Some agencies impose a 50-km daily minimum on their per-km rentals to prevent you from traveling *too* slowly; most rentals are for a minimum of 24 hours. If you want to circle the island in one day and pack as many sidetrips in as you can, an unlimited mileage rental may be for you (from US$60). With four people sharing the costs it's not a bad deal.

Check with Avis and Budget for Tahiti specials before leaving home. Sometimes you can reserve a car with unlimited kilometers from Australia or the U.S. for less than you'd pay upon arrival.

Of the eight car rental agencies on Tahiti, **Hertz** (tel. 42-04-71), beside Peugeot near Uranie Cemetery, is the most expensive (from f.2500 a day, plus f.35 a km, or f.7500 with unlimited mileage). Their CDW insurance is valid only on paved roads. Not recommended.

The cheapest rates on a per-km basis are offered by **Pacificar** (B.P. 1121, Papeete; tel. 41-93-93) on Pont de l'Est at the east end of rue Paul Gauguin. Their smallest car is f.1500 a day, plus f.30 a km, plus f.900 insurance. They're open 24 hours a day—if the main office is closed the watchman in the parking lot can give you a car. Pacificar doesn't have unlimited mileage rentals.

Avis, (B.P. 1683, Papeete; tel. 42-96-49), 35 rue Charles Viénot, offers the lowest rates with unlimited mileage (f.6000, minimum two-day rental), although their insurance charges are the highest (f.1200).

On a per-km basis compare prices at **Robert** (B.P. 1047, Papeete; tel. 42-97-20), rue du Commandant Destremeau, **André** (tel. 42-94-04), boulevard Pomare opposite naval headquarters, and **Budget** (B.P. 306, Papeete; tel. 43-80-79), in the flashy Mobil Oil Australia building north of downtown.

Garage Daniel (B.P. 1445, Papeete; tel. 42-30-04) at PK 5.5 across the highway from the airport terminal has competitive per-km rates, but no unlimited mileages. Many car rental companies have kiosks inside Faaa Airport, and most offer a free pickup and dropoff service to the hotels and airport for clients.

Due to insurance problems and kamakaze traffic, it's not possible to rent a motorcycle or bicycle on Tahiti. **Garage Bambou** (B.P. 5592, Papeete; tel. 42-80-09) on Ave. Georges Clemenceau just beyond Hospital Mamao sells new bicycles for f.22,000 and does repairs.

Local Tours

Aroma Tours (B.P. 4477, Papeete; tel. 42-97-22) at Hotel Tahiti offers a five-hour circle-island tour, including visits to Point Venus, Faarumai Falls, and the Gauguin Museum for f.3500 pp (admissions and lunch extra). The manager, Jean-Paul Aromaiterai, also specializes in making arrangements for film crews shooting in Polynesia.

William Leeteg of **Adventure Eagle Tours** (B.P. 6719, Faaa; tel. 41-37-63) takes visitors to the top of Mt. Marau (1,372 meters) by 4WD jeep for f.5000 pp at 0930 and 1430 (four hours). A visit to Vaimahuta Falls is included but the trip is canceled on rainy days. William speaks good English and will arrange special guided tours for small groups of up to eight. Freddie Pansi of **Terai Tours** (tel. 42-27-50) and Aline Bernard of **Marau Tours** (tel. 42-61-83) also offer these trips.

GETTING AWAY

The **Air Tahiti** office (tel. 42-24-44) is upstairs in Fare Tony, the building behind Acajou off boulevard Pomare. **Air Moorea** (tel. 42-44-29) is at Faaa International Airport. Interisland services by air and sea are covered in the main Introduction to this book.

The ferry to Moorea departs from the landing just north of the tourist office downtown. The *Raromatai Ferry* to the Leeward Islands also leaves from there, as do cruise ships and a few other small boats. All other interisland ships, including the popular *Taporo IV* and *Temehani*, leave from the interisland wharf or Tuamotu wharf in Motu Uta, across the harbor from downtown Papeete. You can catch a *truck* directly to Motu Uta from rue Albert Leboucher beside Papeete market. The ticket offices of some of the vessels are in Fare Ute just north of downtown (addresses given in the main Introduction to this book).

OTHER WINDWARD ISLANDS

Mehetia is an uninhabited high island (435 meters) about 100 km east of Tahiti. It's less than two km across with no lagoon and landing is difficult. Fishermen from the south coast of Tahiti visit occasionally.

Maiao or Tapuaemanu, 70 km southwest of Moorea, is a low coral island with an elongated 154-meter-high hill at the center. On each side of this hill is a large greenish blue lake. Around Maiao is a barrier reef with a pass on the south side accessible only to small boats. Some 250 people live on 8.3-square-km Maiao, all Polynesians. Europeans and Chinese are not allowed to reside on the island as a result of problems with an Englishman, Eric Trower, who attempted to gain control of Maiao for phosphate mining in the 1930s.

There are no tourist accommodations; an invitation from a resident is required to stay. There's no airstrip. For information on the monthly supply ship from Papeete contact the **Compagnie Française Maritime de Tahiti** (B.P. 368, Papeete; tel. 42-63-93) at Fare Ute. A roundtrip voyage on this ship would at least give you a glimpse of Maiao.

TETIAROA

Tetiaroa, 42 km north of Tahiti, is a low coral atoll with a turquoise lagoon and 13 deep green coconut-covered islets totaling 490 hectares. Only small boats can enter the lagoon. Tahuna Iti has been designated a seabird refuge, the lagoon a marine reserve. On three-km-long Rimatuu islet may be seen the remains of Polynesian *maraes* and giant *tuu* trees.

Once a Tahitian royal retreat, in 1904 the Pomare family gave it to the British dentist Walter Williams to pay their bills. Dr. Williams, who was also the British consul from 1923 to 1935, had a daughter who sold Tetiaroa to actor **Marlon Brando** in 1962. Brando came to Tahiti in 1960 to play Fletcher Christian in the MGM film *Mutiny on the Bounty* and ended up marrying his leading lady, Tarita Teriipaia. She and her family still run the small tourist resort on Tetiaroa. Tarita and Marlon have two children, a son Teihotu born in 1965 and a daughter Cheyenne born in 1970.

The gunshot death of Dag Drollet, Cheyenne's ex-boyfriend and father of her son Tuki, at the Brando residence in Los Angeles in 1990 resulted in a 10-year prison sentence for Cheyenne's half-brother, Christian Brando, on a plea bargain. The incident continues to haunt the Brando family as a French examining magistrate pursues his investigation of Cheyenne's complicity in the affair. Until this tragic case is closed Marlon is unable to visit Tahiti, as he was home at the time of the 1990 shooting and could be detained as a material witness.

Getting There

A reservation office (B.P. 2418, Papeete; tel. 42-63-03) in the Air Moorea terminal at Faaa International Airport arranges flying visits to Tetiaroa. A seven-hour day-trip including airfare, bird island tour, and lunch is f.25,000 pp. If you arrange this trip through your hotel their commission will boot the price up to f.29,000 pp. To spend the night at the **Tetiaroa Village Hotel** in a rustic bungalow with private bath and all meals add f.10,000 s, f.14,000 d, f.12,000 t, to the per-person tour price. A second night is f.5000 pp extra. An attempt has been made to keep things as natural as possible, so—though the price may suggest it—don't expect a luxury resort. The hotel is often closed for extended periods and is in need of major renovations.

Less expensive visits to Tetiaroa can be arranged at **Tahiti Mer et Loisirs** (B.P. 3488, Papeete; tel. 43-97-99), in a houseboat on the Papeete waterfront opposite the post office. Their yacht cruises to the atoll are f.14,500 pp for one day, f.24,000 pp for two days, including snorkeling gear, trips ashore, and all meals. Longer stays are possible at f.9500 pp for each additional day, all inclusive. Scuba diving is available at f.4500.

MOOREA
INTRODUCTION

Moorea, Tahiti's heart-shaped sister island, is clearly visible across the Sea of the Moon just 16 km northwest of Papeete. This enticing island offers the white-sand beaches rare on Tahiti, plus long, deep bays, lush volcanic peaks, and a broad blue-green lagoon. Dino de Laurentis filmed *The Bounty* here in 1983. Tourism is concentrated along the north coast around Paopao and Club Med; most of the locals live in the south. Much more than Tahiti, Moorea is the laidback South Sea isle of the travel brochures. With a population of just 9,000, Moorea lives a quiet, relaxed life-style; coconut, pineapple, and vanilla plantations alternate with pleasant resorts and the vegetation-draped dwellings of the inhabitants.

Tourism in Moorea is highly competitive and you can often get good deals by shopping around for rooms, car rentals, tours, etc. When things are slow (such as in Sept. and from mid-Jan. to Feb.) some hotels really slash their rates. Even if you're staying at one of the luxury hotels, you'll do better dealing with a kiosk on the highway for rental cars and circle-island tours; reservations desks inside the hotels are run by exactly the same companies but tack on a commission for the hotel. *Le truck* circles this easily accessible island. The accommodations are good and plentiful, while weekly and monthly apartment rentals make even extended stays possible. Don't try to see it as a day-trip: this is a place to relax!

Orientation
If you arrive by ferry you'll get off at Vaiare, four km south of Temae Airport. Your hotel may be at Maharepa (Bali Hai Hotel, Coconut House), Paopao (Bali Hai Club, Motel Albert), Pihaena (Moorea Lagoon Hotel, Chez Marie Blandine), or Tiahura (Club Med, Chez Nelson et Josiane,

Moorea Village Hotel), all on the north coast. The Paopao hotels enjoy better scenery, but the beach is far superior at Tiahura.

The PKs (kilometer stones) on Moorea begin at the post office opposite the access road to Temae Airport. They're numbered up to PK 35 along the north coast via Club Med and up to PK 24 along the south coast via Afareaitu, meeting at Haapiti halfway around the island. Our circle-island tour below begins at Temae Post Office and travels counterclockwise. The Moorea accommodations and restaurant listings below begin at Vaiare wharf and also go counterclockwise in each category.

THE LAND

This triangular island is actually the surviving south rim of a volcano once 3,000 meters high.

Moorea is twice as old as its Windward partner Tahiti, and weathering is noticeably advanced. The two spectacular bays cutting into the north coast flank Mt. Rotui (899 meters), once Moorea's core. The jagged grandeur of the crescent of peaks facing these northern bays is scenically superb.

Shark-tooth-shaped Mouaroa (880 meters) rising behind Cook's Bay is a visual triumph, but Mount Tohivea (1,207 meters) is higher. Polynesian chiefs were once buried in caves along the cliffs. Moorea's peaks protect the north and northwest coasts from the rain-bearing southeast trades; the drier climate and scenic beauty explain the profusion of hotels along this side of the island. Moorea is surrounded by a coral ring with several passes into the lagoon. Three *motus* enhance the lagoon, one off Afareaitu and two off Club Med.

Moorea's interior valley slopes are unusually rich, with large fruit and vegetable plantations and human habitation. At one time or another coconuts, sugar cane, cotton, vanilla, coffee, rice, and pineapples have all been grown in the rich soil of Moorea's plantations. Stock farming and fishing are other occupations. Vegetables like taro, tomatoes, cucumbers, pumpkins, lettuce, and fruit such as bananas, oranges, grapefruit, papayas, star apples, rambutans, avocados, mangos, limes, tangerines, and breadfruit, make Moorea a veritable garden of Eden.

HISTORY

Legend claims that Aimeho (or "Eimeo" as Capt. Cook spelled it) was formed from the second dorsal fin of the fish that became Tahiti. The present name, Moorea, means "offshoot." A hole right through the summit of Mt. Mouaputa (830 meters) is said to have been made by the spear of the demigod Pai, who tossed it across from Tahiti to prevent Mt. Rotui from being carried off to Raiatea by Hiro, the god of thieves.

Captain Samuel Wallis was the European discoverer of the Windward Islands in 1767. After leaving Tahiti he passed along the north coast of Moorea without landing. He named it Duke of York's Island. The first European visitors were botanist Joseph Banks, Lieutenant Gore, the surgeon William Monkhouse, Herman Sporing, and half a dozen sailors sent over there by Capt. Cook on 1 June 1769 to observe the transit of Venus. (The main observatory was, of course, on Point Venus, but it was also observed by officers on Moorea and on a small islet off the east coast of Tahiti.) The telescope was set up on the small Motu Irioa, halfway between Club Med and Opunohu Bay, and the observation was duly made on 3 June. Banks landed several times on the north coast at Papetoai. The party returned to Tahiti on 4 June. Captain Cook anchored in Opunohu Bay for one week in 1777, but he never visited the bay which today bears his name! His visit was uncharacteristically brutal as he smashed the islanders' canoes and burned their homes when they refused to return a stolen goat.

In 1792 Pomare I conquered Moorea using arms obtained from the *Bounty* mutineers. Moorea had long been a traditional place of refuge for defeated Tahitian warriors, thus in 1808 Pomare II fled into exile here with a party of English missionaries after his bid to bring all Tahiti under his control had failed. Moorea has a special place in the history of Christianity: here in 1812 the missionaries finally managed to convert Pomare II after 15 years of trying. On 14 Feb. 1815 Patii, high priest of Oro, publicly accepted Protestantism and burned the old heathen idols at Papetoai, where the octagonal church is today. Shortly afterward the whole population followed Patii's example. The *maraes* of Moorea were then abandoned and the Opunohu Valley depopulated. The first Tahitian translation of part of the Bible was printed on Moorea in 1817. From this island Protestantism spread throughout the South Pacific.

After Pomare II finally managed to reconquer Tahiti in 1815, Moorea again became a backwater. American novelist Herman Melville visit-

In June 1769 a party led by Captain Cook's botanist Joseph Banks became the first Europeans to land on Moorea. This fictitious engraving by a contemporary London artist shows "Mr. Banks receiving a Visit from the King of Duke of York's Island."

ed Moorea in 1842 and worked with other beachcombers on a sweet-potato farm in Maatea. His book *Omoo* contains a marvelous description of his tour of the island. Cotton and coconut plantations were created on Moorea in the 19th century, followed by vanilla and coffee in the 20th, but only with the advent of the travel industry has Moorea become more than a beautiful backdrop for Tahiti.

SIGHTS

Around Cook's Bay

On the grounds of the American-owned **Bali Hai Hotel** at PK 5 are historic anchors lost by captains Bougainville and Cook in the 18th century. On the mountain side of the road just past the Bali Hai is the "White House," the stately mansion of a former vanilla plantation, now used as a *pareu* salesroom.

At the entrance to Cook's Bay (PK 7) is the **Galerie Aad Van der Heyde** (tel. 56-14-22), as much a museum as a gallery. Aad's paintings hang outside in the flower-filled courtyard; inside are his black-pearl jewelry, a large collection of Marquesan sculpture, and artifacts from around the Pacific.

At the **Moorea Pearls Center** (admission free; tel. 56-13-13) opposite Club Bali Hai in Paopao (PK 8.5) are exquisite black pearls and more Polynesian woodcarvings.

A rough dirt road up to the Belvédère begins just west of the bridge at Paopao (PK 9). On the west side of Cook's Bay a km farther along is

a **Catholic church** (PK 10); an interesting altar painting with Polynesian angels (1948) was done by the Swedish artist Peter Heyman.

It's possible to visit the Distillerie de Moorea **fruit juice factory** (B.P. 23, Moorea; tel. 56-11-33) up off the main road at PK 12 Tues.-Fri. 0900-1200, the only one of its kind in Tahiti-Polynesia. Aside from the papaya, grapefruit, and pineapple juices made from local fruits, the factory produces apple, orange, and passionfruit juices from imported concentrate with no preservatives added. There're also 40-proof brandies (carambole, ginger, grapefruit, guava, mango, orange, and pineapple flavors) and 25-proof liqueurs (coconut, ginger, and pineapple varieties) made here and sold to the public at the Accueil counter. If you look affluent enough they may invite you to sample their brews.

Opunohu Bay To Le Belvédère

The **Moorea Lagoon Hotel** at PK 14 is the only large hotel between Paopao and Tiahura. Shrimp

an old photo of Mouaroa across Cook's Bay, Moorea

ARCHIVES NATIONALES, SECTION OUTRE-MER FRANCE

underwater attractions of Tahiti-Polynesia (all photos this page courtesy Tahiti Tourist Board)

1. WW II American gun on Bora Bora; **2.** a vanilla house, Maharepa, Moorea; **3.** *le truck* near Papeete Market, Tahiti; **4.** lighthouse, Point Venus, Tahiti; **5.** church at Pueu, Tahiti Iti; **6.** Chinese temple, Papeete, Tahiti (all photos this page by D. Stanley)

are bred in large basins at the head of Opunohu Bay (PK 18). A paved road up the pineapple-filled **Opunohu Valley** to the Belvédère begins here: 1¹/₂ km to the connecting road from Cook's Bay, another two km to Marae Titiroa, then one more steep km up to the lookout. On the way pass Moorea's agricultural high school. This worthy institution, with students from all the islands of Tahiti-Polynesia, has hundreds of hectares planted in pineapples, vanilla, coffee, fruit trees, decorative flowers, and native vegetables.

Marae Titiroa, high up near the geographical center of Moorea, is the largest of a group of Polynesian temples restored in 1969 by Prof. Y.H. Sinoto of Honolulu. The small platform or *ahu* at the end of this *marae* (and the others) was a sacred area reserved for the gods. Stone backrests for chiefs and priests are another feature of the *marae*. Here the people offered gifts of tubers, fish, dogs, and pigs, and prayed to their gods, of whom many were deified ancestors. Just 50 meters northwest of Marae Titiroa near the water tanks is a long council platform, and 50 meters farther are two smaller *marae*

surrounded by towering Tahitian chestnut trees *(mape)*. The most evocative of the group is four-tiered **Marae Ahu o Mahine,** about 250 meters down the trail.

Some 500 ancient structures have been identified in this area and, if you're keen, you should be able to find a few in the forest across the stream, evidence of a large population with a highly developed social system. With the acceptance of Christianity in the early 19th century, the Opunohu Valley's importance declined sharply. Naturalists will enjoy the natural vegetation in there (you must bushwhack).

Continue up the main road about 300 meters from Marae Titiroa and watch for some stone archery platforms on the left. Here kneeling noblemen once competed to see who could shoot their arrow the farthest. The bows and arrows employed in these contests were never used in warfare. Less than 100 meters farther up on the left is access to another archery platform and **Marae Afareaito.** The slabs you see sticking up in the middle of the *marae* were backrests for participants of honor.

Above is the **Belvédère** or Roto Nui, a viewpoint from which much of northern Moorea is visible. From here it's easy to visualize the great volcano that was Moorea. Mt. Rotui in front of you was once the central core of an island more than three times as high as the present one. The north part is now missing but the semicircular arch of the southern half is plain to see.

Papetoai To Club Med

Return to the main circuminsular highway and continue west. The **octagonal Protestant church** behind the post office at Papetoai (PK 22) was built on the site of the temple of the god Oro in 1822. Despite having been rebuilt several times the church is known as "the oldest European building still in use in the South Pacific."

As the road begins to curve around the northwest corner of Moorea one passes a number of large resort hotels, the **Beachcomber Parkroyal** (PK 24), **Club Med** (PK 27), and the **Moorea Village Hotel** (PK 28); only Club Med forbids you to walk through their grounds to the beach. It's possible to snorkel out to Tarahu and Tiahuru *motus* from this beach. The recreation people at the Beachcomber Parkroyal and Moorea Beach Hotel could also ferry you over for f.500 pp roundtrip. Try feeding bread to the fish. There's excellent reef-break surfing here, too. In **Le Petit Village** shopping mall across the street from Club Med is a grocery store. **Carole Boutique** beside Hotel Hibiscus (PK 27) lists good prices on T-shirts, etc.

Southern And Eastern Moorea

The south coast of Moorea is much quieter than the north. You'll drive for kilometers through the open coconut plantations with several unspoiled villages and scenic vistas. At PK 31 is **Tiki Theater,** described below under "Entertainment." **Résidence Linareva** (PK 34) is a nice place to stop for lunch or a drink (see below). At PK 35/24, Haapiti, the kilometer numbering begins its descent to Temae Airport.

Afareaitu (PK 9), the administrative center of Moorea, has a hospital, police station, etc. Tiny Motu Hahi lies just off Afareaitu. The London Missionary Society originally had its Academy of the South Seas here. On 30 June 1817, at the original missionary printing works at Afareaitu, King Pomare II ceremonially printed the first page of the first book ever published on a South Pacific island, a Tahitian translation of the Gospel of St. Luke. Before the press was moved to Huahine a year later over 9,000 books—over half a million pages—had been printed at Afareaitu!

Hike an hour up the **Afareaitu Valley** from the old Protestant church (1912) to a high waterfall which cascades down a sheer cliff into a pool. Keep straight on the main track till it becomes a footpath, and you're almost there (keep looking). Tohivea towers to one side.

Vaiare Wharf (where you may have landed) is at PK 4, then comes the **Sofitel Ia Ora** (PK 1.5). If you have your own transport, stop for a look around Moorea's most sophisticated resort. It's enjoyable to walk north along the beach from this hotel or even to go snorkeling. At PK 1 on the main road high above the Ia Ora ia a fine **lookout** over the deep passage romantically named the Sea of the Moon between Tahiti and Moorea. **Temae Post Office** (PK 0) and the airport mark the end of our 59-km circle-island tour.

Hiking

An excellent three-hour hike along a shaded trail takes you from Vaiare up across the moun-

Moorea's Rotui rises above a country road.

tains to Paopao. The way, partly marked by red, white, and green paint dabbed on tree and rock, is much easier to follow from the Vaiare side. Take the road inland about·50 meters south of the first bridge just south of the Vaiare ferry wharf. At the fork, cross a creek on the right and look for the first red marks. The way requires a little concentration to follow, however, as the Tahiti Tourist Board hasn't done any trail maintenance for many years. After rains it can be muddy.

When you reach the divide, go a short distance south along the ridge past some barbed wire to a super viewpoint over the pineapple plantations behind Paopao. On a clear day the rounded double peak of Orohena, Tahiti's highest, is visible, plus the whole interior of Moorea. If you're fresh off the ferry, no other introduction to the island could be more spectacular. This rigorous hike is also worth doing simply to see a good cross section of the vegetation. Don't miss it, but take water.

PRACTICALITIES

ACCOMMODATIONS

Inexpensive Accommodations

The **Tiaia Village** (Chez Gisele et Raymond, B.P. 266, Moorea; tel. 56-16-84) near Maharepa has four bungalows with cooking facilities on the mountain side facing the highway. Each bungalow (up to four persons) is f.5000 daily, f.50,000 monthly. There's a store nearby.

The locally owned **Hotel Baie de Cook** (B.P. 30, Paopao; tel. 56-10-50), formerly the Ibis Moorea, is a mock-colonial building by the highway at the entrance to Cook's Bay. The 76 standard rooms are good value at f.4000 s or d (children under 12 free), but the Baie de Cook has a false-front Waikiki feel. Call ahead to check prices and availability. Neither this hotel nor the two mentioned below are on the beach.

Motel Albert (Albert Haring; tel. 56-12-76), up on the hill above Club Bali Hai at Paopao (PK 8.5), catches splendid views across Cook's Bay. The eight older units with double beds are f.3000 s or d, f.4000 t (two-night minimum stay). The 11 larger houses accommodating up to four persons are f.6000. Monthly rates are f.70,000 d. Each unit has cooking facilities and several stores are nearby. No reservations are accepted. Don't ask Albert for permission to pitch your tent on the grounds—he doesn't care for campers. Giant cockroaches take over the motel at night.

The three bungalows behind **Boutique Dina** (tel. 56-10-39) a km east of the Moorea Lagoon Hotel are f.3000 t, f.4000 for up to five; subtract f.500 a day for the weekly rate. Cooking facilities are provided and the bathroom is communal.

Several places near the Moorea Lagoon Hotel (PK 14) rent more expensive bungalows. **Chez Nani** (B.P. 67, Papeete, tel. 42-79-37) on the west side of the hotel has three thatched bungalows with kitchenettes for f.7000 s or d. The signposted **Faimano Village** (B.P. 1676, Papeete, tel. 56-10-20) next to Chez Nani has four bungalows with cooking facilities at f.10,500 for up to six persons with private bath, f.7500 d or t with shared bath. **Chez Francine** (tel. 56-13-24) 400 meters farther west has one house with kitchenette at f.5000 d. There's no grocery store near the Moorea Lagoon—the nearest is by the bridge in Paopao.

Motel Maeva (tel. 56-20-51), all by itself at PK 20 on the north side of Opunohu Bay, has a couple of studios with cooking facilities at f.4000 for up to three people.

Hotel Résidence Tiahura (B.P. 1068, Papetoai; tel. 56-15-45), at PK 25 Tiahura on the mountain side just east of Club Med, a five-minute walk from the beach. One of the 18 bungalows without kitchenette is f.3500 s or d, one of the six with kitchenette f.4000 s or d, f.5500 t. By the month it's f.45,000 s or d, f.55,000 t. All units have fridge and private bath. Their restaurant is reasonable—nice people, friendly service, good reports.

The **Hibiscus Hotel** (B.P. 1009, Papetoai; tel. 56-12-20) right beside Club Med might be a good choice for families. Two adults and two children can stay in one of the 29 garden bungalows beneath the coconut palms for f.5000. At this price it's reasonable and weekly rates are available, but there's a two-night minimum stay. Canoes and snorkeling gear are extra.

If you have a tent *the* place on Moorea to pitch it is the **Moorea Backpackers' Club** (tel. 56-15-18), beside the Hibiscus Hotel just south of Club Med (PK 27). This campground, also known as "Chez Nelson et Josiane," is beautifully set in a coconut grove right on the beach. The charge is f.500 pp, toilets, showers, refrigerator, and basic cooking facilities provided. No tents are for rent, but a bunk in the six-bed hostel is f.1500. The four small rooms with shared bath are f.3000 d; the three larger bungalows with kitchen and private bath are f.4000 d. Ask about getting one free day if you stay over a week.

A second campground (also f.500 pp) has sprung up just a little south of Chez Nelson et Josiane near the Moorea Village Hotel. Known variously as **Moorea Camping** (tel. 56-14-47) or "Backpackers' Paradise," it also faces a white-sand beach, has four six-bed dorms (f.800 pp), and another 12 double rooms (f.2000 d). Communal kitchen and washing facilities are provided. They'll loan you snorkeling gear, a canoe, and even organize trips around the island for f.800 pp if there are at least six people willing to go. Campground residents get a 10% discount on scuba diving with Scubapiti, transport included. As at Chez Nelson et Josiane, the eighth night is free. Both these campgounds are rather basic, but great for young budget travelers.

Billy Ruta Bungalows (tel. 56-12-54) is at the south end of the west coast strip, right on the beach at PK 28, Tiahura. The 11 thatched A-frame bungalows begin at f.3000 d without kitchenette, f.4000 d with kitchenette.

Fare Matotea (B.P. 1111, Papetoai; tel. 56-14-36) on the beach just south of Billy Ruta (PK 29) is okay if you're in a group: f.7200 for four, f.8300 for six (minimum stay two nights). Monthly rates are f.70,000. All eight bungalows on spacious grounds have full cooking facilities and private bath.

Chez Pauline (Pauline Teariki; tel. 56-11-26) at PK 9, Afareaitu, is between the two stores opposite the gendarmerie. The seven rooms with double beds and shared bath in this old colonial house run f.2500 s, f.3500 d or t. The five-bed dorm is f.1000 pp. You may get a discount if you arrive late or leave early! A picturesque restaurant (closed Sun.), with Pauline's tikis on display, rounds out this establishment which would have great atmosphere if it weren't for the abrupt manner of the proprietress. Dinner here is around f.2000 (fish and Tahitian vegetables).

Chez Coco and Madou (B.P. 390, Afareaitu; tel. 56-17-16) is on Motu Temae, 1 1/2 km down the road opposite the post office near Temae Airport. The contact person is at the Chez Helene shop nearby. Camping is f.500 pp (tent rental f.700, if required) and sleeping in the dorm is f.1000 pp with cooking facilities provided. It's a little off the beaten track; in fact, the easiest way to get there from the wharf is to walk north along the beach from the Sofitel la Ora. Coco's is a good base for surfers awaiting those big righthanders on the nearby Temae reef.

Expensive Accommodations

The **Sofitel la Ora** (B.P. 28, Temae, Moorea; tel. 56-12-90) at PK 1.5 between Vaiare and the airport is *the* place if you want luxury and don't give a damn about the price. The 80 deluxe thatched bungalows begin at f.20,700 s or d (children under 12 free). This French-owned hotel has class! Breakfast and dinner are f.4000 pp extra together. See Tahitian dancing in the la Ora's La Pérouse Restaurant on Mon., Wed., and Sat. at 2030. On the shore is another restaurant-cum-disco in a converted interisland schooner. The beach (topless) is one of the best on the island, with a splendid view of Tahiti.

profile of Moorea

The 63-room **Bali Hai Hotel** (B.P. 26, Moorea; tel. 56-13-59) at PK 5, Maharepa, caters mainly to American tour groups staying three, four, or seven nights. The cheapest rooms are f.11,800 s or d, f.14,300 t (children under 12 free), bungalows two or three times that. The rooms near the highway are noisy. For breakfast and dinner add f.4100 pp extra. There's a Tahitian feast with Polynesian dancing Sundays at lunchtime (f.4000)—see it all for free from the bar. Rides on the Bali Hai's thatched catamaran *Liki Tiki* are also free for guests. This hotel and its namesakes on Huahine and Raiatea were founded by the so-called Bali Hai Boys, Hugh, Jay, and Muk. The happy-go-lucky tale of this gang of three's arrival on Moorea in 1959 is posted in the lobby, if you're interested.

At the **Kaveka Beach Club** (B.P. 13, Temae, Moorea; tel. 56-18-30), nearby at PK 7.5, Paopao, the 24 thatched garden bungalows run f.9500 s, f.11,000 d or t; the breakfast and dinner meal plan is f.3600 pp extra. Some nautical activities such as sailboarding, snorkeling, and paddling are offered free, and scuba diving is available nearby with M.U.S.T.

Club Bali Hai (B.P. 8, Temae, Moorea; tel. 56-13-68) at PK 8.5, Paopao, is f.14,000 s or d, f.16,500 t for a room with a view of spectacular Cook's Bay. The Club's restaurant is worth checking out and the snack bar down by the dock serves a wicked hot dog for f.300! Many of the 19 units with cooking facilities have been sold to affluent Americans on a time-sharing basis with each owner getting two weeks a year at the Club.

The **Moorea Lagoon Hotel** (B.P. 11, Moorea; tel. 56-14-68) at PK 14 is f.11,000 s, f.12,000 d, f.15,000 t for one of the 45 thatched garden bungalows. Ask about the Sat. night Tahitian dancing. This hotel, along with the Hotel Baie de Cook seven km down the road and the Te Puna Bel Air on Tahiti, are owned by the local Rey family. The beach is fine—have fun if your tour company dropped you here.

The 150-room **Moorea Beachcomber Parkroyal** (B.P. 1019, Papetoai; tel. 56-19-19) at PK 24, the former Sofitel Tiare, takes the cake as the most expensive hotel on Moorea. Rooms in the main building start at f.24,000 s, f.26,000 d, f.29,000 t—much too much. For an overwater

bungalow tack on an additional 50%. There's a Tahitian show here on Sat. night. The Beachcomber Parkroyal, built in 1987, was purchased in 1989 for US$13.5 million by Japanese interests, which have since spent further millions of dollars upgrading the place. If you want to see how Moorea is being spoiled by tourism, look no further.

The **Moorea Beach Club** (B.P. 1017, Papetoai; tel. 56-15-48), formerly the Climate de France, is the first hotel on the white sandy shores of Tiahura tourist strip. The 83 a/c rooms with fridge go for f.9500 s, f.11,000 d or t, plus f.3600 pp extra for breakfast and dinner (if desired). The more expensive bungalows have cooking facilities. Prices have increased sharply here in recent years, though outrigger canoes, sailboarding, tennis, snorkeling, and fishing gear may still be loaned free.

Résidence Les Tipaniers (B.P. 1002, Moorea; tel. 56-12-67) is cramped around the reception but better as you approach the beach. The 14 rooms are f.7500 s, f.10,000 d, f.11,700 t, while eight thatched bungalows with kitchen are a few thousand francs extra. They'll shuttle you over to a *motu* for snorkeling, free. The hotel's Italian restaurant is not recommended.

Club Méditerranée (B.P. 1010, Moorea; tel. 56-15-00) at PK 27 has been renovated and expanded to 350 fan-cooled bungalows. You can reserve one by paying f.14,000 pp a day (double occupancy) at the Club Med office in the Vaima Center, Papeete (B.P. 575, Papeete; tel. 42-96-99). The price includes breakfast and dinner, and a wide range of regimented activities, but no transfers. Unlimited beer and wine come with lunch and dinner, but other drinks are expensive and laundry charges will knock your socks off! If you're not a member, the Club Med initiation fee (US$30) and annual dues (US$50) are extra. One of only two full PADI scuba diving centers in the South Pacific is here, for guests only. Club Med's for you if non-stop activity amid an "ambience indigène" is your aim. Otherwise, all the canned entertainment can be to the detriment of peace at night and occasional helicopter landings beside the Tiki Restaurant often interrupt afternoon naps. Clocks inside the village are set ahead to give guests an extra hour in the sun. Club Med's G.O.s *(gentils organisateurs)* tend to resist the unusual or non-routine (such as requesting a specific room), so try to go with the flow. It's not a swinging singles club anymore, but rather a haven for couples where singles can be found. No visitors are allowed.

The 48-unit **Moorea Village Hotel** (B.P. 1008, Moorea; tel. 56-10-02) at PK 28 has nice fan-cooled thatched bungalows for f.5000 s or d, f.7500 for up to four people. For a kitchen in your unit add f.3000 to the price. To be on the beach is another f.5000. The 35 kitchenless garden bungalows are one of the best buys on Moorea and nudism is possible on a small off-shore *motu*. Saturdays at 1900 there's a veal barbecue; the Tahitian feast with Polynesian dancing is Sunday at 1300. There are lots of free activities. For those seeking a resort with middle-range prices, this is a winner.

Résidence Linareva (B.P. 205, Moorea; tel. 56-15-35), amid splendid mountain scenery at PK 34 on the wild side of the island, is designed for long stays. Reservations are recommended. Prices begin at f.8800 s or d, f.9800 t, with 25% weekly discounts. Each of the 11 housekeeping units is unique. Large cozy rooms are available for families or groups (for example, a very pleasant eight-bed bunkroom with kitchenette is f.22,000). The scuba facilities make this residence a natural for divers. Linareva's floating seafood restaurant, the *Tamarii Moorea I*, is an old ferryboat which once plied between Moorea and Tahiti. Colorful reef fish are kept in an enclosure by the dock. It's a good place to have lunch (1200-1400) on the way around the island; specials are marked on a blackboard. Other times the restaurant has a pub atmosphere.

FOOD

Aside from the hotel restaurants, a mixed bag of eateries caters to table hoppers. **Restaurant Chez Michel et Jackie** (closed Mon.; tel. 56-11-08) on the main road just east of the Bali Hai Hotel features French cooking and big two-person pizzas (f.2000).

The **Manava Nui Restaurant** (closed Sun.; tel. 56-22-00) on the east side of Cook's Bay serves Cantonese and European dishes. Mediocre food, poor service, no smiles.

Le Bonne Table du Hakka Restaurant (closed Thurs. or Fri.; tel. 56-12-19) on the island side of the road by Cook's Bay a few hundred meters south of Club Bali Hai (PK 8.5) is one of the old established places. Its moderately expensive French cooking with a Chinese air is reputed to be the best on the island. Fresh fish and shrimp are specialties.

Snack Te Honu Iti (tel. 56-19-84) at PK 9 near the head of Cook's Bay dispenses inexpensive hamburgers, tuna burgers, and a *plat du jour* on their airy terrace. The papaya, coconut, and banana milkshakes are served warm!

Restaurant Fare Manava (closed Wed.; tel. 56-14-24) opposite the Pharmacie in Paopao has a pleasant dining room overlooking Cook's Bay. Prices are reasonable with mahimahi around f.1000 and excellent Chinese food too. Check this one out!

French-operated **Tropical "Snack"** in Le Petit Village shopping mall opposite Club Med serves pizza and light meals for f.500-900. The food is good, a bargain if you only drink water. **Moorea Glaces** in the same mall serves good ice cream (f.120 a scoop), fresh poisson cru, and tasty salads (f.600-800).

Snack Eimeo (tel. 56-20-14) just south of Pauline's at Afareaitu (PK 9) has hamburgers, omelets, salads, steak, *frites,* and lobster specials. They're open for lunch daily.

If you've access to cooking facilities be aware that fresh produce is much harder to obtain on Moorea than it is on Tahiti. Buy things when you see them and plan your grocery shopping carefully. Ask the stores what time the bread arrives, then be there promptly. The hybrid lime grapefruit being developed on Moorea has a thick green skin and really unique taste.

ENTERTAINMENT

Most of the hotel bars have happy hour 1800-1900.

Moorea has its own instant culture village, the **Tiki Theater** (B.P. 1016, Moorea; tel. 56-18-97) at PK 31, Haapiti (closed Wed.; admission f.600). Doors open at 1030, with traditional dances performed at 1130. Line fishing on the reef from a pirogue takes place at 1330 and is

a charming Polynesian woman

included in the price. Lunch is f.2000 extra and features local foods, with beer and wine on the house. Tuesday and Fri. nights at 1800 there's a big sunset show with a *tamaraa* buffet and open bar (f.5000, reservations required). Pirogue transportation from the hotels to Tiki Theater is f.1000. The guided tour of the village is informative and the staff enthusiastic. If you've got US$995 to blow, a royal Tahitian wedding can be arranged at the village (bring your own husband/wife). The ceremony lasts two hours, from 1600 to sunset, and is a private party with the village closed to the public. The bridegroom arrives by canoe and the newlyweds are carried around in procession by four "warriors." Yes, it's kinda tacky, but that's show biz. Many readers have written in to say they liked Tiki Theater.

SPORTS AND RECREATION

Scuba diving is offered by Catherine and Jean-Luc Untz of **Scubapiti** at Résidence Linareva (B.P. 1072, Moorea; tel. 56-20-38), Haapiti, with trips daily except Wed. at 0900 and 1430. Linareva guests get a 10% discount on the f.4500 tariff (f.35,000 for 10 dives). The price

includes transport from the hotels and all equipment. PADI scuba certification is possible. Child divers aged five and up are welcome. Scubapiti frequents the sheltered waters off southern Moorea.

The choppier waters of northern Moorea are the realm of **M.U.S.T. Plongée Scuba Diving** or "Moorea Underwater Scuba diving Tahiti" (B.P. 336, Moorea; tel. 56-17-32), on the dock behind the Hotel Baie de Cook. They offer diving at 0900 and 1400 daily except Mondays for f.4500 for one dive, f.20,000 for five dives. Rental of snorkeling gear is f.300. Divemaster Philippe Molle, author of a well-known French book on scuba diving, knows 15 different spots in and outside the reef. He also runs a two-room guesthouse, **M.U.S.T. Hérbergement**, at PK 15, 1 1/2 km west of the Moorea Lagoon Hotel. Only divers are accommodated: f.6000 pp with all meals and free transfers to the dive shop. Philippe's slogan is: "Diving with M.U.S.T. is a must!"

Bernard and Collette Begliomini's **Bathy's Club** (B.P. 1019, Papetoai; tel. 56-21-07), at the Beachcomber Parkroyal, offers scuba diving for f.4500, plus PADI certification courses. Both the M.U.S.T. and Bathy's Club dive shops specialize in underwater fish, eel, and shark feeding. Sometimes the swarm of fish becomes so thick the guide is lost from sight, yet as the resident shark scatters the mass of fish to steal the bait, the divemaster is seen again patting *le requin* as it passes! Scubapiti foregoes these spectacles in order to present marinelife in its natural state.

The "Activities Nautiques" kiosk (tel. 56-19-19, extension 1140) on the wharf at the **Beachcomber Parkroyal** has a glass-bottom boat (f.1500 pp) which leaves at 0900 and 1400. For more excitement hire a lagoon jet boat for f.6500 an hour (maximum four passengers) or try your hand at parasailing. A tour of both bays on northern Moorea is f.9500 by lagoon jet; a trip around the island f.16,000.

For some horseback riding try **Rupe-Rupe Ranch** (tel. 56-17-93 or 56-22-10) on the mountain side just south of the Hibiscus Hotel. To take one of their 16 horses along the beach for an hour is f.2500. Rides commence at 0800, 1000, 1430, and 1600, but it's best to call ahead.

SERVICES

Most of the **banks** (Banque Socredo included) are near the Bali Hai Hotel at Maharepa, although a branch of the Westpac Bank is in Le Petit Village shopping mall opposite Club Med. **Lav'matic** laundromat, also in Le Petit Village, is absurdly expensive at f.800 to wash, f.800 to dry.

The **Moorea Visitors Bureau** has an office (usually padlocked) opposite Club Bali Hai. A **newsstand** opposite Club Bali Hai has books and magazines in French. The **pharmacy** is near the bridge at Paopao.

TRANSPORT

Air Moorea (tel. 56-10-34) and **Air Tahiti** (tel. 56-10-34) are based at Moorea Temae Airport. Details of the air and ferry services from Tahiti are given in the main Introduction to this book. *Trucks* (f.200 to anywhere on the island) meet the ferries at Vaiare five times a day. Although they don't go right around the island, the northern and southern routes meet at Club Med, so you could theoretically effect a cimcumtruck-navigation by changing there provided you caught the last boat *truck* back (around 1400).

Hitching is wearing thin with Moorea motorists, although still possible. If you really need the ride you'll probably get it, just be prepared to do some walking. Taxis on Moorea are actually minibuses with a white letter "T" inside a red circle. The maximum speed limit is 60 km an hour.

Arii Rent-A-Car (B.P. 104, Moorea; tel. 56-11-03), the Hertz representative on Moorea, has eight locations along the north coast of Moorea including Vaiare Wharf and opposite the Bali Hai Hotel. Their scooters are f.3000 for four hours, f.3500 for eight hours; f.4500 for 24 hours; unlimited mileage cars are f.6000 for eight hours, f.7000 for 24 hours, plus f.1200 insurance. Gas is extra. Bicycles, some in bad condition, are f.1500 for the whole day. Arii doesn't rent to people under age 25.

Pierre Rent-A-Car (Pierre Danloue; tel. 56-12-58), which represents Avis, has an office at the Total service station on the airport access road (and elsewhere). Unlimited mileage cars are f.4500 for four hours, f.6000 for eight hours, f.7000 for 24 hours, plus f.1000 insurance.

The lowest rates for rental cars, bicycles, and circle-island tours (f.1600) are obtained at **Albert Activities Center** (B.P. 77, Moorea; tel. 56-13-53), with locations opposite the Bali Hai Hotel, Club Bali Hai, and the Moorea Lagoon Hotel. Unlimited mileage cars begin at f.6000 for eight hours including insurance and 10 liters of gasoline. Their island tour is recommended but the other rolling stock is in rough shape, so check carefully before turning the key.

Moorea Airport

Moorea Temae Airport (MOZ) is at the northeast corner of the island. No *trucks* serve the airport, so unless you rent a car you'll be stuck with a high taxi fare in addition to the airfare: f.1000 to the Bali Hai Hotel or Vaiare wharf, f.1700 to the Moorea Lagoon Hotel, f.3000 to Club Med. You could also walk out to the main highway and wait for the boat *truck* (f.200) or hitch. Thanks to intimidation from the taxi drivers, none of the hotels offer airport pickups. This considered it might be just as well to take the ferry to/from Moorea and skip the planes. The Moorea Visitors Bureau has a brochure counter at the airport.

SOCIETY ISLANDS
The Leeward Islands
Huahine, Raiatea, Tahaa, Bora Bora, Maupiti

Mount Temanu, Bora Bora

an early 19th-century view of Fare, Huahine

HUAHINE

Huahine, 170 km northwest of Papeete, is the first Leeward Island encountered on the ferry ride north from Tahiti. This friendly, inviting island is an easy escape from busy Papeete. In many ways lush, mountainous Huahine has more to offer than overcrowded Bora Bora. The variety of scenery, splendid beaches, archaeological remains, and characterful main town all call on you to visit. Huahine is a well-known surfing locale with excellent lefts and rights in the passes off Fare.

It's claimed that the island got its name because, when viewed from the sea, Huahine has the shape of a reclining woman—very appropriate for such a fertile, enchanting place. *Hua* means "phallus" (from a rock on Huahine Iti) while *hine* comes from *vahine* (woman). The almost entirely Polynesian population numbers under 5,000. Some of the greatest leaders in the struggle for the independence of Polynesia, Pouvanaa a Oopa among them, have come from this idyllic spot.

Huahine has finally been discovered by international tourism with two new deluxe hotels, the Sofitel Heiva and the Hotel Hana Iti, already operating, big expansions underway at the Relais Mahana and Huahine Beach Club near Parea, and another major bungalow-style hotel, the Te Tiare O Huahine, being developed on the west side of the island. Luckily Huahine is able to absorb these new properties fairly painlessly as it's a much larger island than Bora Bora and the resorts are well scattered and tastefully constructed in the traditional Tahitian style. The island also seems destined to soon join the other main Society Islands as a major port of call for locally chartered or cruising yachts. Backpackers pioneered Huahine in the mid-1980s and there are still good facilities for them.

HUAHINE

AIRPORT

LAKE FAUNA NUI

MARAE MANUNU

MAEVA

LA PETITE FERME

HOTEL BALI HAI

AVAMOA PASS

FARE

HUAHINE NUI

SOFITEL HEIVA

MOTU MAHARE

TIARE PASS

AVAPEIHI PASS

MT. TURI (710 m)

FAIE

MOTU VAVARATEA

FITII

BELLEVUE HOTEL

FARErEA PASS

MAROE BAY

MOTU MURIMAHORA

MAROE

BOURAYNE BAY

HUAHINE ITI

TEFARERII

MOTU VAIOREA

HOTEL HANA ITI

MT. POHUERAHI (485 m)

HAAPU

MAHUTI BAY

PAREA

HUAHINE BEACH CLUB

RELAIS MAHANA

MOTU ARAARA

MARAE ANINI

ARAARA PASS

-N-

0   3 km

Orientation

The little town of Fare, with its tree-lined boulevard along the quay, is joyfully peaceful after the roar of Papeete. A beach runs right along the west side of the main street. There isn't a lot to do in Fare so you're able to stop and relax. The seven other villages on Huahine are joined by winding, picturesque roads. For bicycle riders the roads of Huahine are fairly flat and easily managed. A narrow channel crossed by a bridge slices Huahine into Huahine Nui and Huahine Iti (Great and Little Huahine, respectively). The story goes that the demigod Hiro's canoe cut this strait. The airstrip sits on an elevated barrier reef north of Lake Fauna Nui. White beaches line this cantaloupe- and watermelon-rich north shore.

HISTORY

Archaeologists have found that human habitation goes back 1,300 years on Huahine. In 1925 Dr. K.P. Emory of Hawaii's Bishop Museum recorded 54 *marae* on Huahine, most of them built after the 16th century. In 1968 Professor Yosihiko Sinoto found another 40. Huahine Nui was divided into 10 districts with Huahine Iti as a dependency. As a centralized government complex for a whole island, Maeva is unique in Tahiti-Polynesia. Both the great communal *maraes* at Maeva and Parea have two-stepped platforms *(ahu)* which served as raised seats for the gods. Since 1967 about 16 *marae* have been restored and can be easily visited today. The archaeological area on the south shore of Lake Fauna Nui is one of the five most important in Oceania (along with those on Easter Island, Tongatapu, Pohnpei, and Kosrae). Maeva was occupied as early as A.D. 900. During construction of the Hotel Bali Hai just north of Fare in 1972 a *patu* hand club was uncovered, proving that New Zealand's Maoris originated in this area.

History Of The Leeward Islands

Roggeveen, coming from Makatea in the Tuamotus, discovered (but did not land on) Bora Bora and Maupiti on 6 June 1722. Captain Cook discovered the other Leeward Islands in July 1769, which was quite easy since the Tahitians knew them well. Cook had the Raiatean priest Tupaia on board the *Endeavour* as a pilot. Cook wrote: "To these six islands, as they lie contiguous to each other, I gave the names of Society Islands." In 1773 a man named Omai from Huahine sailed to England with Cook's colleague, Capt. Furneaux, aboard the *Adventure;* he returned to Fare in 1777.

During the 19th century American whalers spent their winters away from the Antarctic in places like Huahine, refurbishing their supplies with local products such as sugar, vegetables, oranges, salted port, and *aito* or ironwood. These visits enriched the island economy and the New England sailors presented the islanders with foreign plants in token of appreciation for the hospitality received.

The Leeward Islands remained independent until 1887; armed resistance to France was only overcome in 1897. The French sent packing the English missionary group which had been there 88 years. Today 80% of the population of the Leewards remains Protestant.

SIGHTS

Near Fare

After you've had a look around Fare, walk inland on the road which begins beside the third house east of the post office to see the beautiful *mape* (chestnut) forest up the valley. After the road becomes a trail, follow the small stream into a forest laced with vanilla vines. By the stream is a long bed-like rock known as Ofaitere, or "Traveling Rock." With a guide you could continue right to the summit of Mt. Turi (710 meters) in about three hours, but it's rough going.

Maeva

Maeva is one of the few Tahitian villages to retain its ancient pattern. In round-ended **Fare Potee** (1974), a replica of an old communal meeting house on the shores of Lake Fauna Nui, is a historical exposition providing much

1. fortification walls
2. Marae Fare Roi
3. Marae Fare Tai
4. Marae Vaitotaha
5. Fare Potee
6. Marae Haumaru
7. Marae Rauhuru
8. Marae Fare Ie
9. *truck* drivers' house
10. Marae Oavauru
11. Marae Faretou
12. Marae Avaroa
13. Protestant church
14. fish traps
15. Marae Manunu (Mataotoerau)
16. monument with cannon
17. grocery stores
18. Marae Matairea
19. Marae Matairea Rahi
20. Marae Paepae Ofata
21. Marae Ofata
22. Marae Tamata Uporu
23. Marae Te Ava
24. Marae Fare Miro
25. Marae Tahaa

Marae Fare Miro at Huahine's Maeva

information on the Maeva archaeological site. Each of the 10 district chiefs of Huahine Nui had his own *marae;* many are strewn along the lakeshore and in the nearby hills. The plentiful small fish in the lake were able to support large chiefly and priestly classes. Under the bridge at the east end of the village are ancient stone fish traps. Huge stone walls were erected to defend Maeva against invaders from Bora Bora (and later France). Many of the structures were restored by Prof. Y.H. Sinoto of Hawaii in the 1970s.

One way to organize a visit to Maeva is to follow the road around to **Marae Te Ave,** then cut up into the foothills on a trail which leads between stakes planted with vanilla (follow the map). **Marae Ofata** gives a magnificent view over the whole northeast coast of Huahine. The ruins of **Marae Tefano** are engulfed by an immense banyan tree. **Marae Matairea Rahi** was the most sacred place on Huahine, dedicated to Tane, god of light. The backrests of Huahine's eight principal chiefs are in the southernmost compound of the *marae,* where the most important religious ceremonies took place.

When you get back down to the road, return to the bridge, across which is a monument guarded by seven cannon. Underneath are buried the French soldiers killed in the Battle of Maeva (1846) when the islanders successfully defended their independence against French marines sent to annex the island. A few hundred meters farther along toward the ocean and to the left is two-tiered **Marae Manunu,** the community *marae* of Huahine Nui. In its base is the grave of Raiti, the last great priest of Huahine. When he died in 1915, a huge stone fell from the *marae.*

Maeva is easily accessible by *truck* from Fare (six km, f.160), and there are two small stores where you can get cold drinks. From Faie, south

This bridge links Huahine Nui to Huahine Iti

of Maeva, a steep track crosses the mountains, making a complete circuit of Huahine Nui possible.

Huahine Iti

Though the "July Bridge" joins the two islands, Huahine Iti is far less accessible than Huahine Nui. *Trucks* to **Parea** village (f.450) run only once a day, so you'll have to stay the night unless you rent a bicycle, scooter, or car. The hotels are very expensive so you may want to bring a tent.

On a golden beach on Point Tiva, one km south of Parea, is **Marae Anini**, the community *marae* of Huahine Iti. Look for petroglyphs on this two-tiered structure dedicated to the god Oro where human sacrifices once took place. If you decide to camp near the *marae,* don't leave a mess. Search for the water tap by the road at the end of the path. Be aware of theft by dogs at night and small boys by day. The only grocery store on Huahine Iti is at **Haapu**, but a grocery truck circles the island several times daily; the locals can tell you when to expect it. Another nice beach with better swimming is a couple of km west. Surfing is possible in Araara Pass beside the *motu* just off Marae Anini.

Haapu village was originally built entirely over the water for lack of sufficient shoreline to house it. Over the centuries the move has gone ashore. From the water Bourayne Bay to the west of the interisland bridge is one of the loveliest spots on the island.

PRACTICALITIES

ACCOMMODATIONS

Inexpensive Lodgings

Several inexpensive lodgings await you in Fare. **Guynette's Lodging** (B.P. 87, Fare; tel. 68-83-75), on the waterfront to the left as you get off the boat, has a nine-bed f.1000 dorm (single night f.1500), three shared four-bed rooms for f.1250 pp, and three doubles for f.3000, minimum two nights, maximum one month. Mosquito nets are provided and a fan is f.300 extra. On departure day you can use the hostel facilities all day for an extra f.350 (the Papeete boat leaves in the evening). You can cook your own meals in the communal kitchen here. Mask and snorkel may be rented at f.600 a day. It's a clean place: no shoes or radios allowed in the house. Upon arrival peruse the list of rules and rates—applied rigorously.

Nearby on the waterfront is decrepit three-story **Hotel Huahine** (tel. 68-82-69), overpriced at f.3000 s, f.4500 d, f.5500 t. The price drops to f.2500 s, f.3000 d, f.4000 t if you stay three nights. It's not possible to lock the rooms. They have water problems, and don't order any meals here as the food is lousy and far too expensive.

Pension Martial et Enite (B.P. 37, Fare; tel. 68-82-37) is an eight-room European-style boarding house at the west end of the waterfront beyond the snack bar. A room here with breakfast and dinner is f.5200 pp (two-day minimum stay, shared bath). Middle-of-the-night arrivals mustn't knock on the door before 0700. They're often full or closed. Martial and Enite also serve meals to outsiders in their thatched cookhouse on the beach for f.2300, or f.3300 if shellfish are on the menu. Advance notice must be given, but the food is good (closed on Sundays).

Anyone wishing to pitch a tent should head for **Chez Lovina** (B.P. 173, Fare; tel. 68-81-90) a km beyond the Bali Hai toward the airport. Camping is f.1200 s, f.2000 d and there are also three small *fares* with TV and shared bath at f.2500 s, f.4000 d, f.4500 t. Dormitory accommodations are f.1500 pp. Cooking facilities (and mosquitos) for all of the above are provided in a separate building. For families and larger groups Chez Lovina has four oversized bungalows with cooking and bathing facilities at f.4000 s, f.6000 d or t, f.7000 for up to five persons, f.11,000 for eight people, etc. By the month it's f.120,000 for one of these larger units and other discounts may be negotiable. The minimum stay is two nights. Airport pick-ups for those with reservations are f.400 pp.

In this same area just north of Fare is **Chez Richard** (B.P. 121, Fare; tel. 68-87-86) which also caters to budget travelers. The three rooms

*the back porch at
Guynette's Lodging,
Fare, Huahine*

with shared bath are f.3000 d and a four-bed dorm is available at f.1000 pp. Cooking is possible here too. Owner Richard Bowens will probably pick you up free at the airport if you call ahead.

If you still don't have a place to stay, **Le Petite Ferme** (see below) offers simple accommodations on their ranch halfway to the airport at f.1500 pp. Ask about their f.7500 pp package which includes accommodation, riding lessons, and all meals.

The **Hotel Bellevue** (B.P. 21, Huahine; tel. 68-82-76), six km south of Fare, offers eight rooms in the main building at f.3500 s, f.4500 d, f.5000 t, 15 bungalows for about twice that. There's an expensive restaurant (meals f.3000 each) with a view of Maroe Bay. Roundtrip airport transfers are f.1000. Considering the expense, isolation, and absence of a beach (there is a swimming pool), the Bellevue has little going for it except the view.

Expensive Hotels

The American-owned **Bali Hai Hotel** (B.P. 2, Fare; tel. 68-84-77) is probably the nicest of the four-hotel Bali Hai chain, with 10 rooms in the main building and 34 lakeside bungalows. The Bali Hai closed in Nov. 1988 but after an injection of fresh Japanese capital the ailing hotel was due to reopen in mid-1992. Visit to see the showcase in the lobby displaying artifacts found here by Dr. Yosihiko H. Sinoto of the Bishop Museum, Hawaii, who excavated the site during construction of the hotel in 1973-75. Marae Tahuea has been reconstructed on the grounds.

The 12-unit **Relais Mahana** (B.P. 30, Huahine; tel. 68-81-54) on a wide white beach near Parea charges f.14,000 s or d, f.17,000 t, for a garden bungalow, f.2000 more for a beach bungalow. For breakfast and dinner add another f.3500 pp; roundtrip airport transfers are an extra f.1600 pp. In early 1992 the Relais Mahana was still closed for renovation and expansion, so the above information may have changed. Reader David Miles of Denver, Colorado, had this comment:

I must say that the Relais on Huahine was the most unbelievably snobbish hotel I've ever been to. The French staff were rude, obnoxious, and flippant, not to mention obviously racist toward the Tahitian people. The Relais Mahana was, indeed, an extremely poor hotel and we were treated poorly. Please don't recommend this bastion of sloppiness and prejudice to anyone.

The 16-unit **Huahine Beach Club** (B.P. 39, Huahine; tel. 68-81-46) at Parea is f.14,500 s, f.17,000 d or t for a garden bungalow, considerably more for a beach bungalow. Breakfast and dinner are f.3600 pp. Saturday night there's a Tahitian buffet with traditional dancing (f.3000). This well-constructed resort sits on a fine white beach between Parea village and Marae Anini. Facilities are being developed to provide visiting yachts with moorings, showers, etc.

In Oct. 1989 the **Sofitel Heiva Huahine** (B.P. 38, Huahine; tel. 68-86-86) opened in a coconut grove on a *motu* just east of Maeva. Striking neo-Polynesian paintings by the late artist/singer Bobby Holcomb highlight the decor in public areas and ancient *marae* are preserved in the gardens. Unspoiled white beaches are all along this section of lagoon and the Maeva archaeological area is within walking distance. The 58 tastefully decorated rooms are f.21,000 s or d, the nine thatched beach bungalows 50% more. The breakfast and dinner plan is f.4000 pp. Polynesian dancing takes place here on Mon., Thurs., and Sat. nights.

Hauhine's newest resort is the US$9 million **Hotel Hana Iti** (B.P. 185, Fare; tel. 68-85-05) which opened in 1992 on a verdant hill above Bourayne Bay. A three-room thatched bungalow complete with whirlpool spa will set you back f.57,500 s, f.70,000 d, f.88,000 t, all meals, drinks, activities, taxes, and airport transfers included. Each of the 26 traditional *fare* units is unique. Some perch on rocks, more stand on stilts, and a few are built into huge trees. The Hana Iti is owned by American marine biologist Thomas C. Kurth who bought the property

from Spanish singer Julio Iglesias. If you're a Hollywood star in search of an exotic hideaway, this is it.

OTHER PRACTICALITIES

Food
Fare doesn't have a good, cheap eatery. The only reasonable places to fill your stomach are the food trailers, which congregate at the wharf when a ship is due in. One trailer is there every afternoon making *crêpes breton*. The numerous Chinese stores sell groceries and cold beer. What you'd pay for the cheapest item on the menu at the "snack bar" will get you the makings of fine sandwiches. The tap water on Huahine can be clouded after heavy rains.

Snack Te Marara at the west end of the waterfront charges similar prices to the deluxe hotel restaurants, which is a little ridiculous. Te Marara does have an unpretentious terrace built over the lagoon, so drop in for an afternoon coffee or a sunset beer. On Fri. evening the place is crowded with Polynesians enjoying *kaina* (folkloric) music.

The **Tiare Tipanie Restaurant**, just south of Fare beyond the *mairie,* serves a good chicken dinner with mushroom and wine sauce for f.800, plus shrimps (f.1100), lobster (f.1800), and hamburgers (f.500). There are also the **Te Manu Restaurant** and **Snack Tiare** in Fare.

the view across the bay from Guynette's Lodging, Fare, Huahine

Recreation

Dominique Tempie's **Pacific Blue Adventure** (tel. 68-87-21) at Fare offers scuba diving at f.5000 a dive (night diving f.6000) and PADI certification courses. Trips leave at 0930 and 1430, depending on demand.

Le Petite Ferme (B.P. 12, Huahine; tel. 68-82-98), between Fare and the airport, offers riding with Jerome, Connie, and their 10 small, robust Marquesan horses. A two-hour ride along the beach is f.2800 (offered at 0800 and 1600). They also offer a two-day ride and camp-out in the mountains for f.13,500, meals included. A three-day ride right around the island is f.19,500. Call ahead to let them know you're coming. This is the best horseback riding operation in Tahiti-Polynesia.

Services

The **Mairie de Huahine** (town hall) provides an excellent free ice water fountain to the left in the courtyard. Public toilets and wash basins are in one of the yellow buildings on the waterfront (if open). **Banque Socredo** (tel. 68-82-71) is on the first street back from the Fare waterfront. The **gendarmerie** is opposite the hospital at the south end of town over the bridge. Yachts anchor just off the Bali Hai. Don't leave valuables unattended on the beach on Huahine.

Transport

The **Air Tahiti** agent (tel. 68-82-65) is wedged in between the Chinese stores on the Fare waterfront. For information on flights to Huahine from Papeete, Moorea, Raiatea, and Bora Bora see the main Introduction to this book. The airport (HUH) is four km north of Fare. Make arrangements for the airport minibus (f.300 pp) at Pension Enite.

The Papeete ships tie up to the wharf in the middle of town. *Taporo IV* and *Temehani* arrive from Papeete around 0200 on Tues., Thurs., and Sat., returning from Raiatea on their way to Papeete Tues., Thurs., Fri., and Sun. afternoons. The *Raromatai Ferry* arrives from Papeete at the slightly more convenient hour of 0430 on Wed. and Sat., departing for Papeete again at 1900 on Wed. and Sunday. Tickets are sold on the wharf as the ships are loading.

Getting around Huahine is not easy. You'll find *trucks* to anywhere on Huahine when a ship arrives; otherwise they're irregular. Only one truck a day runs to Maeva, leaving Fare at 0830 (f.160).

Kake Rent-A-Car (B.P. 34, Fare; tel. 68-82-59) beside the entrance to the Bali Hai Hotel rents small cars (from f.5500 plus f.1000 for insurance and f.1000 for gas for eight hours), scooters (f.3500 plus f.500 insurance for eight hours), and bicycles (f.1000 for eight hours). If you can get a small group together, consider renting a six-passenger Subaru minibus from Kake for f.8000, plus f.1300 insurance, plus f.1000 gas for eight hours. This would work out to around f.1750 pp for a complete island tour at your own pace. **Pacificar Huahine** (tel. 68-81-10) charges similar rates.

M.G.L. DOMENY DE RIENZI

an early 19th-century view of Raiatea

RAIATEA AND TAHAA

RAIATEA

Raiatea, 220 km northwest of Tahiti, is the second-largest, and perhaps the friendliest, high island of Tahiti-Polynesia. Uturoa is a pleasant, unspoiled town, much like Papeete was long ago. Yet this relaxed port is the business and administrative center of the Leeward Islands. The rest of the population of about 9,000 lives in eight flower-filled villages around the island: Avera, Opoa, Puohine, Fetuna, Vaiaau, Tehurui, Tevaitoa, and Tuu Fenua. The west coast of Raiatea south of Tevaitoa is old Polynesia through and through. Raiatea is traditionally the ancient Havai'i, the sacred isle from which all of eastern Polynesia was colonized.

Orientation
Everything is easy to find in Uturoa (pop. 3,200). The double row of Chinese stores along the main drag opens up onto a colorful market. On Wed. and Fri. mornings the Tahaa people sell their products here; the Sun. market is over by 0700. Beyond this is the harbor, with a pleasant park alongside. By the souvenir stalls opposite the wharf is a tourist information stand (B.P. 707, Raiatea; tel. 66-23-34). All of the stores in Uturoa close for lunch from 1200-1400.

The Land
Raiatea, 220 km northwest of Tahiti, shares a protected lagoon with Tahaa three km away. Legends tell how the two islands were cut apart by a mythical eel. About 30 km of steel-blue sea separate Raiatea from both Huahine and Bora Bora. Mount Temehani on mountainous Raiatea rises to 772 meters, and some of the coastlines are rugged and narrow. The highest mountain is Toomaru (1,017 meters). All of the people live on a coastal plain planted in coconuts where cattle graze. No beaches are found on hulking big Raiatea itself. Instead, picnickers are taken to picture-postcard *motus* in the lagoon. Surfing is possible at the eight pass-

RAIATEA AND TAHAA

TEHUTU I.

TAHAA

TUUVAHINE I.

MOTU TAUTAU

PATIO   HIPU

TAPUAMU
WHARF
MT. OHIRI
(590 m)   FAAHA

TIVA
HAAMENE   FAAHA BAY

HUREPITI BAY   HIBISCUS
HOTEL   HAAMENE BAY
TOAHOTU PASS

TIAMAHANA PASS

POUTORU   VAITOARE

APU BAY   HOTEL
MARINA ITI

AIRPORT
TERMINAL   UTUROA

APOOITI BAY   HOTEL BALI HAI

TAPIOI   TUPUA BAY
(294 m)   TEAVAPITI PASS

PUFAU

RAUTOANUI PASS

OROTAIO
TUU FENUA   (497 m)

IRIRU PASS

TAINUU   TEMEHANI
(TEVAITOA)   RAHI PLATEAU   AVERA
(772 m)

TEMEHANI
UTE   FAAROA BAY

PENSION
GREENHILL

TETOOROA BAY

TOOMARU
(1,017 m)   TE AVA MOA PASS

TEHURUI BAY   FAAROA
TEHURUI   VALLEY   OPOA

TOAMARO PASS   MARAE TAPUTAPUATEA
VAIAAU

VAIAAU BAY   RAIATEA

OROPIRO
(824 m)

VAIHUTI BAY   PUOHINE

PUNAEROA PASS
FAATEMU BAY

FETUNA

-N-

NAO NAO I.   NAO NAO PASS

0   5 km

es that open onto the Raiatea/Tahaa lagoon, and sailboarders are active. The Leeward Islands (Îles Sous le Vent) are the most popular sailing area in Tahiti-Polynesia and most of the charter boats are based at Raiatea.

History

Before European encroachment, Raiatea was the religious, cultural, and political center of Tahiti-Polynesia. Tradition holds that the great Polynesian voyagers to Hawaii and New Zealand departed from these shores.

Raiatea was Capt. Cook's favorite island; he visited three times. During his first voyage in 1769 he called first at Opoa from 20 to 24 July. After having surveyed Bora Bora from the sea, he anchored for a week in the Rautoanui Pass on the northwest coast of Raiatea, near the village of Tuu Fenua. During his second voyage Cook lay at anchor twice, first from 8 to 17 Sept. 1773 and again from 25 May to 4 June 1774, both times at Rautoanui. His third visit was from 3 Nov. to 7 Dec. 1777, again at Rautoanui. It can therefore be said that Rautoanui (which he calls "Haamanino Harbour" in his journals) was one of Cook's favorite anchorages.

The last resistance to the French takeover on Raiatea lasted until 1897 when French troops and warships used arms and guns to conquer the island. The native leader of the resistance, Teraupoo, was deported to New Caledonia.

SIGHTS

For a view of four islands climb **Tapioi Hill** (294 meters), the one topped by a TV antenna behind Uturoa. Take the road beside the Gendarmerie Nationale up past the locked gate and ignore any bad dogs you encounter: visitors are allowed. The fastest time on record for climbing Tapioi is 17 minutes! There's good swimming in a large pool open to the sea at the Centre Nautique *("la piscine")* on the coast north of Uturoa.

It takes 4-10 hours to ride a bicycle around Raiatea (97 km), depending on how fast you go. A **waterfall** may be visited up the valley from the Chinese store near PK 9, Avera. The road down the east coast circles fjord-like **Faaroa Bay,** associated with the legends of Polynesian migration. The Apoomau River, which drains the Faaroa Valley, is the only navigable river in Tahiti-Polynesia (for two km by dinghy). From the popular yacht anchorage in the middle of the bay there's a fine view of Toomaru, highest peak in the Leeward Islands.

On the point just beyond Opoa, 32 km from Uturoa, is **Marae Taputapuatea,** one of the largest and best preserved in Polynesia. Its mighty *ahu* is 43 meters long, 7.3 meters wide, and between two and three meters high. Before it is a rectangular courtyard paved with black volcanic rocks. A small platform in the

Marea Taputapuatea on Raiatea is among the most sacred sites in Polynesia

middle of the *ahu* once bore the image of Oro, god of war; backrests still mark the seats of high chiefs on the courtyard. Marae Taputapuatea is directly opposite Te Ava Moa Pass, and fires on the *maraes* may have been a beacon to ancient navigators. Human sacrifices and fire-walking once took place on the *marae*.

Marae Taputapuatea is said to retain its psychic power. Test this by writing down all your negative emotions, bad habits, unhappy memories, and self-doubts on a piece of paper. Then burn the paper(s) on the *marae*. The catharsis works best when done solo, beneath a full moon or the three following nights. The *tupapau* (spirits) are most active at this time, often taking the form of dogs, cats, pigs, etc.

The setting of the village of **Fetuna** on the south coast is attractive and there are two Chinese stores. **Tevaitoa church,** on the west side of Raiatea, is the oldest on the island. Petroglyphs on a broken stone by the road at the entrance to the church show a turtle and some other indistinguishable figure. Behind the church is **Marae Tainuu** dedicated to the ancient god Taaroa.

HIKING

According to Polynesia mythology the fertility god Oro was born from the molten rage of **Mt. Temehani,** the cloud-covered plateau that dominates the north end of the island. *Tiare apetahi,* a sacred white flower which not only exists nowhere else on earth but also resists transplantation, grows on the slopes around the summit. The fragile blossom represents the five fingers of a beautiful Polynesian girl who fell in love with the handsome son of a high chief, but couldn't marry him due to her lowly birth. These flowers are now rare, so don't pick any! Small pink orchids also grow by the way.

Temehani can be climbed from Pufau, the second bay south of Marina Apooiti. Note a series of concrete benches by the road as you come around the north side of the bay. The jeep track inland is about 200 meters south of the bridge. You climb straight up through pine reforestation till you have a clear view of Temehani Rahi and Temehani Ute, divided by a deep gorge. Descend to the right and continue up the track you see on the hillside opposite. It takes about three hours from the main road to the Temehani Rahi Plateau. A guide up Temehani should charge about f.5000 for the group. Friday and Sat. are the best days to go; long pants and sturdy shoes are required.

ACCOMMODATIONS

Places Near Uturoa

Campers are catered for at the friendly **Sunset Beach Motel Apooiti** (Jean and Elianne Boubee, B.P. 397, Uturoa; tel. 66-33-47) in a

JOHN WEBBER

Poetua, daughter of chief of Raiatea, as painted by Capt. Cook's artist John Webber

coconut grove five km from Uturoa (no sign). Look on the point across the bay from Marina Apooiti, about two km west of the airport. The 16 well-spaced bungalows with cooking facilities and private bath (hot water) are f.5000 s, f.6000 d, f.7000 t—highly recommended for families. Discounts of 10% a fortnight and 20% a month are available. Camping is f.1000 pp here and there's a large communal kitchen. If you stay only one night there's a f.1000 surcharge. Bicycles are for rent at f.100 an hour. The helpful proprietors will pick you up at the airport or harbor if you reserve.

Hotel Le Motu (B.P. 549, Raiatea; tel. 66-34-06) is above the noisy pool hall on the main street in the center of Uturoa. The seven rooms (f.5000 s or d, f.6500 t) have private bath, but cross your fingers for hot water. The location is convenient, the adjoining restaurant excellent, and the management convivial, which helps compensate for the tariff. If you're here on business it's ideal. Le Motu arranges picnics on a reef island for f.5000 pp and waterskiing across the lagoon.

The scuba diver's headquarters on Raiatea is **Pension Marie-France** (B.P. 272, Uturoa; tel. 66-37-10) by the lagoon just beyond Chez Andre Chinese store, a km south of the Bali Hai Hotel (yellow sign). There's a clean modern dormitory with full cooking facilities at f.1200 pp. Four neat private rooms with shared bath are f.3800 s or d in back or f.4500 s or d facing the lagoon. You're charged f.500 more if you stay only one night. Bicycles and a washing machine are for rent and there's even hot water. The lagoon off Pension Marie-France is good for sailboarding and you're expected to sign up for the half-day minibus tour of the island (f.3000). Don't come here expecting to rest.

Marie-France's husband, Patrice Philip, runs **Raiatea Safari Tours** and pension residents get reduced rates: f.3500 for a one-tank dive (regular f.5000). He'll take you to the century-old, 100-meter wreck of a Dutch coal boat sunk off the Bali Hai, the top of which is 18 meters down. The coral life is rather poor but there's ample marinelife, including sharks, moray eels, barracudas, manta rays, and countless tropical fish. A trip right around Tahaa by motorized canoe with visits to two *motus* is f.4000, snorkeling in a pass is f.3500, or you can just be

dropped off on a nearby *motu* for f.600. The boat trip up the Faaroa River (f.2500) is not recommended as the boat can only proceed a couple of hundred meters. PADI scuba certification (four dives) is f.16,000 for residents, f.20,000 for nonresidents. A swimming pool on the premises is used for the lessons and the course is highly personalized. This is a good opportunity to learn scuba diving while enjoying the beauty of Raiatea!

Places Around Raiatea

Pension Ariane Brotherson (B.P. 236, Uturoa; tel. 66-33-70) is a km up the valley from PK 8 near Avera School. The two rooms with shared bath go for f.3000 s, f.6000 d, but that includes breakfast and dinner, airport transfers, and sightseeing excursions. (The meals are too spicy and the trips short.) One of Raiatea's best guides, Johnny Brotherson, can be contacted through this pension.

Pension Yolande Roopinia (B.P. 298, Uturoa; tel. 66-35-28), near the Raiatea Village Hotel at PK 10, Avera, is a large thatched bungalow with four rooms at f.5000 s or d (private bath). Cooking facilities are provided but you may be asked to take demi-pension (f.6000 s, f.11,000 d).

The 12-unit **Raiatea Village Hotel** (B.P. 282, Uturoa; tel. 66-31-62) at the mouth of Faaroa Bay (PK 10) is laid out like a real Tahitian village. A garden bungalow with kitchenette is f.5000 s or d, f.8000 for four. Airport transfers are f.1000 pp extra.

Pension Greenhill (B.P. 598, Raiatea; tel. 66-37-64), at PK 12 overlooking serene Faaroa Bay, is an exquisite little hideaway nestled among flowers and birds. Greenhill caters to a select crowd. The five cheerful rooms with private bath are f.6500 s, f.8000 d, including all meals at the host's table (minimum stay two nights). Children under 10 are half price. Sightseeing trips and occasional boat rides are also included, though a minimum of four persons is required before they'll go. Getting into town is no problem—the pension minibus makes several trips a day and will arrange to pick you up later. Bicycles are at your disposal. Gourmet chef Jason makes dining a delight, while hostess Marie-Isabelle loves to sit and chat with guests. They'll pick you up free at the airport or wharf if you call ahead. Recommended.

Expensive Hotel

The 36-room, American-owned **Bali Hai Hotel** (B.P. 43, Uturoa; tel. 66-31-49) just south of Uturoa is Raiatea's only luxury hotel. The nine overwater bungalows run f.23,500 s or d, but you can get a standard room for f.9300 s or d. Their breakfast and dinner meal plan is f.4100 pp extra. Airport transfers are f.2400 pp RT.

Unlike the accommodations, the Bali Hai's bar (shaped like a Polynesian canoe) is reasonable and a nice place to stop for coffee or a drink. One or two ukulele-strumming Tahitians might host happy hour and there's Polynesian dancing once or twice a week. **Firewalking,** once commonly practiced on Raiatea, is now a dying art. The pit is just across the street from the Bali Hai, so ask there if they'll be lighting anyone's fire.

FOOD AND SERVICES

Food

Restaurant Au Motu (closed Sun., tel. 66-34-06) is up a stairway overlooking the park in the center of Uturoa. Their specialty is seafood, cooked as only the French can. Fish of the day is an entire reef fish grilled and served with rice

(f.1000). Proprietor Roger Bardou adds to the breezy, informal atmosphere by trading gossip with his clientele.

The **Jade Garden Restaurant** (open Wed.-Sat.; tel. 66-34-40) on the main street serves exquisite Chinese dishes at about f.1000 a plate (reasonable for Polynesia), but it's pretentious. Climb to the upstairs dining room for more privacy.

Le Quai des Pécheurs (tel. 66-36-83) on the wharf offers pizza with a view of the port. If you stick to the pizza this is one of the cheapest places to eat, and large Hinano beer is available. They don't mind if you linger all evening (the informative cook might join you at your table now and then).

To escape the tourist scene try **Bar Restaurant Maraamu** (Chez Remy; tel. 66-31-08) in what appears to be an old Chinese store between the park and the small boat harbor. The few minutes it takes to locate will net you the lowest prices in town. Coffee and omelets are served in the morning, while the lunch menu tilts toward Chinese food. There's also *poisson cru* and a good selection of other dishes—even cheap carafes of wine!

Snack Moemoea (tel. 66-39-84) on the harbor in the former Hotel Hinano building has hamburgers. **Coconut's Restaurant** at the south end of the waterfront has a complete daily menu for f.1250 and ice cream.

Services

Of Uturoa's four banks only **Banque Socredo** (tel. 66-30-64) doesn't levy a f.350 commission. The large modern post office is just north of town, with the **gendarmerie** about 50 meters beyond on the left. There are free public washrooms *(sanitaires publics)* on the wharf behind Le Quai des Pécheurs restaurant.

TRANSPORT

Getting There And Away

The **Air Tahiti** office (tel. 66-32-50) is at the airport. Flights operate from Raiatea to Maupiti (f.5350) three times a week. For information on flights from Papeete, Huahine, and Bora Bora see the main Introduction to this book.

You can catch the *Temehani, Taporo IV,* and *Raromatai Ferry* to Bora Bora or Huahine twice weekly. Consult the schedule in the main Introduction. Several village boats run between Raiatea and Tahaa on Wed. and Fri. mornings (f.350).

The *Taporo I,* a small cargo/passenger ship, shuttles weekly between Raiatea and Maupiti, departing Raiatea Tues. or Thurs. at midnight (f.1000 deck, f.1600 berth). Once every three months the *Taporo I* makes a six-day roundtrip Raiatea-Scilly-Bellingshausen-Mopelia-Raiatea (f.9000 deck). Meals are not included. For information write: Société Taporo Teaotea, B.P. 68, Uturoa, Raiatea (tel. 66-32-30). Exact times of all boats should be verified locally as they change constantly.

Bareboating
The Moorings (B.P. 165, Uturoa; tel. 66-35-93), a bareboat charter operation with 19 yachts, is based at Marina Apooiti two km west of the airport. Leeward Island charter rates begin at US$311 a day with food and drink extra. This may seem like a lot but split among a nautical-minded group it's a much better deal than hotel rooms. Charterers are given a complete briefing on channels and anchorages, and provided with a detailed set of charts. All boats are radio-equipped and a voice from The Moorings is available to talk nervous skippers in and out. Travel by night is forbidden, but by day it's easy sailing. For more information on bareboat chartering see the main Introduction to this book.

Another yacht charter operation, **A.T.M. South Pacific** (B.P. 331, Uturoa; tel. 66-23-18), is slightly cheaper than The Moorings. The huge power-cruiser *Manavaroa* (B.P. 377, Uturoa) is also based at Marina Apooiti. This monster rents for US$1500 a day, plus US$100 per cruising hour, plus US$60 a day pp for room and board.

Getting Around
Trucks depart Uturoa for Fetuna (f.220) and Opoa every afternoon, but never on Sunday.

The gentleman barber, Mr. Charles Brotherson of **Apetahi Location** (B.P. 99, Uturoa; tel. 66-39-04), rents mopeds out of his barbershop (open Mon., Wed., and Fri.) adjacent to the jeweler beside Hotel Le Motu (*not* the one directly below the hotel beside the pool hall). Other times find Charles at the Mobil service station between Uturoa and the airport. His Vespa motor scooters are f.4500 for eight hours, f.7500 for 24 hours, insurance included (f.5000 deposit). No special motorcycle driver's license is required. Charles is the most knowledgeable person on Raiatea and speaks good English.

Garage Motu Tapu (Guirouard Rent-A-Car, B.P. 139, Uturoa; tel. 66-33-09) across the road from the airport has cars at f.8000 for 24 hours, insurance and km included. **Hotel Le Motu** (tel. 66-34-06) also rents cars at f.8000 a day, mileage and insurance included.

The **Centre Équestre** (tel. 66-22-46) at PK 7, Avera, charges f.1500 an hour for horseback riding. You must reserve 24 hours in advance and there's a two-person minimum.

Airport
The airport (RFP) is three km northwest of Uturoa. A taxi from the Uturoa market taxi stand to the airport is f.600 (double tariff late at night). Most of the hotels pick up clients at the airport free upon request.

DIANA LASICH HARPER

frangipani
(Plumeria obtusa)

TAHAA

Raiatea's lagoonmate, 90-square-km Tahaa is shaped like a hibiscus flower. It's a quiet island with little traffic and few tourists. Mt. Ohiri (590 meters), highest point on the island, gets its name from the demigod Hiro who was born here. There aren't many specific attractions other than a chance to escape the crowds and hurried life on the other Society islands. Notice the vanilla plantations. Beaches are scarce on the main island so the pension owners arrange picnics on *motus* such as Tautau off Tapuamu. The *motus* off the northeast side of Tahaa have the finest white-sand beaches. The Tahaa Festival in late Oct. includes stone fishing with a line of canoes herding the fish into a cove by beating stones on the surface of the lagoon. The 4,000 Tahaa islanders are a little wary of outsiders. Tahaa is well off the beaten track.

Orientation
The administrative center is at Patio on the north coast, where the post office, *mairie* (town hall), and police station share one compound. The ship from Papeete ties up to the wharf at Tapuamu. There's a large covered area at the terminal where you could spread a sleeping bag in a pinch. A new road crosses the mountains from Patio direct to Haamene.

Sights
Several large sea turtles are held captive in a tank by the lagoon behind the community hall near the church in Tiva. You could walk right around the main part of Tahaa in about eight hours with stops, passing villages every couple of kilometers. Haamene Bay, the longest of Tahaa's four fjords, catches the full force of the southeast trades.

ACCOMMODATIONS AND FOOD

Lodging With The Inhabitants
The most convenient place to stay is **Chez Pascal** (tel. 65-60-42). From the Tapuamu ferry wharf you'll see a small bridge at the head of the bay. Turn left as you leave the dock and head for this. Chez Pascal is the first house north of the bridge on the inland side. Bed, breakfast, and dinner is f.4000 pp. You may be able to negotiate a price without meals. Boat trips to a *motu* (f.4000 pp) and the loan of the family bicycle are possible.

Farther south at Tiva is **Chez Francette** (B.P. 142, Haamene; tel. 65-63-75) with three rooms at f.5500 pp including all meals. Their terrace overlooks Hurepiti Bay and there's a beach nearby.

About two km south of the Tapuamu ferry wharf is **Chez Anna** (tel. 65-61-18), also known as the Tahaa Village Hotel, operated by Mr. Petit Tetuanui. There are five small bungalows on the lagoon at f.5000 each (up to five persons), with a 50% reduction if you stay a week. You can cook. A trip to a *motu* is f.3000 for a group or f.2000 for one person.

In Patio ask for Simeon Chu (B.P. 1, Tahaa; tel. 67-65-27) in the Conseiller Technique office behind the post office. If his house is full he'll direct you to Madame Tamariera Marae (tel. 65-64-08), who lives near the large Protestant church nearby. Both rent rooms with shared bath at about f.3000 s or d, half pension another f.2000 pp.

Expensive Hotels

The **Hotel L'Hibiscus** (B.P. 184, Tahaa; tel. 65-61-06) or "Tahaa Lagon" is run by Leo and Lolita on the northeast side of windy Haamene Bay. Get there from Raiatea on the Haamene launch (Wed. and Fri. mornings) and ask to be dropped near the hotel. L'Hibiscus has two classes of accommodations: three small bungalows with private bath at f.6500 for up to three persons, or a small house nearby called Le Moana accommodating four persons for f.4500.

Although the accommodations are satisfactory, the trick is that virtually everything you consume—even the water you drink—is charged extra at resort prices. Common drinking water is not available at L'Hibiscus; bottled water is f.250. The prices of the meals are fixed at f.500 for breakfast, f.2000 for lunch or dinner (not possible to order à la carte). Don't accept a "free welcome drink" from Leo or Lolita unless you don't mind having it added to your bill. There are no cooking facilities and the nearest store is three km away in Haamene (bring food and bottled water). The running water in the house may be turned off, although you can usually use the communal shower behind the restaurant. Lighting in the house could consist of a kerosene lamp.

The **Hotel Marina Iti** (B.P. 888, Uturoa, Raiatea; tel. 65-61-01) sits at the isolated south tip of Tahaa opposite Raiatea on Tahaa's only sandy beach. Their four clean, pleasant bungalows, which accommodate three persons, are f.18,000 by the lagoon or f.12,000 in the garden. Use of bicycles, canoe, and snorkeling gear is included, but meals are f.6600 extra for all three. Scuba diving is f.5000. Credit cards are not accepted.

As you'll have guessed, the Marina Iti caters to an upmarket crowd here in connection with yacht cruises from Raiatea. The Marina itself offers bareboat yacht charters beginning at f.33,000 a day (up to six persons), plus f.10,000 a day extra for a skipper (if required). There are discounts in the yachting off-season Jan. to March. In the U.S. these charters can be arranged through The Moorings and Ocean Voyages (see "Yacht Tours" under "Getting There" in the main Introduction). Numerous cruising yachts anchor in the calm waters offshore (f.500 a day to use the facilities).

Food

The only restaurant on Tahaa is **Snack Melanie** in Patio. A grocery truck passes the L'Hibiscus around 1000 on Mon., Tues., Thurs., and Sat.; the same truck calls at the Marina Iti about noon daily except Sundays.

TRANSPORT

There's no airport on Tahaa. Seven of the eight villages on Tahaa have small passenger launches which leave for Raiatea at 0500 on Wed. and Fri. only, returning to Tahaa at 1000 these same days (f.500 OW). Make sure your boat is going exactly where you want to go.

Temehani and *Taporo* from Papeete call at Tahaa on Thurs. and Sun., the *Raromatai Ferry* on Wed. (northbound) and Sun. (southbound). There's a telephone booth at Tapuamu wharf where you could call your hotel to have them come pick you up.

Trucks on Tahaa are for transporting school children only, so you may have to hitch to get around. It's not that hard to hitch a ride down the west coast from Patio to Haamene, but there's almost no traffic along the east coast. Even car rentals are difficult on Tahaa.

BORA BORA

Bora Bora, 260 km northwest of Papeete, is everyone's idea of a South Pacific island. Dramatic basalt peaks soar 700 meters above a gorgeous, multicolored lagoon. Slopes and valleys blossom with hibiscus. Some of the most perfect beaches you will ever see are here, complete with topless sunbathers. Among the population of 4,500 are many skilled dancers. To see them practicing in the evenings follow the beat of village drums to their source.

The uncontrolled expansion of tourism continues to throw up luxury resorts around the island, creating the illusion of Hawaii or some West Indies hot spot. Yet many of the US$250-a-night hotels stand almost empty. Construction of a huge Hyatt Regency proceeded on a swampy shore at the far north end of the island opposite the airport, until halted by skyrocketing costs. Today the crumbling Hyatt ruins stand as an ugly monument to bad planning and the perils of high-impact development.

The Land
Seven-million-year-old Bora Bora is made up of a 10-km-long main island, a few smaller high islands in the lagoon, and a long ring of *motus* on the barrier reef. Pofai Bay marks the center of the island's collapsed crater with Toopua and Toopuaiti as its eroded west wall. Mt. Pahia's gray basalt mass rises 649 meters behind Vaitape and above it soar the sheer cliffs of Otemanu's mighty volcanic plug (727 meters). The wide-angle scenery of the main island is complemented by the surrounding coral reef and numerous *motus,* one of which bears the airport. Tiny Motu Tabu of the travel brochures was popularized in Murnau's 1928 film *Tabou.* Te Ava Nui Pass is the only entry through the barrier reef. Watch for dolphins near this channel as your ship enters Bora Bora's lagoon; whole colonies sometimes race the boats.

BORA BORA

MOTU MUTE AIRPORT
HOTEL MARINA
AIRPORT LAUNCH
MOTU OME
TEVAIROA
TAIHI POINT
RUINS OF HYATT REGENCY
TEREIA POINT
AMERICAN GUN
MOTU TOFARI
OLD AMERICAN WHARF
MARE FARE OPU
FAANUI BAY
MATAIHUA (314 m) ▲
REVATUA CLUB
FAANUI
MOTU AHUNA
FAREPITI WHARF
MARAE MAROTETINI
MARAE FARE-RAI
MARAE AEHAUTAI
AMERICAN GUNS
FITIIU POINT
POWER PLANT
MARAE TAIANAPA
MARAE NONOHAURA
SHIPPING ROUTE
TE AVA NUE PASS
AMERICAN GUNS
CLUB MED
PAHIA (649 m) ▲
OTEMANU (727 m) ▲
VAIROU BAY
MOTU TABU
HOTEL OA OA
HOTEL ROYAL
VAITAPE
ANAU STORE
CHEZ AIME MARE
WHARF
FREDOS
NUNUE
BLUE LAGOON
MATAPUPU (235 m) ▲
POFAI BAY
ABANDONED MUSEUM
ANAU CAMPING "CHEZ STELEO"
TOOPUA I.
BLOODY MARY'S
SOFITEL MARARA
PAOAOA POINT
MOTU VAIVAHIA
TOOPUAITI
HOTEL BORA BORA
AMERICAN GUNS
BEACH HOTEL MATIRA
MATIRA BEACH PARK
MATIRA POINT
MATIRA TOURS
TAURERE POINT

0   2 km

-N-

History

The letter "B" doesn't exist in Tahitian, so Bora Bora is actually Pora Pora (First Born). Bora Borans of yesteryear were indomitable warriors who often raided Maupiti, Tahaa, and Raiatea. "Discovered" by Roggeveen in 1722, Bora Bora was visited by Capt. James Cook in 1777. In 1895 the island was annexed by France.

In Feb. 1942 the Americans hastily set up a refueling and regrouping base code-named "Bobcat" on the island to serve shipping between the U.S. west coast or Panama Canal and Australia/New Zealand. You can still see remains from this time, including eight huge naval guns to defend the island against a surprise Japanese attack that never materialized.

The big lagoon with only one pass offered a secure anchorage for as many as 100 U.S. Navy transports at a time. A road was built around the island and an airfield constructed. The 4,400 American army troops also left behind 130 half-caste babies, 40% of whom died when the base closed in 1946 and the abandoned infants were forced to switch from their accustomed American baby formulas to island food. The survivors are now approaching ripe middle age. Novelist James A. Michener, a young naval officer at the time, left perhaps the most enduring legacy by modeling his "Bali Hai" on this "enchanted island," Bora Bora.

Orientation

You can arrive at Motu Mute airport and be pleasantly carried to Vaitape wharf by launch, or disembark from a ship at Farepiti wharf, three km north of Vaitape. Most of the stores, banks, and offices are near Vaitape wharf. The best beaches are at Matira at the island's southern tip. *Trucks* link these places and you'll have the choice of staying at a hotel near Vaitape or at Matira.

SIGHTS

South Of Vaitape

Behind the Banque de Tahiti at Vaitape Wharf is the **monument to Alain Gerbault**, who sailed his yacht, the *Firecrest,* around the world from 1925 to 1929—the first Frenchman to do so solo. Gerbault's first visit to Bora Bora was from 25 May to 12 June 1926. He returned to Polynesia in 1933 and stayed until 1940. To get an idea how the Bora Borans live take a stroll through the village: go up the road that begins beside the Banque Socredo nearby.

The good, level 32-km road around the island makes it easy to see Bora Bora by rented bicycle. On the north side of Pofai Bay is a large white mansion built as the residence for the governor of American Samoa for the Dino de Laurentis film *Hurricane* starring Mia Farrow. At the head of Pofai Bay notice the odd assortment of looted war wreckage across the road from **Boutique Alain Linda,** remnants of an abandoned A-frame museum. The seven-inch American gun dragged here from Tereia Point is hard to miss. The locations of the other seven MK II naval guns remaining on Bora Bora are given below. An overgrown track up over the saddle and across the island departs from opposite the forlorn, violated gun.

From **Bloody Mary's Restaurant** there's a spectacular view across Pofai Bay to the island's soaring peaks. An unmarked road near the restaurant leads up to a TV tower with a spectacular view (ask). Photographer Erwin Christian's **Moana Art Boutique** just north of Hotel Bora Bora has a good selection of post-cards. The finest beach on the island stretches east from Hotel Bora Bora to Matira Point. Off the small point at **Hotel Bora Bora** is some of the best snorkeling in the world, with a varied multitude of colorful tropical fish. **Martine's Créations** just east of Hotel Bora Bora has finely crafted black-pearl jewelry and designer beachwear.

Two naval guns sit on the ridge above Hotel Matira. The trail behind the hotel leads right to them (10 minutes): keep straight ahead up to the top of the ridge for good views of the lagoon and neighboring islands. A **public beach** is opposite the **Moana Beach Hotel** on Matira Point. At low tide you can wade from the end of Matira Point right out to the reef.

The East Coast

Continue north to the **Sofitel Marara,** a good place for a beer. Farther up the east side of Bora Bora past Anau is Vairou Bay. An unmarked jeep track crosses the mountains from behind François Temanua's house at the head of Vairou Bay to Faanui.

Just a little farther along, the *ahus* of three *maraes* can be seen by the water. A short distance down a side track off the main road is the best of these, **Marae Aehautai,** from whence there's a stupendous view of Otemanu. From here you'll be able to pick out Te Ana Opea cave far up on the side of Otemanu. It's possible to climb up to the cave in about three hours.

Two more American **seven-inch guns** sit atop Fitiiu Point. To get to them continue east *one of eight U.S. naval guns left behind in 1945*

along the shore from Marae Aehautai till the way becomes constricted and you are forced onto a black rocky outcrop. Go back just a little and look for a trail up to the ridge and guns. Once again, the view alone makes the visit worthwhile. Other than the Hyatt Regency ruins, little of interest is found farther north on this side of the island. Stop at the **Revatua Club** for a drink at the bar.

North Of Vaitape
One American **naval gun** remains on the hillside above the rectangular water tank at Tereia Point. The housing of a second gun, vandalized in 1982, is nearby. The remains of several American concrete wharfs can be seen along the north shore of Faanui Bay. **Marae Fare Opu**, just east of a small boat harbor, is notable for petroglyphs of turtles carved into the stones of the *ahu*. Turtles, a favorite food of the gods, were often offered to them on the *marae*.

Most of the wartime American occupation force was billeted at Faanui, and Quonset huts can still be found in the bush. Just east of the coconut husk-fueled electricity-generating plant between Faanui and Farepiti wharf is **Marae Taianapa**; its long *ahu* is clearly visible from the road.

The most important *marae* on Bora Bora was **Marae Marotetini** on the point near Farepiti wharf—west of the wharf beyond a huge

banyan tree. The great stone *ahu,* 50 meters long and up to three meters high, was restored by Prof. Sinoto in 1968 and is visible from approaching ships.

The last two **American guns** are on the ridge above Club Med, a 10-minute scramble from the main road. At the end of the ridge there's a good view of Te Ava Nui Pass, which the guns were meant to defend. Maupiti is farther out on the horizon.

HIKING

If you're experienced and determined, it's possible to climb **Mt. Pahia** in about three hours. Take the road inland beside the Banque Socredo at Vaitape and go up the depression past a series of mango trees, veering slightly left. Circle the cliffs near the top on the left side, and come up the back of Snoopy's head and along his toes. (These directions will take on meaning if you study Pahia from the end of Vaitape's wharf.) There's no set trail; you must bushwhack. Avoid rainy weather when the way will be muddy and slippery. Christian Pons (tel. 67-70-80) offers three-hour hikes up Pahia at f.8000 pp.

Note that Otemanu has *never* been climbed because clamps pull right out of the vertical, crumbly cliff face. Its name means "Sea of Birds."

1. Tetiaroa atoll (Tahiti Tourist Board); **2.** sunset over Moorea (Paul Bohler)

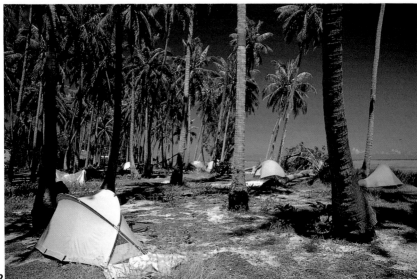

1. pier at Residence Linareva, Moorea (D. Stanley);
2. tents at Chez Nelson et Josiane, Moorea (Don Pitcher)

EVENTS

The *Fêtes de Juillet* are celebrated at Bora Bora with special fervor. The canoe and bicycle races, javelin throwing, flower cars, singing and dancing competitions run until 0300 nightly. A public ball goes till dawn on the Sat. closest to 14 July.

Try to participate in the 10-km foot race to prove that all tourists aren't lazy, but don't take the prizes away from the locals. If you win, be sure to give the money back to them for partying. You'll make good friends that way and have more fun dancing in the evening. The stands are beautiful because the best decorations win prizes, too.

PRACTICALITIES

ACCOMMODATIONS

Nearly a quarter of Tahiti-Polynesia's hotel rooms are on Bora Bora and overbuilding has produced a glut. Except at holiday times, it's not necessary to book a room in advance. In the off season many hotel owners meet the boats. If there isn't anyone from the hotel of your choice at the dock when you arrive, get on the blue *truck* marked "Vaitape-Anau" (f.300 pp, plus f.100 for luggage).

Stay in Vaitape if you're interested in observing the life of the inhabitants, hiking, or frequenting the local bars. You're better off at Matira if the beach is what you came for and you prefer the company of other travelers/tourists. Since most travelers choose to stay at the beach, the budget places at Matira may be overcrowded while those in Vaitape are almost empty, a factor to consider. Bora Bora suffers from serious water shortages, so use it sparingly.

Inexpensive Places Near Vaitape
As you disembark you may be offered a room by someone from the **Hotel Royal Bora Bora** (B.P. 202, Vaitape; tel. 67-71-54). Their minibus meets all boats. This establishment consists of nine bungalows with private bath on the lagoon beside Ets. Loussan supermarket, a few hundred meters north of the wharf in Vaitape. At last report they were asking f.4500 pp in a bungalow including breakfast and dinner, though the price fluctuates according to what the traffic will bear. Avoid the bungalows near the restaurant or shower block—noisy. Hotel Royal also offers beds in small double rooms with shared bath near the restaurant at f.1500 pp with reductions

if you stay two or more nights, worth considering only if everything else is full. No cooking facilities are available. Unfortunately, the elderly Tahitian hotel owner has a rather unpleasant manner and manages to cast a shadow over this hotel.

Chez Aime Mare, a km south of Vaitape pier, used to be the budget traveler's favorite but since the places at Matira Beach opened up it's been largely deserted. Check with the owners across the street to find out if they're still renting rooms.

Four or five houses south down the road from Chez Aime past the Jehovah's Witnesses Church is **Chez Alfredo Doom** (tel. 67-70-31; no sign) with a f.1200 pp dorm (minimum stay two nights). Fredo also has a few duplex bungalows with kitchens (f.5000 d, f.6000 t) if you want more privacy. Cooking and bicycles are available.

Marama Bungalows (B.P. 11, Vaitape; tel. 67-72-97) is by the lagoon between Chez Aime and Vaitape wharf. The two units have private bath and fridge but no kitchens (f.5500 d). The distance from the beach and its high price put this place at the bottom of the list.

Inexpensive Places On The Beach

On the Matira peninsula are two excellent alternatives to the hotels. **Chez Nono** (Noël Leverd, B.P. 282, Vaitape; tel. 67-71-38) is beside the beach park across from the Moana Beach Hotel. They have one large bungalow with cooking facilities (f.12,000), two smaller bungalows with private bath (f.6000), and a three-bedroom guesthouse with shared kitchen at f.4000 s, f.5000 d per room. Ventilation spaces between the ceilings and walls mean you hear *everything* in the other rooms but the atmosphere is amiable and all guests soon become good friends. Their boat tour around the island with shark feeding and an excellent fish lunch is f.4000. This is a fine choice for families.

Chez Robert et Tina (tel. 67-72-92) has two houses with cooking facilities at the tip of Matira Point beyond the Moana Beach Hotel. Rooms are f.3000 s, f.6000 d. Robert's company, Matira Tours, (see below) offers excellent lagoon trips, but Robert himself has acquired a taste for female visitors so let him know right away if you're not interested.

Fare Toopua (Annie Muraz, B.P. 87, Vaitape; tel. 67-74-46) is only inexpensive if you're part of a small group. The main feature is the location—near a white-sand beach on Toopua Island across the lagoon from Vaitape. The four thatched bungalows with cooking facilities are f.9000 d, f.10,200 t, or f.11,400 for four, and that includes an aluminum dinghy with outboard motor for shopping or exploring the lagoon (f.15,000 security deposit). The minimum stay is three nights and monthly rates are available. If you can afford it, this is a great little getaway.

Camping

Most backpackers stay at **Chez Pauline** (Pauline Youssef, B.P. 215, Vaitape; tel. 67-72-16), a perfect campsite in a coconut grove right on a white-sand beach. It's between the Moana Beach and Sofitel Marara hotels, eight km from Vaitape. Pauline charges f.1000 pp to camp (own tent), f.1700 in the 10-bed dorm, or f.4000 d in one of her six simple beach cabins. The two thatched bungalows with kitchens are f.9000 d, f.11,500 t. There are cooking facilities for campers too and although it's quite a hike to the nearest grocery store, the food truck circling the island passes daily around 1100. If you stay a week the eighth night is free. It can get crowded here and falling coconuts can be a hazard during winds.

A less expensive campground is **Chez Steleo** (tel. 67-71-32) at Anau on the east side of the island. Look for the blue "Vaitape-Anau" *truck* at the wharf—transfers are f.300 pp plus f.100 for luggage. Steleo, a helpful, laid-back sort of guy, owns the *truck* so once you're staying there, additional rides are free. Camping is f.800 pp and there's a 10-bed dormitory at f.1300 pp. You can cook. Unlike Pauline's there are no water problems, but it's not on the beach. Steleo owns land on idyllic Motu Vaivahia: for f.1000 pp he'll drop you off there for a few days (take food and water). If you know how to swim ask him about renting an outrigger canoe (pirogue). He also rents bicycles at f.800 a day. A shortcut trail straight across the island begins opposite the campground (follow the power lines). Bora Bora is overrun by land crabs, funny little creatures which make camping exciting.

Yachties Special

Cruising yachties are catered to by two hotels on Bora Bora, both with atmospheric restaurants serving good food, but no beaches. The **Hotel Oa Oa** (B.P. 10, Vaitape; tel. 67-70-84) between Farepiti and Vaitape has long been a yachtie hangout, though in 1992 the 14-room hotel was reported closed. In the past, visiting boats have had free use of the eight moorings, hot showers, garbage disposal, water supply, etc. Check whether they've reopened.

The **Bora Bora Yacht Club** (B.P. 17, Vaitape; tel. 67-70-69) near Farepiti Wharf allows boats free use of their 17 moorings and provides fresh water and showers. Their three floating bungalows with cooking facilities and solar electricity (f.20,000 for four persons) can be towed out and moored off a *motu*. The three garden bungalows are f.9000 for four.

Expensive Hotels

Hotel Bora Bora (B.P. 1, Bora Bora; tel. 67-70-28), which opened in June 1961, was the island's first large resort. At f.49,000 s or d for an overwater bungalow or one-bedroom suite, it's one of the most hyperpriced set-ups in the South Pacific. Standard rooms in this stuffy 79-unit snobs' paradise begin at f.28,000 s or d, f.33,500 t. Breakfast and dinner are f.5800 pp extra. Though you may not wish to shell out those funds, it's worth dropping into this oasis to watch the privileged few consuming—a sightseeing experience. Some 257 coconut trees surround the hotel and any of the gardeners will be happy to crack a nut.

Hotel Matira (B.P. 31, Vaitape; tel. 67-70-51) is one of the only deluxe places offering cooking facilities. Their 28 thatched bungalows with kitchenettes on the mountain side of the road are f.9300 s, f.11,200 d, f.13,600 t. A few units are without kitchens—ask beforehand. The hotel annex is more attractive: thatched bungalows with kitchenettes right on the lagoon at the neck of Matira peninsula (f.10,200 s, f.13,200 d, f.15,700 t). The Matira's Chinese restaurant (closed Mon.) is moderately priced and the beach is excellent.

It's hard to recommend Japanese-owned **Hotel Moana Beach** (B.P. 156, Bora Bora; tel. 67-73-73) on Matira Point, a sterile, life-less luxury resort on a white-sand beach. One of the 10 beachfront bungalows will set you back f.36,800 s or d; the 30 overwater bungalows an additional f.15,400 (children under 19 free). Even the meals are overpriced: f.5500 pp extra for breakfast and dinner. Skip the Moana Beach until it develops a little character (and an extra zero is added to the end of your weekly paycheck).

The **Bora Bora Beach Club** (B.P. 252, Nunue; tel. 67-71-16), which in previous incarnations has been the Climate de France and Ibis Bora Bora, shares the same white beach with the Sofitel Marara. Nine four-unit shingle-roof blocks total 36 rooms which begin at f.12,500 s, f.15,000 d (garden); f.15,000 s, f.18,000 d (beach)—rather overpriced. A breakfast and dinner package is f.3600 pp extra. This hotel loans outrigger canoes and sailboarding, fishing, and snorkeling gear to guests free. Their restaurant serves Mexican food.

Hotel Sofitel Marara (B.P. 6, Bora Bora; tel. 67-70-46) is in the same top-end price range as Hotel Bora Bora, but it's a lot more open and informal. Instead of the boring types you hear at Hotel Bora Bora, the Marara caters to an international mix of tourists. Their bar and restaurant are fairly reasonable for such a swank place and the beach doesn't have the policed look of the Bora Bora's. The Marara was built in 1978 to house the crew filming Dino de Laurentis' *Hurricane;* the name means "Flying Fish." This is the place to stay if you don't give a damn how much it costs: the 64 bungalows begin at f.24,800 s, d, or t. It's the only hotel on the island with a swimming pool (the other resorts don't have them due to the water shortage). Happy hour is 1700-1800 daily.

The 41 fan-cooled rooms at **Club Méditerranée Bora Bora** (B.P. 34, Bora Bora; tel. 67-70-57) just north of Vaitape are f.14,000 pp, double occupancy, including meals and recreational activities. Due to the cramped location, all of the units are built on stilts over the lagoon! Though smaller, quieter, and more intimate, this Club Med isn't as well situated as the one on Moorea. It's more like a regular hotel, with the restaurants and bars open to the general public. To see the Tahitian dancing here costs f.900 but this includes a few drinks.

The 16-room **Revatua Club** (B.P. 159, Vaitape; tel. 67-73-31) on the northeast side of the island is isolated, beachless, and expensive: f.7420 for up to three persons. The mock-Victorian architecture is right out of Hollywood. Its only draws are the excellent overwater French restaurant **Chez Christian,** which offers free transport for diners, and the bar.

FOOD

The assorted snack bars in Vaitape need no introduction. **Bar Teave** (no sign) opposite the Banque de Polynésie near Vaitape wharf is a great place to mix with the locals (open daily till midnight). Beer prices here are the cheapest on the island and Fri. and Sat. afternoons you can get steak *frites* and *poisson cru* to go with the brew. This place has been going for 50 years now, so it should still be around when you get there.

Chez Madam Chou (tel. 67-71-18) next to the pharmacy in Vaitape has Chinese and Tahitian dishes at reasonable prices. Open daily till 2200, dining is on a pleasant outdoor terrace.

The **Blue Lagoon Restaurant** (closed Tues.; tel. 67-70-54) on the north side of Pofai Bay claims to be "the leading French restaurant on Bora Bora," which is something of an overstatement. The French owner masquerades as a Spaniard and will prepare *paella Valenciana* (f.3000 pp) if given two hours' advance notice. It's all a bit of a come-on, but American tourists with thick wallets eat it up. Hotel pick-ups for clients with dinner reservations are at 1845. Blue Lagoon also offers a five-hour reef tour with shark feeding and lunch on a *motu* for f.4900 pp—it's said to be quite good. Their three-hour lagoon excursion without lunch is f.3200, transfers included.

Bloody Mary's Seafood Restaurant (closed Sun.; tel. 67-72-86) used to be the "in" spot on Bora Bora: a board outside lists "famous guests" including Jane Fonda and Baron George Von Dangel. It's still good, with pizza for lunch (1100-1500) and dinner (1830-2100), plus filet of fish, lobster, and a vegetarian plate. Free transportation for diners is available at 1830 or 1930 if you call for pick-up. Beer is on tap all day, so it's worth a stop at any time on your way around the island.

On the inland side of the road opposite Musée Jean Masson at Matira look for the sign "Cuisine Vietnamiene." The lady in this tiny hut serves delicious meals for about f.1200 afternoons (1200-1700). The handwritten menu changes daily. A snack bar near Pauline's also serves good cheap meals (but no beer).

ENTERTAINMENT

Witness the Polynesian dancing at **Hotel Bora Bora** (tel. 67-70-28) for free by grabbing a barside seat before it starts at 2100 on Wed. and Sun. nights. This hotel has a "tropical hour" with free hors d'oeuvres and exotic cocktails for half price on Tues., Thurs., and Sat. 1700-1800. Better traditional dancing occurs after dinner Tues., Thurs., and Sat. nights at the **Moana Beach Hotel** (tel. 67-73-73).

You'll feel more at home watching the Tahitian dance show at the **Hotel Sofitel Marara** (tel. 67-70-46) every night at 2030; see it all for the price of a draft beer. On Sat. at 1830 they open the earth oven and a Tahitian feast begins.

Le Récife Bar (B.P. 278, Vaitape; tel. 67-73-87) between Hotel Oa Oa and Farepiti wharf is Bora Bora's after-hours club, open Fri. and Sat. from 2230. Disco dancing continues almost until dawn and there are large, clean rooms with shared bath for rent (f.3000 s, f.4000 d) if you can't make it back to your hotel or just want to be near the action.

SPORTS AND RECREATION

Claude Sibani's **Bora Bora Calypso Club** (B.P. 259, Bora Bora; tel. 67-74-64), at the Bora Bora Beach Club, offers scuba diving at normal prices: f.5500 for a lagoon dive, f.6500 for an ocean dive. They go out daily at 0900 and 1400 from the Beach Club dock.

Noted photographer Erwin Christian of **Moana Adventure Tours** (B.P. 5, Bora Bora; tel. 67-70-33) also organizes scuba diving (f.7000 in the lagoon, f.7500 in the ocean) and PADI scuba certification. Ask for him at Moana Art Boutique just north of Hotel Bora Bora. Since the pass is far from the large hotels at the south end of the island, most scuba diving at Bora Bora is within the lagoon, and visibility is sometimes limited.

Matira Tours (tel. 67-70-97) runs a round-the-island boat trip (f.4000 pp) on the catamaran *Vehia* departing Matira Point daily at 0930. The price includes a seafood picnic lunch on a *motu*, reefwalking, and snorkeling gear, plus a chance to see giant clams, manta rays, and the hand feeding of small lagoon sharks.

Lagoon trips with other companies vary in price from f.2500 to f.8000 depending on whether lunch is included, length of trip, luxury of boat, etc., so check around. Also see the Blue Lagoon Restaurant and Chez Nono listings above. An excursion of this kind is an essential part of the Bora Bora experience, so splurge on this one.

SERVICES

Air Tahiti and a **tourist information office** (B.P. 144, Bora Bora; tel. 67-76-36) are beside the Banque de Tahiti on the wharf at Vaitape. Local handicrafts are sold in the **Centre Artisanal** hut nearby. The post office, gendarmerie, and health clinic *(infirmerie)* are within a stone's throw of the wharf. **Banque Socredo** (tel. 67-71-11) is behind the basketball court across the street from the clinic. Pharmacie Fare Ra'au is farther north.

Also north of Vaitape wharf is the largest store, Magasin Chin Lee, and the island's Mobil gas station. Chin Lee and another well-stocked grocery store in Vaitape are open Mon. to Sat. 0600-1730. The Total service station is north again, just south of Hotel Oa Oa. The only other place to buy groceries is the general store at Anau, halfway around the island. It closes 1200-1330 and on Sunday. No grocery store is found at Matira although a grocery truck passes this way around 1100 daily (except Sundays).

TRANSPORT

The **Air Tahiti** office (tel. 67-70-35) is opposite the Town Hall *(mairie)* adjoining the wharf. A useful transversal flight direct from Bora Bora to Rangiroa (f.19,000) operates four times a week (but there's no Rangiroa-Bora Bora flight). For information on flights to Bora Bora from Papeete,

Huahine, and Raiatea see the main "Introduction" to this book.

Ships from Raiatea and Papeete tie up at Farepiti wharf, three km north of Vaitape. The shipping companies have no representatives on Bora Bora, so for departure times just keep asking. Drivers of the *trucks* are the most likely to know. You buy your ticket when the ship arrives.

Officially the *Taporo IV* leaves at 1300 on Tues. and 0800 on Sun., while the *Temehani* departs on Thurs. at 1300. The *Raromatai Ferry* is supposed to leave Wed. at 1400 and Sun. at 1200. Beware of ships leaving early.

Getting around is a bit of a headache as *truck* service is irregular. Public *trucks* usually meet the boats but many of the *trucks* you see around town are strictly for guests of the luxury hotels. If you do find one willing to take you, fares between Vaitape and Matira vary from f.150 to f.300 plus f.100 for luggage. Taxi fares are high, so check before getting in (f.1500 is average).

Mautara Rent-A-Bike (tel. 67-73-16) near Chez Aime rents bicycles at f.800 a half day, f.1000 a full day. Other places around Vaitape charge a rip-off f.1300 for a six-hour bicycle rental!

If you have to rent a car, **Bora Rent-A-Car** (B.P. 246, Vaitape; tel. 67-70-03) south of Vaitape wharf rents Renaults at f.6500 for an 0800 to 1700 day, f.7500 for 24 hours. The price includes unlimited km, insurance, and gasoline, valid driver's license required. They also have motor scooters for f.4000 from 0800-1700 or f.4500 for 24 hours. For service and price they're the best on the island. If driving at night watch out for scooters and bicycles without lights. But best is to dispense with motorized transport on little Bora Bora.

The **Bora Bora Yacht Club** (tel. 67-70-69) rents small, two-person dinghies with six-horse power outboard motors for f.3500 a half day, f.6000 a whole day (gas extra). With an early start you could circumnavigate the island.

Otemanu Tours (tel. 67-70-49) between Hotel Oa Oa and Club Med offers a tour around Bora Bora by *truck* daily at 1400 (2¹/₂ hours—f.1500). Avoid the various "jeep safari" tours (f.4000) around the island, which don't offer a lot more.

Airport

Bora Bora's vast airfield (BOB) on Motu Mute north of the main island was built by the Americans during WW II. Until 1961 all international flights to Tahiti-Polynesia arrived here; passengers were then transferred to Papeete by Catalina amphibious or Bermuda Flying Boat seaplanes. Today, arriving air passengers are taken to Vaitape wharf by launch (included in the plane ticket). If you're flying to Bora Bora from Papeete go early in the morning and sit on the left side of the aircraft for spectacular views—it's only from the air that Bora Bora is the most beautiful island in the world.

DIANA LASICH HARPER

strand morning glory (Ipomoea pes-caprae)

scorpion fish

MAUPITI

Majestic Maupiti (Maurua), 44 km west of Bora Bora, is the least known of the accessible Society Islands. Maupiti's mighty volcanic plug soars from a sapphire lagoon. Vegetation-draped cliffs contrast with magnificent *motu* beaches. Almost every bit of level land on the main island is taken up by fruit trees, while watermelons thrive on the surrounding *motus*. Maupiti abounds in native seabirds including frigate birds, terns, and others. The absence of Indian mynahs allows you to see native land birds almost extinct elsewhere.

The 1,000 people live in the adjacent villages of Vaiea, Farauru, and Pauma. Tourism is not promoted because there aren't any hotels, which can be an advantage! Maupiti was once famous for its black basalt stone pounders, and fishhooks made from the seven local varieties of mother-of-pearl shell.

Sights
It takes only three hours to walk right around the island. The nine-km crushed coral road lined with breadfruit, mango, and banana trees, and hibiscus bushes passes crumbling *maraes,* freshwater springs, and a beach.

Marae Vaiahu by the shore a few hundred meters beyond Hotuparaoa Massif is the largest *marae*. Once a royal landing opposite the pass into the lagoon, the king's throne and ancient burials are still on the *marae*. Nearby is the sorcerers' rock: light a fire beside this rock and you will die. Above the road are a few smaller *marae*.

Terei'a Beach at the west tip of the Maupiti is the only good beach on the main island. At low tide you can wade across from Terei'a to Motu Auira in waist-deep water. **Marae Vaiorie** is a double *marae* with freshwater springs between.

As many as two dozen large *marae* are hidden in Maupiti's mountainous interior and the island is known for its ghosts. A local guide will lead you to the 372-meter summit of Maupiti for around f.2500. With the proper encouragement he/she may show you the *marae* and tell the legends.

Accommodations

Several of the 963 inhabitants take paying guests at about f.3000 pp, including all meals. The guesthouse owners meet the flights and boats in search of clients. The absence of a regular hotel on Maupiti throws together an odd mix of vacationing French couples, backpackers, and "adventuresome" tourists in the guesthouses. You could camp on the white sands of Terei'a Beach but water and *nonos* (insects) would be a problem. If you're set on camping, get across to the airport *motu* and hike south looking for a campsite there—you'll have to befriend someone to obtain water. Maupiti, like Bora Bora, experiences serious water shortages during the dry season.

Chez Mareta (Tinorua and Mareta Anua; tel. 67-80-25) in the center of Vai'ea village, is the house with the sloping blue roof a few minutes' walk from the Mairie. They offer mattresses on the floor in the upstairs double rooms for f.1000 pp, or f.3000 pp including breakfast and a good dinner. A very pleasant sitting room faces the lagoon downstairs. Upon request they'll drop you

DIANA LASICH HARPER

A clown- or damselfish (Amphiprion clarkii) nestles among the venomous tentacles of an anemone. A mucous secretion protects the fish from the creature's stinging cells, providing it with a safe refuge. Anemones gather plankton from the water, but also feed on mussels, snails, or barnacles that fall their way.

on a *motu* for the day (beware of sunburn). It's okay for a couple of days, but not for an extended stay. Agree on the price beforehand and check your bill when you leave.

At **Pension Tamati** (Chez Paparoro; tel. 67-80-10) a single room with breakfast costs f.2000. Unfortunately tourists are usually given the inside rooms without proper ventilation. Other places to stay in the village are **Chez Floriette** (tel. 67-80-85) at f.4000 pp with half pension and **Pension Huranui** (tel. 67-81-07) which charges f.6000 pp including all meals for the six rooms.

Fare Pae'ao (Jeannine Tavaearii, B.P. 33, Maupiti; tel. 67-81-01) on Motu Pae'ao is quiet and offers a superb white beach. It's f.6000 pp including all meals in a screened two-bedroom bungalow. Reservations are required to ensure airport pick-up (f.1000 pp RT) and a room. (In 1962 Kenneth Emory and Yoshiko Sinoto excavated a prehistoric cemetery on Pae'ao and found 15 adzes of six different types, providing valuable evidence for the study of Polynesian migrations.)

Hotel Auira (Edna Terai and Richard Tefaatan, B.P. 2, Maupiti; tel. 67-80-26) on

Motu Auira, the *motu* opposite Terei'a Beach, has nine thatched bungalows. The garden variety with shared bath are f.7500 pp a day including all meals; those on the beach, with private bath, are f.8500 pp. Both food and beach are excellent. Boat transfers from the airport are f.2000 pp.

Services
No bank exists on Maupiti, so bring money. The **post office** is at the Mairie. The bakery is in the power plant on the edge of town and the baguettes are baked and sold around 1100 and 1500. The island's youth hang out here from 1000 on. There's a village disco in Fararuu village Fri. and Sat. nights with no cover charge, and canned beer is sold.

Getting There
Air Tahiti has flights to Maupiti from Raiatea (f.5350 OW) three times a week. Reconfirm with the Air Tahiti agent (tel. 67-80-20) at the Mairie. Here you board the launch to the airport (f.400 pp OW).

The 20-meter interisland boat *Taporo I* motors weekly between Raiatea and Maupiti, leaving Raiatea on Tues. or Thurs. (f.1000 deck, f.1600 *couchette*). The boat returns to Raiatea from Maupiti on the afternoon of the arrival day. The pass into Maupiti is narrow. When there's a southeast wind it can be dangerous—boats have had to turn back. Ships must enter the channel during daylight, thus the compulsory morning arrival and afternoon (or morning) departure. *Taporo I* has only six bunks and in rough weather it can be a rough six-hour trip. The coming and going of this tiny ship is a major event in the otherwise unperturbed weekly life of the Maupitians. If you arrive by boat you'll be treated with more respect than if you arrive by plane. (A recent reader's letter claims this boat no longer accepts passengers.)

Airport
Like Bora Bora, Maupiti's airport (MAU) is on a small *motu*. You must take a launch to the main island (f.400).

OTHER LEEWARD ISLANDS

Tupai

Tupai or Motu Iti ("Small Island"), 13 km north of Bora Bora, is a tiny privately owned coral atoll measuring 1,100 hectares. The facing horse-shoe-shaped *motus* enclose a lagoon. Ships must anchor offshore. The few dozen people here live by making copra. Opposition by tradi-tional landowners blocked resort development on the atoll by a Japanese corporation in 1990.

Maupihaa

To approach 360-hectare Maupihaa (Mopelia) in stormy weather is dangerous. The unmarked pass is a mere 10 meters wide and can only be found by searching for the strong outflow of lagoon water at low tide. No fresh water is avail-able on the uninhabited atoll. Cruising yachts and copra cutters sometimes call.

In 1917 the notorious German raider *Seeadler* was wrecked on Maupihaa. Count Felix von

Luckner was able to carry on to Fiji where he was captured at Wakaya Island. Count von Luckner's journal, *The Sea Devil,* became a best-seller after the war.

Manuae

Manuae (Scilly) is the westernmost island of the Society Islands. This atoll is 15 km in di-ameter but totals only 400 hectares. Pearl divers once visited Manuae. In 1855 the three-masted schooner *Julia Ann* sank on the Man-uae reef. It took the survivors two months to build a small boat which carried them to safety at Raiatea.

Motu One

Motu One (Bellingshausen) got its second name from a 19th-century Russian explorer. Tiny 280-hectare Motu One is circled by a guano-bearing reef with no pass into the lagoon.

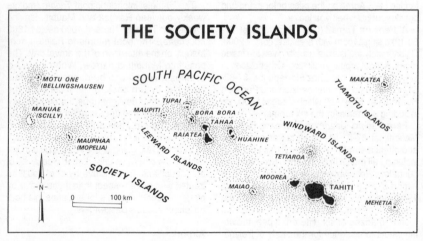

THE SOCIETY ISLANDS

OUTER ISLANDS

Australs, Tuamotus, Gambiers, Marquesas

M.G.L. DOMÉNY DE RIENZI

LES MARQUISES

Ils parlent de la morte comme tu parles d'un fruit
Ils regardent la mer comme tu regardes un puits

Les femmes sont lascives au soleil redouté
Et s'il n'y a pas d'hiver cela n'est pas l'été

La pluie est traversière elle bat de grain en grain
Quelques vieux chevaux blancs qui fredonnent Gauguin

Et par manque de brise le temps s'immobilise
Aux Marquises.

Du soir montent des feux et des points de silence
Qui vont s'élargissant et la lune s'avance

Et la mer se déchire infiniment brisée
Par des rochers qui prirent des prénoms affolés

Et puis plus loin des chiens des chants de repentance
Et quelques pas de deux et quelques pas de danse

Et la nuit est soumise et l'alizé se brise
Aux Marquises.

Leur rire est dans le coeur le mot dans le regard
Le coeur est voyageur l'avenir est au hasard

Et passent des cocotiers qui écrivent des chants d'amour
Que les soeurs d'alentours ignorent d'ignorer

Les pirogues s'en vont les pirogues s'en viennent
Et mes souvenirs deviennent ce que les vieux en font

Veux-tu que je te dise gémir n'est pas de mise
Aux Marquises.

—Jacques Brel

M.G.L. DOMENY DE RIENZI

THE AUSTRAL ISLANDS

The inhabited volcanic islands of Rimatara, Rurutu, Tubuai, Raivavae, and Rapa, plus uninhabited Maria (or Hull) atoll, make up the Austral Group. This southernmost island chain is a 1,280-km extension of the same submerged mountain range as the southern Cook Islands, 900 km farther northwest. The islands of the Australs seldom exceed 300 meters, except Rapa which soars to 650 meters. Their southerly location makes these islands notably cooler than Tahiti. Collectively the Australs are known as Tuhaa Pae, the "Fifth Part" or fifth administrative subdivision of Tahiti-Polynesia. It's still a world apart from tourism.

History

Excavations carried out on the northwest coast of Rurutu uncovered 60 round-ended houses arrayed in parallel rows, with 14 *marae* scattered among them, demonstrating man's presence here as early as A.D. 900. The ruins of *marae* can also be seen on Rimatara, Tubuai,

and Raivavae. Huge stone *tikis* once graced Raivavae, but most have since been destroyed or removed. The terraced mountain fortifications or *pa* on Rapa are unique.

The Australs were one of the great art areas of the Pacific, represented today in many museums. The best known artifacts are sculptured sharkskin drums, wooden bowls, fly whisks, and tapa cloth. Offerings which could not be touched by human hands were placed on the sacred altars with intricately incised ceremonial ladles. European contact effaced most of these traditions; the carving done today is crude by comparison.

Rurutu was spotted by Capt. James Cook in 1769; he found Tubuai in 1777. In 1789 Fletcher Christian and the *Bounty* mutineers attempted to establish a settlement at the northeast corner of Tubuai. They left after only three months, following battles with the islanders in which 66 Polynesians died. The European discoverer of Rapa was Capt. George Vancouver in

1791. Rimatara wasn't discovered until 1813 by the Australian captain Michael Fodger.

English missionaries converted most of the people to Protestantism in the early 19th century. Whalers and sandalwood ships introduced diseases and firearms which decimated the Austral islanders. The French didn't complete their annexation of the group until 1900. Since then the Australs have gone their sleepy way.

The People

The 6,500 mostly Polynesian inhabitants are fishermen and farmers who live in attractive villages with homes and churches built of coral limestone. The rich soil and temperate climate stimulate agriculture, with staple crops such as taro, manioc, Irish potatoes, sweet potatoes, leeks, cabbage, carrots, corn, and coffee. The coconut palm also thrives except on Rapa. Today many Austral people live in Papeete.

Getting There

Air Tahiti has three flights a week to Rurutu and Tubuai, the only islands with airports. One flight operates Papeete-Tubuai-Rurutu-Papeete, the other two Papeete-Rurutu-Tubuai-Papeete. One-way fares from Tahiti are f.17,350 to Rurutu and f.19,450 to Tubuai. Rurutu-Tubuai is f.7900.

All the other Austral Islands are accessible only by boat. For information on the twice-monthly sailings of the *Tuhaa Pae II* from Papeete, see the main Introduction to this book.

RURUTU

This island, 572 km south of Tahiti, is shaped like a miniature of the African continent. For the hiker, mountainous, 32-square-km Rurutu is a more varied island to visit than Tubuai. Taatioe (389 meters) and Manureva (384 meters) are the highest peaks. A narrow fringing reef surrounds Rurutu but there's no lagoon. The climate of this northernmost Austral island is temperate and dry. The history of Rurutu revolves around three important dates: 1821 when the gospel arrived on the island, 1970 when Cyclone Emma devastated the three villages, and 1975 when the airport opened.

In Jan. and July Rurutuans practice the ancient art of stone lifting or *amoraa ofai*. Men get three tries to hoist a 130-kilogram boulder up onto their shoulder, while women attempt a 60-kilogram stone. Dancing and feasting follow the event. The women of Rurutu weave fine pandanus hats, bags, baskets, fans, lamp shades, and mats. Rurutu's famous Manureva ("Soaring Bird") Dance Group has performed around the world. The main evening entertainment is to watch dancers practicing in the villages.

Sights

The pleasant main village, Moerai, boasts a post office, four small stores, two bakeries, and two banks. Two other villages, Avera and Hauti, bring the total island population to about 2,000.

Electricity functions 24 hours a day. Neat fences and flower gardens surround the coral limestone houses. This is the Polynesia of 50 years ago: though snack bars have appeared, *trucks* have yet to cover the 30-km coastal road. Beaches, waterfalls, valleys, and limestone caves beckon the explorer.

At Moerai village lies the tomb of French navigator Eric de Bisschop whose exploits equaled but are far less known than those of Thor Heyerdahl. Before WW II de Bisschop sailed a catamaran, the *Kaimiloa,* from Hawaii to the Mediterranean via the Indian Ocean and the tip of Africa. His greatest voyage was aboard the *Tahiti Nui,* a series of three rafts, each of which eventually broke up and sank. In 1956 the *Tahiti Nui* set out from Tahiti to Chile to demonstrate the now-accepted theory that the Polynesians had visited South America in prehistoric times. There, two of his four crewmen abandoned ship but de Bisschop doggedly set out to return. After a total of 13 months at sea the expedition's final raft foundered on a reef in the Cook Islands and its courageous leader, one of the giants of Pacific exploration, was killed.

Accommodations

Chez Catherine (tel. 94-03-11), a concrete building behind the Protestant church in Moerai, has 10 rooms (f.3500 s, f.5000 d). Chil-

RURUTU

Eric de Bisschop

dren under 12 are free. A restaurant and bar are on the premises.

Chez Metu Teinaore (tel. 94-04-93), across the street from Moerai's Protestant church, is a large white house with four rooms, shared cooking facilities and bath. Rates are f.50,000 a month. **Chez Maurice** at Avera takes guests in a large 13-bed house.

The **Rurutu Village Hotel** (B.P. 6, Unaa, Rurutu; tel. 94-03-92), on a beach just west of the airport, is Rurutu's only regular hotel. The 16 bungalows go for f.9500 s, f.17,000 d, including all meals. Facilities encompass a restaurant, bar, and swimming pool. The hotel owner, Iareta Moeau, is a dance leader and a very nice fellow. For reservations call 42-93-85 in Papeete.

Services And Transportation
Banque Socredo (tel. 94-04-75) is at Moerai.

Unaa Airport (RUR) is at the north tip of Rurutu, four km from Moerai. **Air Tahiti** can be reached at 94-03-57. The supply ship from Papeete ties up at Moerai.

TUBUAI

Ten-km-long by five-km-wide Tubuai, largest of the Australs, is 670 km south of Tahiti. Hills on the east and west sides of this oval 45-square-km island are joined by low land in the middle; when seen from the sea Tubuai looks like two islands. Mount Taitaa (422 meters) is its highest point. Tubuai is surrounded by a barrier reef; a pass on the north side gives access to a wide turquoise lagoon bordered by brilliant white-sand beaches. Picnics are often arranged on the small reef *motus* amid superb snorkeling grounds.

The brisk climate permits the cultivation of potatoes, carrots, oranges, and coffee, but other vegetation is sparse. Several *marae* are on Tubuai, but they're in extremely bad condition with potatoes growing on the sites. The *Bounty* mutineers attempted unsuccessfully to settle on Tubuai in 1789. Mormon missionaries arrived as early as 1844 and today there are active branches of the Church of Latter-day Saints in all the villages. The islanders weave fine pandanus hats and some woodcarving is done at Mahu.

Most of the 1,900 inhabitants live in Mataura and Taahuaia villages on the north coast, though houses and hamlets are found all along the 24-km road around the island. A red dirt road cuts right across the middle of Tubuai to Mahu village on the south coast.

Mataura is the administrative center of the Austral Islands. The two stores at Mataura bake bread. The **Manu Patia Restaurant** is just outside Mataura. Banque Socredo (tel. 95-04-86) is also at Mataura. *Trucks* haven't reached this island yet.

Accommodations

Several people rent rooms to visitors at about f.2500 pp, meals extra. Monthly rates are much less. **Chez Caro** (Caroline Chung Thien, B.P. 94, Mataura; tel. 95-03-46) next to Chung Tien store in Mataura may have housekeeping rooms at this price.

Chez Taro Tanepau (tel. 95-03-82), by the lagoon near a small beach between Mataura and the wharf, has small bungalows with cooking facilities at f.2500 pp daily or f.40,000 for the entire four-bed unit per month. On the monthly basis f.5000 extra is charged to cover electricity and gas. For advance reservations call 43-87-32 in Papeete.

Chez Ah Sing (tel. 95-03-52), a two-bedroom house with cooking facilities in Taahuaia, is f.2200 pp or f.35,000 d a month.

Chez Turina Victor (B.P. 7, Mataura; tel. 95-03-27) is near the beach at Taahuaia, three km east of Mataura. A room with cooking facilities is f.2200 pp or f.33,000 a month.

Chez Terii Turina (tel. 95-04-98) behind Chez Turina Victor in Taahuaia, has two houses with cooking facilities. There's no hot water and the baths are shared. Rooms are f.2200 pp.

The **Ermitage Sainte Hélène** (Madame Tehinarii Ilari, B.P. 79, Mataura; tel. 95-04-79) is at Mahu, eight km south of Mataura. The three quiet houses with cooking facilities and private bath are f.2500 pp, or f.40,000 a month. Bicycles are f.1000 a day, airport transfers f.2000 pp return. The Ermitage, named for Napoleon's isle of exile, was created by ex-politico Noel Ilari whose "tomb" sits on the front lawn. Have a chat with him about it after you check in.

Getting There
Tubuai Airport (TUB) in the northwest corner of the island was opened in 1972. **Air Tahiti** (tel. 95-04-76) arrives from Rurutu and Papeete several times a week. Ships enter the lagoon through a passage in the barrier reef on the northwest side and proceed to the wharf at Mataura. Otherwise, the lagoon is too shallow for navigation.

OTHER AUSTRAL ISLANDS

RIMATARA

Without airport, harbor, wharf, hotels, restaurants, bars, or taxis, Rimatara is a place to escape the world. Only a narrow fringing reef hugs Rimatara's lagoonless shore; arriving passengers are landed at Amaru by whaleboat. It's customary for newcomers to pass through a cloud of purifying smoke from beachside fires. The women of Rimatara make fine pandanus hats, mats, and bags, and shell necklaces. *Monoi* (skin oil) is prepared from gardenias and coconut oil.

This smallest (eight square km) and lowest (83 meters) of the Australs is home to about 1,000 people. Dirt roads lead from Amaru, the main village, to Anapoto and Mutuaura. Water is scarce in the dry season. Bring food and drink to Rimatara.

Uninhabited Maria (or Hull) is a four-islet atoll 192 km northwest of Rimatara, visited once or twice a year by men from Rimatara or Rurutu for fishing and copra-making. They stay on the atoll two or three months, among seabirds and giant lobsters.

Accommodations
Local postmistress **Marie Taharia** rents rooms with cooking facilities in a three-bedroom house by the sea across from the school in Mutuaura. Rates are f.2200 pp a day or f.50,000 a month for the house.

The **Mairie of Amaru** offers two small rooms each with one single bed, shared bath, and cooking facilities, in Amaru Town Hall for f.750 pp a day.

RAIVAVAE

This appealing, nine-km-long and two-km-wide island is just south of the Tropic of Capricorn and thus outside the tropics. For archaeology and natural beauty, this is one of the finest islands in Polynesia. Fern-covered Mt. Hiro (437 meters) is the highest point on 16-square-km Raivavae. A barrier reef encloses an emerald lagoon, but the 32 small coral *motus* are mostly located on the southern and eastern portions of the reef. The tropical vegetation is rich: rose and sandalwood are used to make perfumes for local use. A malignant fever epidemic in

RIMATARA

Different teams led by Frank Stimson, Don Marshall, and Thor Heyerdahl have explored the ancient temples and taro terraces of Raivavae. Many two- to three-meter-high stone statues once stood on the island, but most have since been destroyed, and two were removed to Tahiti where they can be seen on the grounds of the Gauguin Museum. One big tiki is still standing by the road between Rairua and Mahanatoa villages.

Annie Flores runs a two-bedroom guesthouse with cooking facilities next to the gendarmerie in Rairua, the main village. The charge is f.30,000 a month for the house. A Chinese shop is nearby, but bring your own bread.

The inhabitants of Raivavae have decided they don't want an airport. If you'll be taking a boat to the Australs anyway, you may as well go to Raivavae where airborne tourists can't follow! Ships enter the lagoon through a pass on the north side and tie up to the pier at Rairua. A boat calls at the island about every 10-14 days.

1826 reduced the number of people on Raivavae from 3,000 to 120. The present population of around 1,250 lives in four coastal villages, Rairua, Mahanatoa, Anatonu, and Vairuru, linked by a dirt road. A shortcut route direct from Rairua to Vairuru crosses a 119-meter saddle with splendid views of the island.

RAPA

Rapa, the southernmost point in Tahiti-Polynesia, is one of the most isolated and spectacular

RAPA ITI

RAPA ITI

PERAU
(650m)

AREA

HUAREI BAY

HIRI
BAY

MORONGO
UTA

HUAREI

- N -

PUKUMARU
(605m)

0   1   2 km

TAUTURU
ISLAND

The present population of about 550 lives at Area and Haurei villages on the north and south sides of Rapa's great open bay, connected only by boat. To arrange a stay on Rapa is difficult. Write to Le Maire, Rapa, Îles Australes, four or five months in advance stating your name, nationality, age, and profession. If you're granted a *certificat d'hebergement,* it means the mayor is willing to arrange room and board for you with a local family, the price to be decided upon your arrival. Then contact the Subdivision Administrative des Îles Australes, B.P. 4587, Papeete (tel. 42-20-00) which may actually grant you a permit to go. The *Tuhaa Pae II* calls at Rapa every four to six weeks, so that's how long you'll be there.

Marotiri or the "Bass Rocks" are 10 uninhabited islets 74 km southeast of Rapa. Amazingly enough, some of these pinnacles are crowned with stone platforms and round "towers." One 105-meter-high pinnacle is visible from Rapa in very clear weather. Landing is difficult.

islands in the Pacific. Its nearest neighbor is Raivavae, 600 km away. It's sometimes called Rapa Iti (Little Rapa) to distinguish it from Rapa Nui (Easter Island). Soaring peaks reaching 650 meters surround magnificent Haurei Bay, Rapa's crater harbor, the western portion of a drowned volcano. This is only one of 12 deeply indented bays around the island; the absence of reefs allows the sea to cut into the 40-square-km island's outer coasts. Offshore are several sugarloaf-shaped islets. The east slopes of the mountains are bare, while large fern forests are found on the west. Coconut trees cannot grow in the foggy, temperate climate.

A timeworn **Polynesian fortress** with terraces is situated on the crest of a ridge at Morongo Uta, commanding a wide outlook over the steep rugged hills. Morongo Uta was cleared of vegetation by a party of archaeologists led by Thor Heyerdahl in 1956 and is still easily visitable. About a dozen of these *pa* are found above the bay, built to defend the territories of the different tribes of overpopulated ancient Rapa. Today the young men of Rapa organize eight-day bivouacs to hunt wild goats which range across the island.

the famous tiki from Raivavae, now at Tahiti's Gauguin Museum

DAVID STANLEY

a Tuamotu outrigger

THE TUAMOTU ISLANDS

Arrayed in two parallel northwest-southeast chains scattered across an area of ocean 600 km wide and 1,200 km long, the Tuamotus are the largest group of coral atolls in the world. Of the 78 atolls in the group 21 have one entrance (pass), 10 have two passes, and 47 have no pass at all. A total of around 12,500 people live on the 45 inhabited islands. Although the land area of the Tuamotus is only 726 square km, the lagoons of the atolls total some 6,000 square km of sheltered water. All are atolls: some have an unbroken ring of reef around the lagoon, while others appear as a necklace of islets separated by channels.

Variable currents, sudden storms, and poor charts make cruising this group by yacht extremely hazardous—in fact, the Tuamotus are popularly known as the "Dangerous Archipelago" or "Labyrinth." Wrecks litter the reefs of many atolls. Winds are generally from the east, varying to northeast from Nov. to May and south-

east from June to October. A series of hurricanes devastated these islands between 1980 and 1983.

The resourceful Tuamotu people have always lived from seafood, pandanus nuts, and coconuts. They once dove to depths of 30 meters and more, wearing only tiny goggles, to collect mother-of-pearl shells. This activity has largely ceased as overharvesting has made the shells rare. Today, cultured pearl farms operate on Aratika, Hikueru, Katiu, Kaukura, Manihi, Raroia, South Marutea, Takapoto, Takaroa, Takume, and Taenga. Cultured black pearls *(Pinctada margaritifera)* from the Tuamotus and Gambiers are world famous.

The scarcity of land and fresh water have always been major problems. Many of these dry, coconut-covered atolls have only a few hundred inhabitants. Though airstrips exist on 12 islands, the isolation has led many Tuamotuans to migrate to Papeete. The only regular ho-

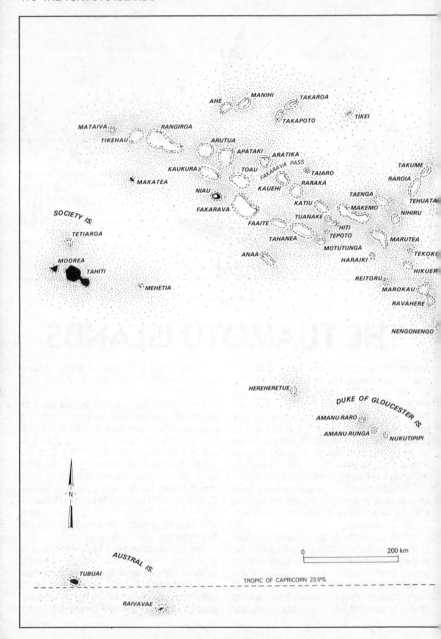

THE TUAMOTU / GAMBIER GROUP

DISAPPOINTMENT IS

TEPOTO

NAPUKA

PUKAPUKA

FANGATAU

FAKAHINA

AUERE

TATAKOTO

AMANU

HAO

PUKA-RUHA

REAO

AKIAKI

VAHITAHI

PARAOA

MANUHANGI

VAIRAATEA

NUKUTAVAKE

PINAKI

AHUNUI

VANAVANA

TUREIA

TENARARO

VAHANGA

TENARUNGA

MARUTEA

MATUREI-VAVAO

BERTERO

TEMATANGI

MORUROA

MARIA

FANGATAUFA

MINERVE

GAMBIER IS.

MANGAREVA

MORANE

TEMOE

TROPIC OF CAPRICORN

23.5°S.

tels are on Rangiroa and Manihi. French military activity has largely closed the eastern Tuamotus to tourism. Beware of fish poisoning all across this archipelago.

HISTORY

The Tuamotus were originally settled around 1000 A.D. from the Society and Marquesas islands, mostly by political refugees. The inhabitants of the atolls frequently warred among themselves or against those of a Society island and even King Pomare II was unable to conquer the group despite the help of the missionaries and European firearms. After Tahiti came under French "protection" in 1842, the Tuamotus remained independent and it was not until the transformation of the protectorate into a French colony in 1880 that the Tuamotu islands gradually submitted to French rule. Since 1923 the group has been administered from Papeete. Two-thirds of the people are Catholic, the rest Mormon.

Magellan sighted Pukapuka on the northeast fringe of the Tuamotus in 1521, but it was not until 1835 that all of the islands had been "discovered." On 2 June 1722, a landing was made on Makatea by Roggeveen's men. To clear the beach beforehand, the crew opened fire on a crowd of islanders. The survivors pretended to be pacified with gifts, but the next day the explorers were lured into an ambush by women and stoned, leaving 10 Dutchmen dead and many wounded. Fourteen European expeditions passed the Tuamotus between 1606 and 1816, but only eight bothered to go ashore. Of these all but the first (Quiros) were involved in skirmishes with the islanders.

Centuries later, a group of Scandinavians under the leadership of Thor Heyerdahl ran aground on Raroia atoll on 7 Aug. 1947, after having sailed 7,000 km from South America in 101 days on the raft *Kon Tiki* to prove that Peruvian Indians could have done the same thing centuries before.

GETTING THERE

Information on the various cargo boats from Papeete is given in the main Introduction.

Permission

Due to French nuclear-testing activities in the area, foreigners require special permission to stay on any of the islands south and east of Anaa. It's okay to go ashore as a passenger on a through ship, but you must leave again with the ship. Since the launching of overt French terrorism in the South Pacific in 1985, it's forbidden for non-French to even be aboard a ship when it stops at the military bases, Hao, Moruroa, and Fangataufa. This creates a problem as Hao is central to the Tuamotus and most ships do call there. Foreigners trying to leave a remote atoll might be sent to Hao! There aren't any ships from Rangiroa or Manihi to Hao, so those atolls are "safe" for foreigners.

If you do wish to spend time on one of the central or southern Tuamotus, apply at a French embassy a year in advance. Once in Papeete, if you find your ship (to the Marquesas or otherwise) will be passing through the forbidden zone, you may require a permit. Ask at the friendly Subdivision Administrative des Tuamotu-Gambier (B.P. 34, Papeete) behind the police station on Ave. Bruat. They'll probably send you back to the Police de l'Air et des Frontières near the tourist office on the harbor or at the airport.

If the police won't help, go to the Direction Réglementation et Controle de Légalité du Haut-Commissariat, upstairs in the Bloc Donald behind Voyagence Tahiti off rue Jeanne d'Arc. With a special permit stamped and signed by them, the police at the harbor will no longer resist granting the disembarkation permit. Allow several days for these difficult formalities and don't be intimidated. You'll need to know a little French—otherwise forget it. Try to remain polite to avoid spoiling things for those who follow. On departure day get to the boat early enough to allow time for last-minute return visits to the above offices—you never know.

RANGIROA

Rangiroa, 200 km northeast of Papeete, is the Tuamotus' most populous atoll and the second largest in the world (after Kwajalein in the Marshall Islands). Its 1,020-square-km aquamarine lagoon is 78 km long, 24 km across (too far to see), and 225 km around—the island of Tahiti would fit inside its reef. The name Rangiroa means "extended sky." Some 240 *motus* sit on this reef.

What draws people to Rangi (as everyone calls it) is the marinelife in the lagoon. You've never seen so many fish. While lagoons in the Society Islands are often murky due to runoff from the main volcanic islands and pollution from coastal communities, the waters of the Tuamotus are clean and fresh with excellent swimming and snorkeling.

Rangiroa's twin villages, each facing a pass 500 meters wide into the lagoon, house 1,400 people. Avatoru village on Avatoru Pass is at the west end of the airport island. A 20-km paved road runs east from Avatoru past the airport and Kia Ora Hotel to Tiputa Pass. Tiputa village is just across the water. Both villages have small post offices and stores; the town hall and

gendarmerie are at Tiputa and the health clinic and marine research center at Avatoru. Avatoru has better facilities, but Tiputa is less touristed and offers the chance to escape by simply walking and wading southeast. No bank is to be found at Rangiroa, so bring money.

Budget Accommodations

A nice place to stay is **Chez Nanua** (Nanua and Marie Tamaehu, B.P. 54, Avatoru; tel. 96-03-88), between the airport and Avatoru village. The three thatched bungalows with shared bath are f.3000 pp including all meals (small). You eat with the owners—a little fish and rice every meal. Camping is f.1000 pp (f.2500 pp with all meals). There's no electricity or running water but you're right on the beach.

A relative of the above family, Punua Tamaehu (tel. 96-04-73) has four bungalows with shared bath at f.2000 pp, or f.3500 pp including all meals. Punua also has eight small huts on Motu Teavahia where one can stay for f.3500 pp including all meals, plus f.3500 pp for boat transfers. This is the solution for those who really want to get away.

A new place for low-budget travelers is **Chez Tamatona** (B.P. 74, Rangiroa; tel. 92-02-85). In late 1991 the bungalows were still in the planning stages but camping space was free for anyone taking their meals there (about f.1000 pp a day). To find it turn left as you leave the airport and after 500 meters you'll see the snack bar on the right. Mr. Tamatona is a good cook and very gregarious.

Chez Marie (Marie Bellais-Richmond, B.P. 51, Avatoru; tel. 96-03-92) on Point Peretue, Avatoru, has seven bungalows with private bath, f.5500 pp complete pension or f.1200 pp for a room only. This family also dedicates itself to drying fish and raising pigs and the "busy" atmosphere can be a little annoying a times.

Rangiroa Lodge (Jacques and Florida Ly; tel. 96-02-13) near the wharf in Avatoru has six rooms with shared bath at f.2000 pp, or f.3500 pp with breakfast and dinner.

Chez Glorine (Glorine To'i; tel. 96-04-05) is on the airport island near Tiputa Pass. The six thatched bungalows with private bath are f.5500 pp including all meals (the specialty is fresh lagoon fish).

Chez Lucien (Lucien and Esther Pe'a, B.P. 69, Tiputa; tel. 96-03-55) in Tiputa village offers three traditional bungalows with private bath at f.5000 pp, including all meals.

Pension Estall (Ronald Estall, B.P. 13, Tiputa; tel. 96-03-16) in Tiputa village has four Polynesian-style bungalows with private bath, f.5000 pp complete pension.

Expensive Hotels

The snobbish, French-operated **Kia Ora Village** (B.P. 1, Tiputa; tel. 96-03-84), near Tiputa Pass about two km from the airport by road, is Rangiroa's top resort. The 30 beach bungalows are f.22,000 s, f.25,000 d, f.28,000 t. Breakfast and dinner are f.4800 pp extra. In 1991 the Kia Ora began offering accommodation in five A-frame bungalows at "Kia Ora Sauvage" on Motu Avaerahi on the far south side of the lagoon with packages costing f.45,000 pp including two nights accommodation, meals, activities, and boat transfers.

La Bouteille à la Mer (B.P. 17, Avatoru; tel. 96-03-34), also on the airport island, has 11 thatched bungalows at f.10,900 s, f.18,375 d, f.24,100 t, including breakfast and dinner.

The **Rangiroa Village** (B.P. 8, Avatoru; tel. 96-03-83) is a nine-bungalow resort near Avatoru village: f.8000 s, f.13,000 d, f.17,000 t, including breakfast and dinner. Extras are a small "bungalow tax" and f.600 pp for airport transfers.

The **Village Sans Souci** (B.P. 22, Avatoru; tel. 42-49-36) is an escapist's retreat on Motu Mahuta, an islet to the west of Avatoru Pass. It offers 14 thatched bungalows with communal shower and toilet stalls. The package rates are f.30,500 s, f.50,000 d, f.69,500 t for three nights, f.6500 pp per additional night, including transfers and all meals. The Sans Souci's restaurant specializes in seafood and there's a self-service bar. Scuba diving is possible. The Sans Souci is the place to get away from it all.

Sports And Recreation

The strong tidal currents *(opape)* through Avatoru and Tiputa passes generate flows of three to six knots. It's exciting to shoot these 30-meter-deep passes on an incoming tide wearing a mask and snorkel, and the hotels offer this activity (f.1500-3000) using a small motorboat. The marinelife is fantastic and sharks may be seen. They're *usually* harmless black-tip reef sharks. Other popular excursions include a picnic to the "blue lagoon" at **Motu Taeoo** (f.5000 pp) and tiny mid-lagoon **Motu Paio**, a bird sanctuary (f.3000 pp).

Scuba diving is arranged by the friendly **Centre de Plongée Raie Manta Club** (Yves and Brigette Lefevre, B.P. 55, Avatoru; tel. 96-04-80) at the Kia Ora Village Hotel in Avatoru— f.4500 pp for one tank including a float through the pass (night diving f.5500). For regular customers the 11th dive is free. Every dive is different: falling, pass, undulating bottom, hollow. Humphead wrasses, manta rays, barracudas, and lots of sharks are seen. A full day-trip to the "Blue Lagoon," two dives included, is f.7000 (five-person minimum). PADI certification courses are offered. Divers come from all parts of the world to dive with Yves and his highly professional team.

Jack's Rent a Boat (B.P. 61, Avatoru; tel. 96-04-69) in Avatoru charges f.3000 pp to float through the pass or f.5000 pp for an all-day excursion to the Blue Lagoon.

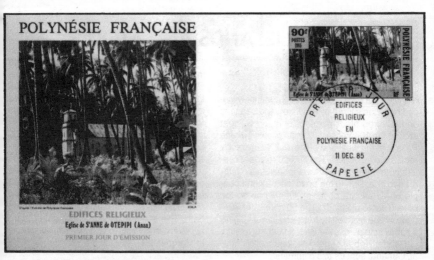

a church among the coconut palms at Anaa, Tuamotu Islands, is featured on this 1985 first-day cover

Getting There

Air Tahiti (tel. 96-03-41) flies Tahiti-Rangiroa daily (f.12,950 OW) using 46-seat ATR 42 equipment. Wednesday and Sun. a flight arrives direct from Bora Bora (f.19,000). Note that this flight is only eastbound: no flight operates *to* Bora Bora from Rangiroa. There's service three times a week from Rangiroa to Manihi (f.8400) and weekly to the Marquesas (f.24,150). All seats on the plane to Hiva Oa are almost always booked in advance.

Schooners *(goelettes)* from Papeete (f.3000 OW) take 22 hours to get there from Tahiti, but 72 hours to return (not direct). Boats making the run include the *Manava II, Manava III, St. Xavier Marie Stella,* and *St. Corentin.* For more information on transport to the Tuamotus see the main Introduction to this book.

Airport

The airstrip (RGI) is about five km from Avatoru village by road, accessible to Tiputa village by boat. Some of the pensions offer free transfers; others charge f.500.

OTHER ISLANDS AND ATOLLS

MANIHI

Manihi is the other Tuamotu atoll commonly visited by tourists lured by its white-sand beaches and cultured black pearls. You can see right around the 10-by-22-km Manihi lagoon; Tairapa Pass is at the west end of the atoll. Many of the *motus* are inhabited. The 50,000 resident oysters outnumber the 500 local inhabitants a hundred to one. Due to the pearl industry, the people of Manihi are better off than those on the other Tuamotu islands. The 50 houses of Turipaoa village, shaded by trees and flowers, share a sandy strip across the lagoon from the airstrip.

Reader Robert Leger Teilelbaum of Montreal, Canada, sent us this comment:

Do not arrive in Manihi without advance reservations. The Air Tahiti staff were the most pernicious, offensive people I met during my entire year traveling in the South Pacific area. This mother/daughter team seem to take particular delight in stranding budget travelers at the airport. I was left, unfortunately, with a profound distaste for this place. Prices generally are exorbitant and having to stay in a crowded, unoriginal village is to be avoided.

Accommodations

The **Hotel Kaina Village** (B.P. 2560, Papeete; tel. 96-42-73) is Manihi's luxury hotel, located on the airport *motu* and owned by Air Tahiti. The 16 overwater bungalows run f.16,500 s, f.22,000 d or t. Breakfast and dinner are f.4700 pp extra. A f.1000 "bungalow tax" and f.500 pp airport transfer charge are additional. Gilles and Wendy Petre of **Manihi Blue Nui** offer scuba diving (f.3500) and PADI certification from the resort.

Cheaper lodging is offered by the inhabitants of Turipaoa village. Advance reservations by mail or telegram are recommended to ensure space and airport pick-ups. Bring money as credit cards and foreign currency are not accepted.

Chez Huri (tel. 96-42-29) in Turipaoa village includes a three-bedroom house with cooking facilities and two bungalows with shared bath at f.2000 pp without food. If you want meals served it's f.3000 pp for them all. Airport transfers are free.

Chez Teiva, also in Turipaoa village, is f.5000 pp for room and board. Each of their five houses with shared bath also has cooking facilities.

Chez Marguerite Fareea (tel. 96-42-40) is on Motu Topiheiri, a *motu* across the lagoon from Turipaoa village. The six bungalows are f.5000 pp including all meals. Five have private bath. This is a friendly place with better-than-average accommodations. There's no telephone at Marquerite's—you must write.

Getting There

You'll need a boat to go from Manihi airport (XMH) to Turipaoa, which can be expensive unless you've arranged to be picked up. All Air Tahiti (tel. 96-42-71) flights from Papeete or Bora Bora are via Rangiroa. Boats from Papeete also call here.

OTHERS

Makatea is an uplifted atoll with a lunar surface eight km long and 110 meters high. Gray cliffs plunge to the sea. Phosphate was dug up here by workers with shovels from 1917 to 1966 and exported to Japan and New Zealand by a transnational corporation which pocketed the profits. At one time 2,500 workers were present. The mining was abandoned in 1966 but many buildings and a railway remain. Numerous archaeological remains were found during the mining.

Ahe, 13 km west of Manihi, is often visited by cruising yachts which are able to enter the 16-km-long lagoon. The village is on the southeast side of the atoll. Facilities include two tiny stores, a post office, and a community center where everyone meets at night. Despite the steady stream of sailing boats, the people are very friendly. All of the houses have solar generating panels supplied after a hurricane in the early 1980s. Only a handful of small children can be seen in the village; most are away at school on Rangiroa or Tahiti. Mama Fana keeps the yachtie log. She or the mayor can arrange accommodations. Many families follow their children to the main islands while they're at school, so you may even be able to rent a whole house. A local government boat runs between Ahe and Manihi on an irregular schedule.

In 1972 the private owner of **Taiaro**, Mr. W.A. Robinson, declared the atoll a nature reserve, and in 1977 it was accepted by the United Nations as a "biosphere reserve." Some 285 areas with unique natural values are included in UNESCO's "Man and the Biosphere Program" and Taiaro is the only South Pacific site so listed! Scientific missions studying atoll ecology sometimes visit Taiaro, the only permanent inhabitants of which are a caretaker family.

The shark-free lagoon at **Niau** is enclosed by an unbroken circle of land. Yachts can enter the lagoon at **Toau**, though the pass is on the windward side. A leper colony once on **Reao** is now closed. **Takapoto** and **Takaroa** atolls are separated by only eight km of open sea and on both the airstrip is within walking distance of the village. On the outer reef near Takaroa's airstrip are two wrecks, one a four-masted sailing ship here since 1906. Due to the fact that all the inhabitants of Takaroa belong to the Mormon church, their village is often called "Little America." Pearl farming is carried out in the Takaroa lagoon which offers good anchorage.

For information on lodging with the inhabitants on **Anaa, Arutua, Fakarava, Kaukura, Takapoto, Takaroa,** and **Tikehau,** ask at the Tahiti Tourist Board in Papeete. All these atolls receive regular Air Tahiti flights from Tahiti and offer a less commercialized experience than heavily promoted Rangiroa and Manihi. Inter-

island boats call about once a week, bringing imported foods and other goods and returning to Papeete with fish. If you go by boat take along a good supply of fresh produce from the bountiful Papeete market, as such things are in short supply here. It's very difficult to change money on the atolls, so bring enough cash. All the Tuamotu atolls offer the same splendid snorkeling possibilities (take snorkeling gear), though scuba diving is only developed on Rangiroa and Manihi. The advantage of the outer atolls is that the people will be far less impacted by packaged tourism. On these it should be easy to hitch rides with the locals across to *le secteur* (uninhabited *motus*) as they go to cut copra or tend the pearl farms. You don't really need maps or guides to these outer atolls—you'll soon know all you need to know.

The Lost Treasure Of The Tuamotus

During the War of the Pacific (1879-83) four mercenaries stole 14 tons of gold from a church in Pisco, Peru. They buried most of the treasure on **Pinaki** or **Raraka** atolls in the Tuamotus before proceeding to Australia where two were killed by aboriginals and the other two were sentenced to 20 years imprisonment for murder. Just prior to his death the surviving mercenary told prospector Charles Howe the story.

In 1913 Howe began a 13-year search which finally located part of the treasure on an island near Raraka. He reburied the chests and returned to Australia to organize an expedition which would remove the gold in secret. Before it could set out, however, Howe disappeared. But using Howe's treasure map, diver George Hamilton took over in 1934. Hamilton thought he found the cached gold in a pool but was unable to extract it. After being attacked by a giant octopus and moray eel Hamilton abandoned the search and the expedition dissolved. As far as is known, the US$1.8 million in gold has never been found.

THE NUCLEAR TEST ZONE

The nuclear test zone (Centre d'Expérimentations du Pacifique) is at the southeastern end of the Tuamotu group, 1,200 km from Tahiti. The main site is 30-km-long Moruroa atoll, but Fangataufa atoll 37 km south of Moruroa is also being used. In 1962 the French nuclear-testing sites in the Algerian Sahara had to be abandoned after the country won its independence. In 1963 French President Charles de Gaulle announced officially that France was shifting the program to Moruroa and Fangataufa. Since 1966 more than 175 nuclear bombs, reaching up to 200 kilotons, have been set off in the Tuamotus. The tests continue at the rate of six per year at a cost to French taxpayers of millions of dollars each. By 1974 the French had conducted 44 *atmospheric* tests, 39 over Moruroa and five over Fangataufa.

Way back in 1963 the U.S., Britain, and the U.S.S.R. agreed in the Partial Test Ban Treaty to halt nuclear tests in the atmosphere. France chose not to sign. On 23 June 1973, the World Court urged France to discontinue nuclear tests, which might drop radioactive material on surrounding territories. When the French government refused to recognize the Court's jurisdiction in this matter, New Zealand Prime Minister Norman Kirk ordered the New Zealand frigate *Otago* to enter the danger zone off Moruroa and on 23 July Peru broke diplomatic relations with France. On 15 Aug. French commandos boarded the protest vessels *Fri* and *Greenpeace III*, attacking and arresting the crews.

In 1974, with opposition mounting in the Territorial Assembly and growing world indignation, French President Giscard D'Estaing ordered a switch to the *underground* tests which continue today. The French support base on Hao atoll (population 1,156), 500 km north of Moruroa, allows the French military to fly materials directly into the area without passing through Faaa Airport. Evidence of the testing is kept well away from the eyes of tourists on Tahiti—you'll find no mention of these tests in any of the official tourist brochures and most travel guides give them only cursory mention.

Moruroa

Obviously, an atoll, with its porous coral cap sitting on a narrow basalt base, is the unsafest place in the world to stage underground nuclear explosions. It's unlikely this was ever intended. Moruroa was chosen for its isolated location, far from major population centers which might be affected by fallout. By 1974 when atmospheric testing had to cease, the French military had a huge investment there. So rather than move to a more secure location in France or elsewhere they decided to take a chance. Underground testing was to be carried out in Moruroa's basalt core, 500-1,200 meters below the surface of the atoll.

On 10 Sept. 1966 President de Gaulle was present at Moruroa to witness an atmospheric test of a bomb suspended from a balloon. Weather conditions caused the test to be postponed and the following day conditions were still unsuitable as the wind was blowing in the direction of inhabited islands to the west instead of toward uninhabited Antarctica to the south. De Gaulle complained he was a busy man and could afford to wait no longer, so the test went ahead—spreading radioactive fallout across Cook Islands, Niue, Tonga, Samoa, Fiji, and Tuvalu. Tahiti itself was the most directly affected island but the French authorities never acknowledged this fact.

Two serious accidents occurred within weeks of each other in 1979. On 6 July 1979, an explosion and fire in a laboratory bunker on Moruroa killed two and injured four others. For two weeks after the accident, workers in protective suits tried to clean up the area contaminated with plutonium by the explosion. On 25 July 1979, a nuclear device became stuck halfway down an 800-meter shaft. When the army engineers were unable to move the device, they exploded it where it was, causing a massive chunk of outer slope of the atoll to break loose. This generated a huge tsunami which hit Moruroa, overturning cars and injuring seven people. After the blast, a crack 40 cm wide and two km long appeared on the surface of the island. As a precaution against further tidal waves and hurricanes, refuge platforms were built at intervals around the atoll. For an hour before and after each test all personnel must climb up on these platforms.

Right from the beginning contaminated debris including scrap metal, wood, plastic, and clothing had carelessly been stored in plastic bags on the north side of the atoll. On 11 March 1981, a hurricane washed large quantities of this nuclear waste into the lagoon and surrounding sea and that Aug. another storm spread more material from the same dump. Enough radioactive debris to fill 200,000 44-gallon drums is still lying on the north side of the atoll.

By 1981 Moruroa was punctured as a Swiss cheese and sinking two cm after every test, or 1½ meters between 1976 and 1981. With the atoll's 60-km coral rim dangerously fractured by drilling shafts, the French switched to underwater testing in the Moruroa lagoon in 1981, to be closer to the center of the island's core. By 1988 the 108 underground blasts had weakened the geological formations beneath Moruroa so severely that French officials announced that henceforth the largest underground tests would take place on nearby Fangataufa atoll, despite the additional cost involved. The military base remains on Moruroa and small groups of work-

ers and technicians are sent over to Fangataufa every time a test is made there.

The French government claims it "owns" Moruroa and Fangataufa because in 1964 a standing committee of the Territorial Assembly voted three to two to cede the atolls to France for an indefinite period. This was never ratified by the full assembly and French troops had occupied the islands before the vote was taken anyway.

Impact
In 1983 the French government invited a delegation of scientists from Australia, New Zealand,

one of 23 huge platforms where the employees at Moruroa seek refuge from hurricanes or tsunamis that sweep the atoll and Papua New Guinea to visit Moruroa. Significantly, they were not permitted to take samples from the northern or western areas of the atoll, nor of lagoon sediments. The scientists reported that "if fracturing of the volcanics accompanied a test and allowed a vertical release of radioactivity to the limestones, specific contaminants would, in this worst case, enter the biosphere within five years."

On 21 June 1987 the famous French underwater explorer Jacques Cousteau was present for a test at Moruroa; the next day he took water samples in the lagoon, the first time such independent tests had been allowed. Two samples collected by Cousteau nine km apart contained traces of cesium 134, an isotope with a half-life of two years. Though French officials claimed the cesium 134 remained from atmospheric testing before 1975, a Sept. 1990 *Review of the Calypso Water Samples* by Norm Buske of Search Technical Services (HCR Box 17, Davenport, WA 99122-9404 U.S.A.) has proved that this is not scientifically feasible and leakage from underground testing is the only possible explanation. In 1990 a computer model of Moruroa developed by New Zealand scientists indicated that radioactive groundwater with a half-life of several thousand years may be seeping through fractures in the atoll at the rate of 100 meters a year and, according to Prof. Manfred Hochstein, head of Auckland University's Geothermal Institute, "in about 30 years the disaster will hit us." Buske's study indicates that the release of contamination into the Pacific from the numerous cracks and fissures may already have started.

Unlike the U.S., which has paid millions of dollars in compensation money to the Marshallese victims of its nuclear testing program, the French government has refused to even acknowledge the already-apparent effects of its 44 atmospheric tests. From 1963 to 1983 no public health statistics were published. Now the rates of thyroid cancer, leukemia, brain tumors, and stillbirths are on the upswing in Tahiti-Polynesia, and the problem of seafood poisoning (ciguatera) in the nearby Gambier Islands is clearly related. French nonresponse to these first side effects demonstrates vividly how they plan to deal with the more serious environmental consequences yet to come.

The Issue

France is the only nuclear state to have conducted tests under a Pacific island. France has not limited itself to testing atomic and hydrogen devices: numerous neutron bombs have also been exploded. The French have maintained that the tests are harmless and that every precaution has been taken. And yet, the underground tests could be carried out much more effectively, safely, and cheaply in France itself! The claim that the tests are "safe" is disproved by the very choice of the test site, on the opposite side of the globe from their homeland.

French radioactivity will remain in the Tuamotus for thousands of years and the unknown future consequences of this program are the most frightening part of it. Virtually every South Pacific country has strongly condemned the tests on numerous occasions and the island people have protested, yet it remains official U.S. government policy not to oppose French nuclear testing in the region. Thus the U.S. must share responsibility with France for this shameful practice. The hope now is that with the Cold War over, and the need for this type of weaponry gone, the Partial Test Ban Treaty will soon be extended to cover all nuclear testing.

Note

For a complete background to this problem, read *Poisoned Reign: French Nuclear Colonialism in the Pacific* by Bengt and Marie-Thérèse Danielsson (Penguin Books, 1986).

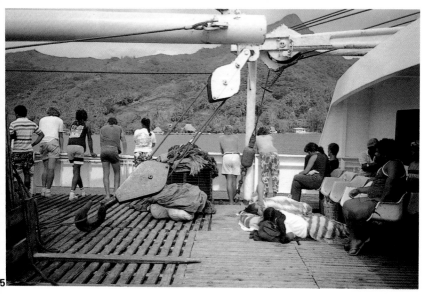

1. approaching Maupiti aboard *Taporo I;* **2.** deck class, *Taporo I;* **3.** the *Raromatai Ferry* at Bora Bora;
4. maintenance, *Raromatai Ferry;* **5.** *Taporo IV* arriving at Fare, Huahine
(all photos this page by D. Stanley)

1. Polynesian girl (Tahiti Tourist Board); 2. flower vendors, Papeete Market, Tahiti (Tahiti Tourist Board photo by Tini Colombel); 3. children, Maupiti (D. Stanley); 4. Tahitian dancer (Tahiti Tourist Board); 5. painter Aad Van der Heyde at his studio on Moorea (D. Stanley); 6. Tuamotu children (Tahiti Tourist Board)

an early 19th-century engraving of Mangarevans aboard a craft with sail

THE GAMBIER ISLANDS

The Gambier (or Mangareva) Islands are just north of the Tropic of Capricorn, 1,650 km southeast of Tahiti. The archipelago, contrasting sharply with the atolls of the Tuamotus, consists of 10 rocky islands enclosed on three sides by a semicircular barrier reef 65 km long. In all, there are 22 square km of dry land. The Polynesian inhabitants named the main island and largest, Mangareva, "Floating Mountain." Unlike the Marquesas where the mountains are entirely jungle-clad, hilltops in the Gambiers are covered with tall *aeho* grass.

Aside from Mangareva, small groups of people live only on Taravai and Kamaka islands. Makaroa is a barren, rugged 136-meter-high island. In a cliffside cave on the island of Agakauitai, the mummies of 35 generations of cannibal kings are interred. A local seabird, the *karako,* crows at dawn like a rooster.

A dramatic intensification of the ciguatera problem in the Gambiers is believed to be linked to reef damage or pollution originating at the nuclear-testing facilities on Moruroa, 400 km east. During the atmospheric testing series (until 1974) Mangarevans had to take refuge in French-constructed fallout shelters whenever advised by the military. Before each of the 41 atmospheric tests French warships would evacuate the 3,000 persons from Moruroa, usually to Mangareva, Hao, and Fakarava. Upon arrival the ships were washed down with seawater, spreading radioactive contamination into the lagoons, and the French never made the slightest attempt to clean up after themselves. Between 1971 and 1980 the annual incidence of ciguatera remained above 30%, peaking at 56% in 1975. Each of the 500-600 inhabitants suffered five to seven excruciating attacks of seafood poisoning. Lagoon fish can no longer be eaten.

Now increasing birth defects, kidney problems, and cancer among the inhabitants are being covered up by authorities, who will not allow foreigners on the islands. It's believed that a deciding reason for the French decision to launch a terrorist attack on Greenpeace's *Rainbow Warrior* in 1985 was a report indicating that the ship intended to proceed to Mangareva with doctors aboard to assess the radiation exposure of residents.

Orientation

The population of the Gambiers is around 650. Rikitea, on 6½-by-1½-km Mangareva, is the main village. A post office, small shops, gendarmerie, infirmary, schools, and a cathedral three times as big as the one in Papeete make up the infrastructure of this administrative backwater. The tomb of the 35th and last king of Mangareva, Gregorio Maputeoa (died 1868), is on a plateau above the village. Nearby is a huge

nuclear-fallout shelter built during the French atmospheric testing at Moruroa. Black pearls are cultured at a farm off Taku on the north coast of Mangareva.

HISTORY

Mangareva, which was originally settled from the Marquesas Islands around A.D. 1100, was shortly afterwards the jumping-off place for small groups which discovered and occupied Pitcairn and Henderson islands. In 1797 Capt. James Wilson of the London Missionary Society's ship *Duff* named the group for the English Admiral Gambier. France made the Gambiers a "protectorate" in 1844 and annexed the group in 1881.

Mangareva was the area of operations for a fanatical French priest, Father Honoré Laval of the Congregation for the Sacred Hearts, who ruled here for nearly 40 years. Upon hearing whalers' tales of rampant cannibalism and marvelous pearls, Laval left his monastery in Chile and with another priest reached the Gambiers in 1834. An old Mangarevan prophecy had foretold the coming of two magicians whose god was all-powerful. Laval toppled the dreaded stone effigy of the god Tu on the island's sacred *marae* with his own hands. He single-handedly imposed a ruthless and inflexible moral code on the islanders, recruiting them as virtual slaves to build a 1,200-seat cathedral, convents, and triumphal arches, with the result that he utterly destroyed this once vigorous native culture, and practically wiped out its people. During Laval's 37-year reign the population dropped from 9,000 to 500. You can still see his architectural masterpiece—the cathedral Rikitea with its twin towers of white coral rock from Kamaka and altar shining with polished mother-of-pearl—a monument to horror and yet another lost culture. In 1871 Laval was removed from Mangareva by a French warship, tried for murder on Tahiti, and declared insane. He lies buried in a crypt before the altar of St. Michael's Cathedral, Mangareva.

For a glimpse of the Gambiers half a century ago and a fuller account of Père Laval, read Robert Lee Eskridge's *Manga Reva: The Forgotten Islands* (see "Booklist").

PRACTICALITIES

Due to the nearby French nuclear-testing facilities, the entry of foreigners to the Gambier Islands is restricted. No cameras or video equipment are allowed in the islands. For information write: Subdivision Administrative des Tuamotu-Gambiers, B.P. 34, Papeete (tel. 42-20-00). Of course, this is unnecessary if you're French.

If you do get there **Chez François Labbeyi** near the wharf in Rikitea provides accommodations for about f.2500 pp. Mr. Jean Anania (nicknamed "Siki") offers speedboat charters and fishing trips.

The airstrip (GMR) is on Totegegie, a long coral island eight km northeast of Rikitea. The twice-monthly Air Tahiti flight from Papeete (f.41,500) is via the huge French military base at Hao, closed to non-French. The monthly supply boat from Papeete also travels via Hao.

The passion flower (passiflora) got its name from a symbolic resemblance between its flower and Jesus's wounds, crown of thorns, etc.

A Marquesan meae at Nuku Hiva in the early 19th century

THE MARQUESAS ISLANDS

The Marquesas Islands are the farthest north of the high islands of the South Pacific, on the same latitude as the Solomons. Though the group was known as Te Fenua Enata ("The Land of Men") by the Polynesian inhabitants, depopulation during the 19th and 20th centuries has left many of the valleys empty. Ten main islands form a line 300 km long, roughly 1,400 km northeast of Tahiti, but only six are inhabited today: Nuku Hiva, Ua Pou, and Ua Huka in a cluster to the northwest, and Hiva Oa, Tahuata, and Fatu Hiva to the southeast. The administrative centers, Atuona (Hiva Oa), Hakahau (Ua Pou), and Taiohae (Nuku Hiva), are the only places with post offices, banks, gendarmes, etc. The total population is just 7,500.

The expense and difficulty in getting there have made visitors rare. Most only visit Nuku Hiva (where the plane from Tahiti lands) and Hiva Oa (where Paul Gauguin is buried). Cruising yachts from California often call on the way to Papeete, even though ocean swells reaching the shorelines make the anchorages rough. This is paradise, however, for surfers and hikers. Multitudes of waterfalls tumble down the slopes. A knowledge of French is an asset. In the smaller villages it's proper to pay a courtesy call on the mayor (or chief), who can arrange paid accommodations (if required). If you enjoy quiet, unspoiled places you'll like the Marquesas, but one month should be enough. The Marquesas have been left behind by their remoteness.

The Land

These wild, rugged islands feature steep cliffs and valleys leading up to high central ridges, sectioning the islands off into a cartwheel of segments which create major transportation difficulties. Reefs don't form due to the cold south-equatorial current. The absence of protective reefs has prevented the creation of coastal plains, so no roads go around any of the islands. Most of the people live in the narrow, fertile river valleys. The interiors are inhabited only by hundreds of wild horses, cattle, and goats, which have destroyed much of the original vegetation. A Catholic bishop introduced the horses from Chile in 1856 and today they're almost a symbol of the Marquesas. The islands are abundant with lemons, tangerines, oranges, grapefruit, bananas, mangoes, and papayas. Taro and breadfruit are the main staples. Birdlife is rich, and the waters around the Marquesas are teeming with lobster, fish, and sharks.

The subtropical climate is hotter and drier than that of Tahiti. July and August are the coolest months. The deep bays on the west sides of the islands are better sheltered for shipping, and the humidity is lower there than on the east sides, which catch the trade winds. The precipitation is uneven with drought some years, heavy rainfall the others. The southern islands of the Marquesas (Hiva Oa, Tahuata, Fatu Hiva) are green and humid; the northern islands (Nuku Hiva, Ua Huka, Ua Pou) are brown and dry.

FIELD MUSEUM OF NATURAL HISTORY, CHICAGO

stilt footrests: The Marquesans once staged races and mock battles on stilts with the participants attempting to knock one another off balance.

THE MARQUESAS

HATUTU
EIAO

NUKU HIVA
TAIOHAE
AIPIVAI

UA HUKA
HANE
VAIPAEE

UA POU
HAKAHAU

FATU HUKU

HIVA OA
PUAMAU
ATUONA
VAITAHU
TAHUATA
MOHOTANI

0 ___ 50 km

FATU HIVA
HANAVAVE
OMOA

HISTORY

Pre-European Society

Marquesan houses were built on high platforms *(paepae)* scattered through the valleys (still fairly easy to find). Each valley had a ceremonial area *(tohua)* where important festivals took place. Archaeologists are still able to trace stone temples *(meae)*, agricultural terraces, and earthen fortifications *(akaua)* half hidden in the jungle, evocative reminders of a vanished civilization. Then as now, the valleys were isolated from one another by high ridges and turbulent seas, yet warfare was vicious and cannibalism an important incentive. An able warrior could attain great power. Local hereditary chiefs exercised authority over commoners.

The Marquesans' artistic style was one of the most powerful and refined in the Pacific. The ironwood war club was their most distinctive symbol, but there were also finely carved wooden bowls, fan handles, and tikis of stone and wood, both miniature and massive. The carvings are noted for the faces: the mouth with lips parted, and bespectacled eyes. Both men and women wore carved ivory ear plugs. Men's entire bodies were covered by bold and striking tattoos, a practice banned by the Catholic missionaries. Stilts were used by boys for racing and mock fighting. This was about the only part of Polynesia where polyandry was common. There was a strong cult of the dead: the bodies or skulls of ancestors were carefully preserved. Both Easter Island (around A.D. 500) and Hawaii (around A.D. 700) were colonized from here.

European Contact

The existence of these islands was long concealed from the world by the Spanish, to prevent the English from taking possession of them. The southern group was found by Alvaro de Mendana in July 1595 during his second voyage of exploration from Peru. He named them Las Marquesas de Mendoza after his benefactor, the Spanish viceroy. The first island sighted (Fatu Hiva) seemed uninhabited, but as Mendana's San Jeronimo sailed nearer scores of outriggers appeared, paddled by about 400 robust, light-skinned islanders. Their hair was long and loose, and they were naked and tattooed in blue patterns. The natives boarded the ship, but when they became overly curious and bold, Mendana ordered a gun fired, and they jumped over the side.

Then began one of the most murderous and shameful of all the white man's entries into the South Pacific region. As a matter of caution, Mendana's men began shooting natives on sight, in one instance hanging three bodies in the shore camp on Santa Cristina (Tahuata) as a warning. They left behind three large crosses, the date cut in a tree, and over 200 dead Polynesians.

The northern Marquesas Islands were "discovered" by Joseph Ingraham of the American trading vessel Hope on 19 April 1791. After that, blackbirders, firearms, disease, and alcohol reduced the population. American whalers called frequently from 1800 onwards. Although France took possession of the group in 1842, Peruvian slavers kidnapped some Marquesans to South America in 1863 to work the plantations and mines. Those few who returned brought a catastrophic smallpox epidemic. The Marquesans clung to their warlike, cannibalistic ways until 95% of their number had died—the remainder adopted Catholicism. (The Marquesas today is the only island group of Tahiti-Polynesia with a Catholic majority.) From 80,000 at the beginning of the 19th century, the population fell to about 15,000 by 1842 when the French "protectors" arrived, and to a devastated 2,000 by 1926.

The Marquesans preserved the skulls of their ancestors.

FIELD MUSEUM OF NATURAL HISTORY, CHICAGO

Madisonville, Nuku Hiva: On 19 Nov. 1813 Capt. David Porter of the U.S. frigate Essex took possession of Nuku Hiva, Marquesas Islands, for the United States

The Marquesas Today

Slowly the Marquesas are catching up with the rest of the world—VCRs are the latest introduced species. Cruise ships are also finding their ways into the group. Yet the islands remain very untouristy. Though there are many negative attitudes toward the French and on Tahiti talk for independence is heard, the Marquesans realize that without French subsidies their economy would collapse and they would become even more distant from the Tuamotus, Tahiti, and "civilization." Making copra would no longer be an economic activity and far fewer supply ships would call at the islands. Hospitalization, drugs, and dental care are provided free by the government and a monthly family allowance of US$50 is paid for each child under 16—quite a bundle if you have eight kids, as many do! If the Marquesans had to give up their cars, videos, and U.S. frozen chicken, many would abandon the already underpopulated islands.

During the Heiva or Tiurai festival in July, races, games, and dance competitions take place on the different islands. The older women prove themselves graceful dancers and excellent singers.

GETTING THERE

To visit the Marquesas requires either lots of money or lots of time or both. An **Air Tahiti** 46-seat ATR 42 flies to Nuku Hiva and Atuona from Tahiti twice a week (f.37,800, four hours). There are also weekly Dornier 228 flights from Rangiroa to Atuona via Napuka in the Tuamotus (f.24,150), but the plane is always full. Stopovers on Napuka cost f.18,500 extra!

Dornier flights between Nuku Hiva and Ua Huka and Ua Pou operate weekly, connecting with the ATR 42 flight from Papeete. Fares from Nuku Hiva are f.4700 to Ua Pou, f.4950 to Ua Huka, and f.8400 to Atuona. No flight goes straight from Ua Pou to Ua Huka—you must backtrack to Nuku Hiva.

All flights are heavily booked. Reserve your seat from Papeete to Nuku Hiva six months in advance! You can do this through your international carrier or Air France, and it's not necessary to pay to make the booking. Get a through ticket to your final destination as flights to both Nuku Hiva and Atuona are the same price from Papeete. Tahuata and Fatu Hiva are without air service.

Three ships, the *Aranui, Tamarii Tuamotu,* and *Taporo V,* sail monthly from Papeete, calling at all six inhabited Marquesas Islands. The *Aranui* is the easiest to use as it follows a regular schedule and no special permission is required. To come on the *Tamarii Tuamotu* and *Taporo V* you may have to go through the procedure described under "Permission" in the introductory pages of the Tuamotu chapter above. Air passengers are also spared these courtesies.

The freighter *Aranui* is also much more comfortable, if you can afford it. The roundtrip voyages designed for tourists flown in from the U.S. and France cost cruiseship prices. See "Getting Around" in the main Introduction to this book for details. The other main interisland boat, *Taporo V,* is cheaper at f.16,000 deck, but it's dirty and unfriendly. Food is included in the passages. It's not necessary to reserve deck passage on these boats. The ships tie up to the wharves at Taiohae, Atuona, Vaipaee, and Hakahau; at Tahauta and Fatu Hiva passengers must go ashore by whaleboat. In stormy weather landings can be dangerous.

NUKU HIVA

Nuku Hiva is the largest (339 square km) and most populous (2,250 inhabitants) of the Marquesas. In 1813 Capt. David Porter of the American raider *Essex* annexed Nuku Hiva for the United States, though the act was never ratified by Congress. Porter built a fort at the present site of Taiohae, which he named Madisonville for the U.S. president of his day. Nothing remains of this or another fort erected by the French in 1842. Sandalwood traders followed Porter, then whalers. Herman Melville's *Typee,* written after a one-month stay in the Taipivai Valley in 1842, is still the classic narrative of Marquesan life during the 19th century.

Hakaui on Nuku Hiva's south coast, home of the Taioa tribe

Taiohae (population 1,500) on the south coast is the administrative and economic center of the Marquesas. It's a modern little town with a post office, hospital, town hall, two banks, five grocery stores, and street lighting. Winding mountain roads lead northeast from Taiohae to Taipivai and Hatiheu villages, where a few dozen families reside. In the center of the island, Mt. Tekao (1,224 meters) rises above the vast, empty Toovii plateau. Though open to the south, Taiohae's deep harbor offers excellent anchorage and cruising yachts are often seen here. A nominal "water fee" is charged (don't take on water if it's been raining).

SIGHTS

Vestiges of an **old prison** can still be seen in Taiohae. Many stone and woodcarvers continue to work on Nuku Hiva, making wooden tikis, bowls, ukuleles, ceremonial war clubs, etc. Some items are on display at the Banque Socredo. Other woodcarvings may be viewed in the **Catholic cathedral** (1974) at Taiohae. Ask to see the small collection of artifacts at the Bishop's residence.

For a good view of Taiohae Bay hike up to **Muake** (864 meters) on the Taipivai road. From there lifts are possible with market gardeners headed for the agricultural station on the **Toovii Plateau** to the west.

Taipivai is a five-hour, 17-km walk from Taiohae. Herman Melville spent a month here with his tattooed sweetheart, Fataway, in 1842. In his novel *Typee* (his spelling for Taipi), he gives a delightful account of the life of the great-grandparents of the present forlorn and decultured inhabitants. The huge *tohua* of Vahangekua at Taipivai is a whopping 170 by 25 meters. Great stone tikis watch over the *meae* of Paeke, also near Taipivai. Vanilla grows wild. At **Hooumi**, a fine protected bay near Taipivai, is a truly magical little church.

Above **Hatiheu** on the north coast are two more tikis and a reconstructed *meae*. **Anaho**, 45 minutes east of Hatiheu on foot, is one of the most beautiful of Nuku Hiva's bays with a fine **white-sand beach** and good snorkeling. Unfortunately, it's infested with *nono* sand flies. Even better white-sand beaches face Haatuatua and Haataivea bays beyond Anaho. No one lives there, though wild horses are seen.

At Hakaui, west of Taiohae, a river rushes down a steep-sided valley. Fantastic 350-meter **Vaipo Waterfall**, highest in the territory, drops from the plateau at the far end of the valley, four km from the coast. It's a two-hour walk from Hakaui to the waterfall. The trail passes many crumbling platforms indicating that the valley was once well populated. A boat from Taiohae to Hakaui costs f.12,500, plus f.3500 for a guide. A switchback trail also crosses the 535-meter ridge from Taiohae to Hakaui.

PRACTICALITIES

Accommodations

The **Keikahanui Inn** (B.P. 21, Taiohae; tel. 92-03-82) on the west side of Taiohae Bay is run by American yachties Rose and Frank Corser (ask to see Maurice's log books). They have three screened Polynesian bungalows with private bath: f.7500 s, f.10,000 d, f.13,000 t with continental breakfast. Meals in the dining room are f.2500 each. The Corsers give much lower rates to locals, so you might try bargaining for a 50% reduction. You can buy Fatu Hiva tapa at the Inn. Frank and Rose have coauthored a *Tahiti Traveler's Guide*.

The **Hotel Moana Nui** (B.P. 9, Taiohae; tel. 92-03-30) in the middle of Taiohae has seven rooms with private bath. Bed and breakfast is f.3000 pp, meals f.2500 each.

Chez Fetu Peterano (B.P. 22, Taiohae; tel. 92-03-66) near the wharf in Taiohae provides rooms in the owner's house at f.2500 pp with breakfast. You can cook.

In Hatiheu **Chez Yvonne Katupa** (tel. 92-02-97) offers three bungalows without cooking facilities or hot water at f.1600 pp, breakfast included. A small restaurant nearby serves fried fish for f.1000, lobster for f.1800.

Chez Clarisse Omitai also provides accommodations (f.1200 pp) in Hatiheu. At Taipivai camp on the football field.

Chez Marie Foucaud, on a white-sand beach at Anaho Bay, has four bungalows at f.2000 pp including breakfast, other meals f.1300.

The **Hotel Moetai Village** (Guy Millon, tel. 92-04-91) near Nuku Ataha Airport has six bungalows with private bath: f.3000 s, f.4000 d for bed and breakfast, other meals f.2500.

Services

Madame Debora Kimitete (B.P. 38, Taiohae; tel. 92-04-04) operates the **Syndicat d'Initiative** information office opposite the wharf at Taiohae. She sells excellent topographical maps of the main islands for f.1250 each. Taiohae has a **Banque Socredo** branch at tel. 92-03-63. Don't have your mail sent c/o poste restante at the local post office as it will be returned via surface after 15 days. Instead have it addressed c/o the Keikahanui Inn.

Get bread at Ropa's Bakery and supplies from Maurice McKitrick's store. Yachties who figure they'll need fuel when they get to the Marquesas should write a letter to Maurice and ask him to order an extra drum or two from Papeete. Things to bring to trade with the locals include perfume, earrings, reggae tapes, T-shirts, and surfing magazines, for which you'll receive tapas, tye-dyed *pareus,* and all the fruit you can carry. A small crafts center is on the ocean side near Maurice's store. War clubs, wooden bowls, and ukuleles are the most popular items. Take care with the drinking water at Taiohae.

Getting Around

The airport *truck* is the only one on Nuku Hiva, though you can hitch fairly easily. Several people in Taiohae arrange horseback riding to Taipivai for about f.4500 pp.

Airport

Nuku Ataha Airport (NHV) is in the "Terre-Deserte" at the northwest corner of Nuku Hiva. A restaurant and hotel are near the terminal. To reach Taiohae (60 km), take a *truck* from the terminal to Haahopu Bay (f.270, 15 minutes), then the launch *Atea* to Taiohae (f.800, two hours). The **Air Tahiti** number is tel. 92-03-41.

HIVA OA

Measuring 40 by 19 km, 315-square-km Hiva Oa (population 1,750) is the second largest of the Marquesas. Mt. Temetiu (1,276 meters) towers above Atuona to the west. The administrative headquarters for the Marquesas group switched back and forth several times: Taiohae was the center until 1904, then it was Atuona until 1944, when Taiohae once more took over. The town may be the center of the southern cluster of the Marquesas but it's quieter still than Taiohae. The Marquesas Festival of Arts takes place in Atuona every December.

Atuona was made forever famous when Paul Gauguin came to live here in 1901. Despite the attentions of his 14-year-old mistress, Vaeoho, he died of syphilis a year later at age 55 and is buried in the cemetery above the town. When Tioka, Gauguin's neighbor, found him stretched out with one leg hanging over the side of his bed, he bit him on the head as the Marquesans do to see if he really was dead. No, there was no doubt. *"Ua mate Koke!"* he cried, and disap-

peared. Gauguin was constantly in conflict with the colonial authorities, who disapproved of his heavy drinking sessions with the locals. Just a week before his death, Gauguin was summarily convicted of "libel of a *gendarme* in the course of his official duties," fined, and sentenced to three months in prison.

The famous Belgian *chanson* singer Jacques Brel and companion Maddly Bamy came to the Marquesas in 1975 aboard his 18-meter yacht, the *Askoy II.* Jacques decided to settle at Atuona and sold his boat to an American couple. Maddly, who had been a dancer on her native Guadeloupe, gave dancing lessons to the local girls, while Jacques ran an open-air cinema. His plane, nicknamed "Jojo," was kept at Hiva Oa airport for trips to Papeete, 1,500 km southwest. The album *Brel 1977* under the Barclay label includes one of his last songs, "Les Marquises." In 1978, chain-smoker Brel died of lung cancer and was buried in Atuona cemetery near Gauguin.

LOUIS GRELET

Marquesan model Tohotaua served as the model for "Girl with a Fan."
The photo was taken by Gauguin's friend Louis Grelet.

SIGHTS

The view of Atuona from the **graveyard** is good (take the first left fork in the road as you climb the hill), but the beach at Atuona is poor. A **lighthouse** on the point looks across Taaoa, or "Traitors'," Bay. Polynesian ruins may be found up the Vaioa River just west of Atuona.

For better swimming take the road five km south along the bay to **Taaoa**. A big *meae* (temple) is found a km up the river from there.

A second village, **Puamau,** is on the northeast coast, about 30 km from Atuona over a winding road. It's a good eight-hour walk from Atuona to Puamau, up and down all the way. Five huge stone tikis and Meae Takaii can be seen in the valley behind Puamau, a 10-minute walk from Chez Bernard. One stands over two meters high.

At **Hanaiapa** ask for William who keeps a yachties' log. He's happy to have his infrequent visitors sign and is generous with fresh fruit and vegetables. **Hanamenu** in the northwest cor-ner of Hiva Oa is now uninhabited but dozens of old stone platforms can still be seen. If you'd like to spend some time here as a hermit ask for Ozanne in Atuona who has a house at Hana-menu he might be willing to rent. To the right of Ozanne's house is a small, crystal-clear pool.

PRACTICALITIES

Accommodations
The **Hanakee Hotel** (B.P. 57, Hiva Oa; tel. 92-71-62) has bungalows at f.22,000 s or d, f.24,000 t. Breakfast and dinner are f.3500 pp extra.

The **Mairie d'Atuona** (tel. 92-73-32) rents out five pleasant bungalows behind the Town Hall at f.1700-2000 pp. The food served is good (ask for *popoi*—fermented breadfruit). You'll be awakened in the very early morning by noisy roosters, dogs, people.

Chez Jean Saucourt (tel. 92-73-33) at Atuona has one bungalow with cooking facilities, f.3500 d, f.4000 t.

Gabriel Heitaa (B.P. 52, Atuona; tel. 92-73-02) has a two-room bungalow at Atuona, f.2200 pp including breakfast. Airport transfers are f.1000 pp roundtrip.

The budget traveler's best friend, **Philippe Robard** (B.P. 46, Atuona; tel. 92-74-73), takes

The tomb of Gauguin at Atuona. Gauguin's wish that his ceramic figure of Oviri, goddess of death, mourning, and destruction, be erected over his tomb has finally been granted, if only in the form of a copy. The name Oviri also means "the savage."

guests in his large bungalow four km southwest of Atuona for f.500 pp. Cooking facilities are available and vegetables can be purchased from Philippe.

In Puamau stay at **Chez Bernard Heitaa** (tel. 92-72-27). The two rooms with cooking facilities and shared bath are f.1700 pp, or f.3500 pp including all meals.

Services

Banque Socredo (tel. 92-73-54) is next to the post office at Atuona. Of the five small stores in Atuona, only Duncan's (the blue one) sells propane; diagonally across the street from Duncan's is a hardware store. The snack bar in Atuona charges f.500 for a Coke. To rent a six-passenger Land Rover from Atuona to Puamau will run you f.12,500. Inquire at Atuona Town Hall.

Yachts anchor behind the breakwater in Tahauku Bay, two km east of the center of town. The copra boats also tie up here. A shower stall and laundry tub are provided on the wharf and there's plenty of good water. Yachties should stock up on fresh vegetables at Atuona.

Airport

The airstrip (AUQ) is on a 441-meter-high plateau 13 km northeast of Atuona. In 1991 the runway was upgraded to allow it to receive direct ATR 42 flights from Papeete (via Nuku Hiva). Weekly flights by the smaller Dornier 228 aircraft continue to arrive from Rangiroa. It's a two-hour walk from the airport to Atuona (or you can hitch). **Air Tahiti** is at tel. 92-73-41.

OTHER MARQUESAS ISLANDS

UA HUKA

Goats and wild horses range across the plateaus and through the valleys of 81-square-km Ua Huka (pop. 550). Mt. Hitikau (884 meters) rises northeast of Hane village. The tiny island of Teuaua off the southwest tip of Ua Huka is a breeding ground for millions of *kaveka* (sternas). Vaipaee is the main village of the island, although the clinic is at Hane.

Archaeological excavations by Prof. Y.H. Sinoto in 1965 dated a coastal site on Ua Huka to A.D. 300, which is the oldest in Tahiti-Polynesia; two pottery fragments found here suggest that the island was probably a major dispersal point for the ancient Polynesians. Small tikis may be visited in the valley behind Hane. In Vaipaee is a small **museum** of local artifacts and seashells. Woodcarvers are active on the island.

Accommodations

Several of the residents provide room and board for visitors. **Joseph Lichtle** (tel. 92-60-72) at Vaipaee has a three-bedroom house with cooking facilities, f.3000 pp meals included. Joseph also has five bungalows ensconced on the white sands of Haavei Beach (same price). Joseph and Laura are reputedly the best cooks in the Marquesas. Their son Leon, mayor of Ua Huka, is extremely helpful. Rent a horse from Joseph for f.2000 a day.

Laura Raioha (tel. 92-60-22), nicknamed "Tati Laura," rents out four rooms in her house with cooking facilities at Vaipaee (f.2000 s, f.3000 d). Also in Vaipaee, **Miriama Fournier** has three rooms with cooking facilities (f.1500 pp, meals f.1000).

In Hane, **Jean and Celina Fournier** (tel. 92-60-68) offer four rooms with shared bath and no cooking at f.2500 s, f.3500 d. Food is avail-

UA POU

able at their restaurant. Also in Hane, **Madame Vii Fournier** rents rooms in a two-bedroom house with cooking facilities at f.20,000 a month.

Getting There
The airstrip (UAH) is on a hilltop between Hane and Vaipaee, closer to the latter. Ships tie up to a wharf at Vaipaee.

UA POU

This island lies about 40 km south of Nuku Hiva. Several jagged volcanic plugs loom behind Hakahau, the main village on the northeast coast of 120-square-km Ua Pou. One of these sugarloaf-shaped mountains inspired Jacques Brel's song "La Cathédrale." Mt. Oave (1,203 meters), highest point on Ua Pou, is often cloud-covered. The population of 2,000 is almost the same as Nuku Hiva. In 1988, 500 French foreign legionnaires rebuilt the breakwater at Hakahau and yachts can now tie up to the concrete pier.

A track goes right around the island. The road leads south from Hakahau to a beach beyond Hohoi. On 112-meter-high Motu Oa off the south coast, millions of seabirds nest. The villages of Hakatao and Hakamaii on the west coast are only reachable on foot, hoof, or by sea. In Haka-

hetau village are two new churches, one Catholic, the other Protestant. The first stone church in the Marquesas was erected at Haka-hau in 1859 and the present church has a fine-ly carved pulpit shaped like a boat.

Accommodations
Chez Yvonne et Jules Hituputoka (tel. 92-53-33) at Hakahau is a three-room guesthouse with cooking facilities, f.2000 pp. They also rent horses at f.3000 a day and operate a taxi service.

Marguerite Dordillon (B.P. 17, Hakahau; tel. 92-53-15) has a two-bedroom house near the wharf at Hakahau. A room with cooking facilities is f.2000 s, f.3000 d.

Other people in Hakahau with rooms at f.2000 pp include **Marguerite Kaiha-Schaffer** (tel. 92-53-76) and **Rosalie Tata** (tel. 92-53-11). Rosalie also operates a restaurant. In Hohoi village there's **Pension Puanea** (tel. 92-51-32).

Services
Banque Socredo (tel. 92-53-63), post office, gendarmerie, and six or seven stores are at Hakahau. A boutique sells some local carvings and beautiful hand-painted *pareus*. Four wood-carvers work in the village—just ask for *les sculpteurs*. If you're buying, shop around at the beginning of your stay as many items are un-finished and there'll be time to have something completed for you; the same carvings cost three times as much on Tahiti. On the right just past the bakery (great baguettes!) is the home of Jacob Teikitutoua, who makes ukuleles.

Ua Pou's Aneou airstrip (UAP) is on the north coast, five km from Hakahau on a very rough road over a ridge. You can reach **Air Tahiti** at tel. 92-53-41.

TAHUATA

Fifteen km long by nine km wide, 61-square-km Tahuata is the smallest of the six inhabited islands of the Marquesas. The population is about 700.

On the west coast is the main village, Vaitahu, where a new Catholic church was completed in 1988. The anchorage at Hana Moe Noa just north of Vaitahu is protected from the ocean his young bride Liv on this southernmost island, and wrote a book called *Fatu Hiva*, describing their far from successful attempt "to return to a simple, natural life." Fatu Hiva (80 square km) is far wetter than the northern islands and the vegetation is lush. Mt. Tauaouoho (960 meters) is the highest point.

Today a revival of the old crafts is taking place in Fatu Hiva and it's again possible to buy not only sculptures but painted tapa cloth. Hats and mats are woven from pandanus. *Monoi* oils are made from coconut oil, gardenia, jasmine, and sandalwood.

This is the most remote of the Marquesas and no French officials are present. With 500 inhabitants, Fatu Hiva has only two villages, Omoa and Hanavave. It takes about five hours to walk the 17-km trail linking the two, up and down over the mountains amid breathtaking scenery. Surfing onto the rocky beach at Omoa can be pretty exciting! Hanavave on the Bay of Virgins offers one of the most fantastic scenic spectacles in all of Polynesia, with tiki-shaped cliffs dotted with goats.

Yachts usually anchor in the Bay of Virgins (from Jan. to Sept.); the swell can be uncom-

swells. The water here is clear as no rivers run into this bay. Archaeological sites exist in the Vaitahu Valley. Hapatoni village farther south is picturesque with a tamanu-bordered road and petroglyphs in the Hanatahau Valley behind. White-sand beaches are found on the north side of the island.

Chez Naani Barsinas (tel. 92-92-26) is a three-room house, f.2000 pp for bed and breakfast, or f.3000 pp for a bed and all meals.

There's no airport on Tahuata. The island is only six km south of Hiva Oa across Bordelais Channel, and you can charter an eight-passenger boat between the islands for f.10,000 (one hour). Small boats leave Hiva Oa for Tahuata almost daily, so ask around at the harbor on Takauku Bay near Atuona. The launch *Te Pua Omioi* belonging to the Commune of Tahautu leaves Atuona on Thurs. and Fri. at 1230. Take supplies with you.

FATU HIVA

Fatu Hiva was the first of the Marquesas to be visited by Europeans (Mendana called in 1595). Thor Heyerdahl spent one year in 1937-38 with *the* Cannilie Kai *at Bay of Virgins, Fatu Hiva*

She also makes tapa cloth and sandalwood oil. **Jacques Tevenino** and **Daniel Pavaouau** rent rooms at f.2000 pp or f.40,000 a month. **Tutai Kohueinui** charges f.1500 pp, while **Lionel Cantois** (tel. 92-80-04) and **Ahutoui Tevenino** are f.2500 pp.

If you plan on staying a while, get some free anti-elephantiasis pills at a clinic. Fatu Hiva doesn't have any *nonos,* but lots of mosquitos. Horses and canoes are for hire in both villages. There's a speedboat or "bonitier" once a week from Fatu Hiva to Atuona (f.3500 OW), leaving Atuona at 1500 on Friday. It takes just over three hours and carries eight people, mail, and video cassettes.

MOTANE

Motane (Mohotani) is an eight-km-long island rising to 520 meters about 18 km southeast of Hiva Oa. The depredations of wild sheep on Motane turned the island into a treeless desert. When the Spaniards "discovered" it in 1595 Motane was well-wooded and populated, but today it's uninhabited.

EIAO

Uninhabited Eiao and Hatutu islands, 85 km northwest of Nuku Hiva, are the most remote of the Marquesas. Eiao is a 40-square-km island, 10 km long and 576 meters high, with landings on the northwest and west sides. The French once used Eiao as a site of deportation for criminals or "rebellious" natives. In 1972 the French Army drilled holes 1,000 meters down into Eiao to check the island's suitability for underground nuclear testing but deemed the basalt rock too fragile for such use. Wild cattle, sheep, pigs, and donkeys forage across Eiao, ravaging the vegetation, and suffering from droughts.

Hatutu, the northernmost of the Marquesas, measures 6.4 square km. Thousands of birds nest here.

fortable at times but the holding is good in about six fathoms. Yachties trade perfume, lipstick, and cosmetics for the huge Fatu Hiva grapefruits. Cruising yachts often make Fatu Hiva their first landfall in Polynesia but this is technically illegal as the island is not a port of entry. If the village chief uses his radio to report your presence to the *gendarme* at Atuona you'll probably pay a f.5000 fine when you check in at Hiva Oa.

Many local families take paying guests and camping is possible. In Omoa, **Joseph Tetuanui** (tel. 92-80-09) and **Kehu Kamia** rent rooms at f.1500 pp, plus another f.1500 for all meals. **François Peters** and **Jean Bouyer** charge f.3500 pp including all meals. Mr. Peters has a room for f.20,000 pp a month. A bakery and four or five small stores are also in Omoa.

In Hanavave, **Veronique Kamia** (tel. 92-80-56) has two rooms at f.2500 pp including meals.

BOOKLIST

GUIDEBOOKS

Bruce, Erroll. *Deep Sea Sailing*. London: Stanley Paul, 1953. The classic text on ocean cruising. Study it beforehand if you're thinking of crewing on a yacht.

Danielsson, Bengt. *Tahiti, Circle Island Tour Guide*. Singapore: Les Editions du Pacifique, 1986. A kilometer-by-kilometer ride around the island with *the* expert.

Davock, Marcia. *Cruising Guide to Tahiti and the French Society Islands*. Stamford, CT: Wescott Cove Publishing, 1985. A large-format, spiral-bound guide for yachties.

Fisher, Jon. *The Last Frontiers on Earth*. Loompanics Unlimited, Box 1197, Port Townsend, WA 98368 U.S.A. This unique book and Dr. Fisher's other work, *Uninhabited and Deserted Islands*, are essential reading for anyone considering relocating in Polynesia.

Hatt, John. *The Tropical Traveler*. Pan Books, 1985. Over a thousand tips covering every aspect of tropical travel.

Hermann-Auclair, Helene, and Alain Durand. *A Tahiti en Polynésie à l'Île de Pâques*. Paris: Hachette. The main French-language guide to the area.

Hinz, Earl R. *Landfalls of Paradise: The Guide to Pacific Islands*. Western Marine Enterprises, 3611 Motor Ave., Suite 102, Los Angeles, CA 90034-5748 U.S.A. The only genuine cruising guide to all 32 island groups of Oceania.

Nude Pacific Travel Guide. Tahanga Research Assn., Box 8714, La Jolla, CA 92038 U.S.A. Dedicated to "trying to uncover approximately 60 islands."

Stanley, David. *South Pacific Handbook*. Chico: Moon Publications, 1992. Covers the entire region in the same manner as the book you're reading. There's also *Fiji Islands Handbook* and *Micronesia Handbook,* by the same author.

Street, Donald. *The Ocean Sailing Yacht*. New York: Norton, 1973. A complete handbook on the operation of a cruising yacht.

DESCRIPTION AND TRAVEL

de Bovis, Edmond. Robert D. Craig, trans. *Tahitian Society Before the Arrival of the Europeans*. Honolulu: University of Hawaii Press, 1980. These observations of a French naval officer on the history, customs, religion, and government of Tahiti were written in 1850.

Childress, David Hatcher. *Lost Cities of Ancient Lemuria and the Pacific*. Adventures Unlimited Press, Box 22, Stelle, IL 60919 U.S.A. The Indiana Jones of Pacific archaeology takes you on a mysterious journey to the pyramids of paradise.

Danielsson, Bengt. *Forgotten Islands of the South Seas*. London: Allen and Unwin, 1957. A fascinating tale of life and love in the Marquesas Islands.

Danielsson, Bengt. *From Raft to Raft*. New York: Doubleday and Co., 1960. The story of one of the greatest sea adventures of modern times: Eric de Bisschop's raft voyage from Tahiti to South America and back, as told by one of the survivors.

Dodd, Edward. *Polynesia's Sacred Isle*. New York: Dodd, Mead and Co., 1976. An excellent account of Raiatea, its culture and history, based on the author's own researches, together with a vivid account of his many sojourns on the island.

Ellis, William. *Polynesian Researches*. Rutland, VT: Charles E. Tuttle Co., 1969. An early missionary's detailed observations of Tahiti during the years 1817-1825.

Eskridge, Robert Lee. *Manga Reva: The Forgotten Islands*. Honolulu: Mutual Publishing, 1986. The autobiography of a wandering American painter in the Gambiers in 1927.

Finney, Ben R. *Hokule'a: The Way to Tahiti*. New York: Dodd, Mead, 1979. The story of the *Hokule'a*'s 1976 voyage from Hawaii to Tahiti.

Heyerdahl, Thor. *Fatu Hiva: Back to Nature*. New York: Doubleday, 1974. In 1936 Heyerdahl and his wife Liv went to live on Fatu Hiva. This book describes their year there.

Heyerdahl, Thor. *Kon Tiki*. F.H. Lyon, trans. Chicago: Rand McNally, 1950. Convinced that the mysterious origin of the Polynesians lies in the equally mysterious disappearance of the pre-Incan Indians of Peru, the author finds that only by repeating their feat of sailing some 6,500 km across the Pacific in a balsa raft can he substantiate his theory.

Kyselka, Will. *An Ocean in Mind*. Honolulu: University of Hawaii Press, 1987. Analyzes the learning techniques of Nainoa Thompson, who successfully navigated the re-created traditional Polynesian sailing vessel, *Hokule'a,* during its second roundtrip journey between Hawaii and Tahiti in 1980, without the use of modern navigational equipment.

Stevenson, Robert Louis. *In the South Seas*. New York: Scribner's, 1901. The author's account of his travels through the Marquesas, Tuamotus, and Gilberts by yacht in the years 1888-90.

Thompson, Rev. Robert. Robert D. Craig, ed. *The Marquesas Islands*. Honolulu: University of Hawaii Press, 1980. Thompson's account, written in 1841, is a valuable record of the Marquesas just before their rapid decline.

GEOGRAPHY

Couper, Alastair, ed. *The Times Atlas of the Oceans*. New York: Van Nostrand Reinhold, 1983. A superb study of the oceans of the world in their contemporary context.

Freeman, Otis W., ed. *Geography of the Pacific*. New York: John Wiley, 1951. Although somewhat dated, this book does provide a wealth of background information on the islands.

Ridgell, Reilly. *Pacific Nations and Territories*. Honolulu: Bess Press, 1988. One of the few high school geography texts to the region.

NATURAL SCIENCES

Bruner, Phillip L. *Field Guide to the Birds of French Polynesia*. Honolulu: Bishop Museum Press, 1972.

DeLuca, Charles J., and Diana MacIntyre DeLuca. *Pacific Marine Life: A Survey of Pacific Ocean Invertebrates*. Rutland, VT: Charles E. Tuttle Co., 1976. An informative, 82-page pamphlet.

Hargreaves, Bob, and Dorothy Hargreaves. *Tropical Blossoms of the Pacific*. Ross-Hargreaves, Box 11897, Lahaina, HI 96761 U.S.A. A handy, 64-page booklet with color photos to assist in identification; a matching volume is titled *Tropical Trees of the Pacific*.

Hinton, A.G. *Shells of New Guinea and the Central Indo-Pacific*. Australia: Jacaranda Press, 1972. A photo guide to identification.

Martini, Frederic. *Exploring Tropical Isles and Seas*. Englewood Cliffs, NJ: Prentice-Hall, 1984. A fine introduction to the natural environment of the islands.

Mayr, Ernst. *Birds of the Southwest Pacific*. Rutland, VT: Charles E. Tuttle Co., 1978. A reprint of the 1945 edition.

Merrill, Elmer D. *Plant Life of the Pacific World.* Rutland, VT: Charles E. Tuttle Co., 1981. First published in 1945, this handy volume is a useful first reference in a field very poorly covered.

Mitchell, Andrew W. *A Fragile Paradise: Man and Nature in the Pacific.* London: Fontana, 1990. Published in the U.S. by the University of Texas Press under the title *The Fragile South Pacific: An Ecological Odyssey.* Andrew Mitchell, an Earthwatch Europe deputy director, utters a heartfelt plea on behalf of all endangered Pacific wildlife in this brilliant book.

Pratt, Douglas. *A Field Guide to the Birds of Hawaii and the Tropical Pacific.* Princeton, NJ: Princeton University Press, 1986. The best of its kind—essential reading for birders.

Tinker, Spencer Wilkie. *Fishes of Hawaii: A Handbook of the Marine Fishes of Hawaii and the Central Pacific Ocean.* Hawaiian Service, Inc., Box 2835, Honolulu, HI 96803 U.S.A. A comprehensive, indexed reference work; $30.

HISTORY

Bellwood, Peter. *Man's Conquest of the Pacific.* New York: Oxford University Press, 1979. One of the most extensive studies of the prehistory of Southeast Asia and Oceania ever published.

Bellwood, Peter. *The Polynesians, Prehistory of an Island People.* London: Thames and Hudson, 1978. A well-written account of the archaeology of Polynesian expansion.

Buck, Peter H. *Vikings of the Pacific.* Chicago: University of Chicago Press, 1959. A popular narrative of Polynesian migrations.

Clark, Thomas Blake. *Omai, First Polynesian Ambassador to England.* Honolulu: University of Hawaii Press, 1969. Catches the atmosphere of the cultural impact of Polynesia on the West, in that pristine dawn before the counterimpact of the West on Polynesia.

Danielsson, Bengt. *What Happened on the Bounty.* London: Allen and Unwin, 1963. A reappraisal of Capt. Bligh, whom Hollywood has unfairly cast as a tyrant. The subsequent fate of the mutineers is also given in depth.

Dole, Paul W. *Seventy North to Fifty South: Captain Cook's Last Voyage.* Englewood Cliffs, NJ: Prentice-Hall, Inc., 1969. A modern annotation of Cook's final journal.

Howarth, David. *Tahiti: A Paradise Lost.* New York: Penguin Books, 1985. A readable history of European exploration in the Society Islands.

Howe, K.R. *Where the Waves Fall.* Honolulu: University of Hawaii Press, 1984. This South Seas history from first settlement to colonial rule maintains a steady and sympathetic focus on the islanders themselves.

Jennings, Jesse D., ed. *The Prehistory of Polynesia.* Cambridge, MA: Harvard University Press, 1979. A comprehensive work on the subject.

Langdon, Robert. *The Lost Caravel.* Sydney: Pacific Publications, 1975. The author proposes that Spanish castaways from Magellan's fleet gave a totally new direction to Polynesian culture, an audacious theory which has met with little approval among professional anthropologists and historians.

Langdon, Robert. *Tahiti, Island of Love.* Australia: Pacific Publications, 1979. A popular history of Tahiti since the European discovery in 1767.

Moorehead, Alan. *The Fatal Impact.* New York: Harper & Row, 1966. European impact on the South Pacific, as illustrated in the cases of Tahiti, Australia, and Antarctica.

Newbury, Colin. *Tahiti Nui: Change and Survival in French Polynesia, 1767-1945.* Honolulu: University of Hawaii Press, 1980. Describes major events while providing many details of the social and economic processes.

Oliver, Douglas L. *Return to Tahiti: Bligh's Second Breadfruit Voyage.* Honolulu: University of Hawaii Press, 1988. Offers insights on the inhabitants of Tahiti and their customs at the time of European contact.

Oliver, Douglas L. *The Pacific Islands.* Honolulu: University of Hawaii Press, 1989. A new edition of the classic 1951 study of the history and economies of the entire Pacific area.

PACIFIC ISSUES

Buske, Norm. *Cesium-134 at Moruroa: Review of the Calypso Water Samples.* Search Technical Services, HCR Box 17, Davenport, WA 99122-9404 U.S.A. This report, dated Sept. 1990 provides clearest proof yet that radiation is leaking from the underground nuclear testing at Moruroa.

Danielsson, Bengt, and Marie-Thérèse Danielsson. *Poisoned Reign: French Nuclear Colonialism in the Pacific.* New York: Penguin Books, 1986. An updated version of *Moruroa Mon Amour,* first published in 1977. This powerful book is probably the best history of Tahiti-Polynesia you can read.

Firth, Stewart. *Nuclear Playground.* Honolulu: University of Hawaii Press, 1987. The story of the nuclear age in the Pacific.

Garrison, Randall, ed. *Readings on Canada and the South Pacific, 1991.* South Pacific Peoples Foundation, 415-620 View St., Victoria, B.C. V8W 1J6, Canada. This 77-page dossier covers a wide range of issues of concern to everyone.

Robie, David. *Blood on their Banner.* London: Zed Books, 1989. Robie's fast-moving account of nationalist struggles in the South Pacific includes a chapter on Tahiti's fight for independence. In the U.S. it's available from Zed Books, 171 First Ave., Atlantic Heights, NJ 07716 U.S.A; in Britain from Zed Books, 57 Caledonian Rd., London

N1 9BU; in Australia from Pluto Press, Box 199, Leichhardt, NSW 2040. Highly recommended.

Robie, David. *Eyes of Fire: The Last Voyage of the Rainbow Warrior.* New Society Publishers, 4527 Springfield Ave., Philadelphia, PA 19143 U.S.A. Robie was aboard the Greenpeace protest vessel sunk at Auckland in 1985 by French terrorists. His photos and firsthand account tell the inside story.

Testimonies: Witnesses of French Nuclear Testing in the South Pacific. Greenpeace International, 1990. A 72-page collection of interviews carried out in Tahiti-Polynesia in 1987 by Dr. Andy Biedermann.

SOCIAL SCIENCE

Danielsson, Bengt. *Love in the South Seas.* Honolulu: Mutual Publishing, 1986. Sex and family life of the Polynesians, based on early accounts as well as observations by the noted Swedish anthropologist.

Danielsson, Bengt. *Work and Life on Raroia.* Danielsson spent 18 months on this atoll observing Tuamotu life, and this book is still the only detailed history of the Tuamotu islands.

Howell, William. *The Pacific Islanders.* New York: Scribner's, 1973. An anthropological study of the origins of Pacific peoples.

Levy, Robert. *Tahitians: Mind and Experience in the Society Islands.* Chicago: University of Chicago Press, 1973. Levy's study, based on several years of field work on Tahiti and Huahine, includes an intriguing examination of the *mahu* (transvestite) phenomenon.

Marshall, Don. *Raivavae.* New York: Doubleday and Co., 1961. The author, who is a professional anthropologist, did field work on this high island in the Austral group in 1957-58 to find out what was left of the old orgiastic pagan religion and sexual rites.

Oliver, Douglas L. *Ancient Tahitian Society.* Honolulu: University of Hawaii Press, 1975. Sets out to describe what Tahitian society was like immediately before, and immediately after, contact with peoples of literate, industrial societies.

Oliver, Douglas L. *Native Cultures of the Pacific Islands.* Honolulu: University of Hawaii Press, 1988. Intended primarily for college-level courses on precontact anthropology, history, economy, and politics of the entire region; an abridged version of Oliver's *Oceania,* listed below.

Oliver, Douglas L. *Oceania: The Native Cultures of Australia and the Pacific Islands.* Honolulu: University of Hawaii Press, 1988. A massive, two-volume, 1,264-page anthropological survey.

Oliver, Douglas L. *Two Tahitian Villages.* Honolulu: University of Hawaii Press, 1983. What is learned about this developing Polynesian society is useful to the study of other human societies.

LANGUAGE

Anisson du Perron, Jacques, and Mai-Arii Cadousteau. *Dictionaire Moderne, Tahitien-Français et Français-Tahitien.* Papeete: Stepolde, 1973.

Tryon, Darrell T. *Conversational Tahitian.* Canberra: Australian National University Press, 1970.

Tryon, Darrell T. *Say It In Tahitian.* Sydney: Pacific Publications, 1977. For lovers of the exotic, an instant introduction to spoken Tahitian.

LITERATURE

Andersen, Johannes C. *Myths and Legends of the Polynesians.* Rutland, VT: Charles E. Tuttle Co., 1969. A massive compilation of Polynesian mythology; fully indexed.

Day, A. Grove. *The Lure of Tahiti.* Honolulu: Mutual Publishing, 1986. Fifteen choice extracts from the rich literature of "the most romantic island in the world."

Day, A. Grove. *Pacific Literature: One Hundred Basic Books.* Honolulu: University Press, 1971. Reviews the most outstanding books to come out of the Pacific experience over the past 400 years.

Hall, James Norman, and Charles Bernard Nordhoff. *The Bounty Trilogy.* New York: Grosset and Dunlap, 1945. Retells in fictional form the famous mutiny, Bligh's escape to Timor, and the mutineers' fate on Pitcairn.

Hall, James Norman. *The Forgotten One and Other True Tales of the South Seas.* Honolulu: Mutual Publishing, 1987. Hall arrived on Tahiti in 1920 and collaborated with Charles Nordhoff in such famous works as *The Mutiny of the Bounty* (1930) and *Hurricane* (1936). He died at his home in Arue in 1951.

Loti, Pierre. *The Marriage of Loti.* Honolulu: University of Hawaii Press, 1976. This tale of Loti's visits to Tahiti in 1872 helped create the romantic myth of Polynesia in contemporary Europe.

Maugham, W. Somerset. *The Moon and Sixpence.* Story of a London stockbroker who leaves his job for Tahiti and ends up leading an artist's primitive life that isn't as romantic as he hoped.

Melville, Herman. *Typee, A Peep at Polynesian Life.* Evanston, IL: Northwestern University Press, 1968. In 1842 Melville deserted from an American whaler at Nuku Hiva, Marquesas Islands. This semifictional work tells of Melville's four months among the Typee people. A sequel, *Omoo,* relates his observations on Tahiti at the time of the French takeover.

Michener, James A. *Return to Paradise.* New York: Random House, 1951. Essays and short stories. Michener's *Tales of the South Pacific,* the first of over 30 books, won the Pulitzer Prize for fiction in 1948. A year later it appeared on Broadway as the long-running musical *South Pacific.*

Stone, William S. *Idylls of the South Seas*. Honolulu: University of Hawaii Press, 1971. Stone uses the same narrator, Tetua, to recount ten myths and legends of Tahiti.

THE ARTS

Barrow, Terence. *The Art of Tahiti*. London: Thames and Hudson, 1979. A concise, well-illustrated survey of works of art from the Society, Austral, and Cook islands.

Danielsson, Bengt. *Gauguin in the South Seas*. New York: Doubleday, 1966. Danielsson's fascinating account of Gauguin's ten years in Polynesia.

Gauguin, Paul. *Noa Noa*. A Tahitian journal kept by this famous artist during his first two years in the islands.

Guiart, Jean. *The Arts of the South Pacific*. New York: Golden Press, 1963. A well-illustrated coffee-table art book. Consideration is given to the cultures that produced the works.

Linton, Ralph, and Paul S. Wingert. *Arts of the South Seas*. New York: Museum of Modern Art, 1946. Although a little dated, this book provides a starting point for the study of the art of Polynesia.

REFERENCE BOOKS

Douglas, Ngaire, and Norman, eds. *Pacific Islands Yearbook*. Australia: Angus & Robertson Publishers. Despite the name, a new edition of this authoritative sourcebook has come out about every three years since 1932. Copies may be ordered through *Pacific Islands Monthly*, GPO Box 1167, Suva, Fiji Islands.

Fenton, Thomas P., and Mary J. Heffron, eds. *Asia and Pacific: A Directory of Resources*. Maryknoll, NY: Orbis Books, 1986. A complete survey of organizations, books, periodicals, pamphlets, articles, audiovisuals, and other resources relating to Pacific issues. Complete names and addresses, plus five indexes, make this work an invaluable contact point.

Fry, Gerald W., and Rufino Mauricio. *Pacific Basin and Oceania*. Oxford: Clio Press, 1987. A selective, indexed Pacific bibliography which actually describes the contents of the books instead of merely listing them.

Jackson, Miles M., ed. *Pacific Island Studies: A Survey of the Literature*. Westport, CT: Greenwood Press, 1986. In addition to comprehensive listings there are extensive essays which put the most important works in perspective.

Oceania, A Regional Study. Washington, DC: U.S. Government Printing Office, 1985. This 572-page volume forms part of the area handbook series sponsored by the U.S. Army and intended to educate American officials. A comprehensive, uncritical source of background information; extensive bibliography and index.

Silveira de Braganza, Ronald, and Charlotte Oakes, eds. *The Hill Collection of Pacific Voyages*. San Diego: University Library, 1974. A descriptive catalog of antique books about the Pacific.

Taylor, Clyde R. *A Pacific Bibliography: Printed Matter Relating to the Native Peoples of Polynesia, Melanesia and Micronesia*. Oxford: Clarendon Press, 1965. Extensive.

The Far East and Australasia. London: Europa Publications. An annual survey and directory of Asia and the Pacific. Provides abundant and factual political, social, and economic data; an excellent reference source.

BOOKSELLERS AND PUBLISHERS

Many of the titles listed above are out of print and not available in regular bookstores. Major research libraries should have a few, otherwise write to the specialized antiquarian booksellers or regional publishers listed below for their printed lists of recycled or hard-to-find books on the Pacific.

Australia, the Pacific and South East Asia. Serendipity Books, Box 340, Nedlands, WA

6009, Australia. The largest stocks of antiquarian, secondhand, and out-of-print books on the Pacific in Western Australia.

Boating Books. International Marine Publishing Co., Box 220, Camden, ME 04843 U.S.A. All the books you'll ever need to teach yourself how to sail.

Books from the Pacific Islands. Institute of Pacific Studies, University of the South Pacific, Box 1168, Suva, Fiji Islands. Their specialty is books about the islands written by Pacific islanders themselves.

Books, Maps & Prints of Pacific Islands. Colin Hinchcliffe, 12 Queens Staith Mews, York, Y01 1HH, England. An excellent source of antique books, maps, and engravings.

Books on Africa, Archaeology and Anthropology, Asia, and Oceania. Michael Graves-Johnson, Bookseller, Box 532, London SW9 0DR, England. Recycled books on the South Pacific.

Books and Series in Print. Bishop Museum Press, Box 19000-A, Honolulu, HI 96817-0916 U.S.A. An indexed list of publications on the Pacific available from the Bishop Museum.

Catalogue of Pacific Region Books. Pacific Book House, 17 Park Ave., Broadbeach Waters, Gold Coast, QLD 4218, Australia. A Queensland source of out-of-print books on the Pacific.

Defense Mapping Agency Catalog of Maps, Charts, and Related Products: Part 2—Hydrographic Products, Volume VIII, Oceania. Defense Mapping Agency Combat Support Center, ATTN: DDCP, Washington, DC 20315-0010 U.S.A. For a copy of this complete index and order form for nautical charts of the South Pacific, send US$2.50.

Hawaii and Pacific Islands. The Book Bin, 2305 NW Monroe St., Corvallis, OR 97330 U.S.A. An indexed mail-order catalog of hundreds of rare books on the Pacific. If there's a particular book about the Pacific you can't find anywhere, this is the place to try (tel. 503-752-0045).

Hawaii and the Pacific. University of Hawaii Press, 2840 Kolowalu St., Honolulu, HI 96822 U.S.A. Lists many new and current titles on Tahiti-Polynesia.

Pacificana. Messrs Berkelouw, "Bendooley," Hume Highway, Berrima, NSW 2577, Australia (tel. 048-77-1370). A detailed listing of thousands of rare Pacific titles. Payment of an annual subscription of A$25 entitles one to 25 catalogs a year.

Pacificana. Books of Yesteryear, Box 19, Mosman, NSW 2088, Australia. Another good source of old, fine, and rare books on the Pacific.

Polynesian Bookshop Catalogues. Box 68-446, Newton, Auckland 1, New Zealand. A wide range of new, in-print books on the South Pacific.

Société des Océanistes Catalogue. Musée de l'Homme, 75116, Paris, France. Many scholarly works (in French) on Polynesia are available from this body.

Tales of the Pacific. Mutual Publishing, 2055 N. King St., Suite 201, Honolulu, HI 96819 U.S.A. The classics of Pacific literature available in cheap paperback editions.

The "Nesias" and Down Under: Some Recent Books. The Cellar Book Shop, 18090 Wyoming, Detroit, Michigan 48221 U.S.A. The best American mail-order list of new books on the South Pacific.

The Peoples of the Pacific. AMS Press Inc., 56 East 13th St., New York, NY 10003 U.S.A. Reprinted editions of many classic works of Polynesian anthropology.

PERIODICALS

Bulletin of Concerned Asian Scholars. 3239 9th St., Boulder, CO 80302-2112 U.S.A. The Vol. 18, No. 2, 1986 issue is devoted entirely to the antinuclear movement in the Pacific.

Commodores' Bulletin. Seven Seas Cruising Assn., 521 South Andrews Ave., Suite 10, Fort

Lauderdale, FL 33301 U.S.A (US$29 a year worldwide by surface mail). This monthly bulletin is chock-full of useful information for anyone wishing to tour the Pacific by sailing boat. All Pacific yachties and friends should be Seven Seas members!

German Pacific Society Bulletin. Feichmayrstr. 25, 8000 München 50, Germany. At DM70 a year, Society membership is a good way for German speakers to keep in touch.

Globe Newsletter. The Globetrotters Club, BCM/Roving, London WC1N 3XX, England. This informative travel newsletter, published six times a year, provides lots of practical information on how to tour the world "on the cheap." Club membership (US$18 plus a US$5 joining fee) includes a subscription to *Globe,* a globetrotter's handbook, a list of other members, etc. This is "the" club for world travelers.

Globetrotter-Magazine. Postfach, 8023 Zürich, Switzerland. If you read German you won't find a more informative travel magazine than this and its companions, *Ticket-Info* and *Travel-Info,* all published quarterly. A subscription to all three is included in the Globetrotter Club membership fee (Fr.20 in Switzerland, DM20 elsewhere).

Islands Business. Box 12718, Suva, Fiji Islands (annual airmailed subscription US$38 to North America, US$50 to Europe, A$32 to Australia, NZ$40 to New Zealand). A monthly newsmagazine, with the emphasis on political, economic, and business trends in the South Pacific.

Journal of Pacific History. Division of Pacific and Asian History, RSPacS, Australian National University, GPO Box 4, Canberra, ACT 2601, Australia (annual subscription US$35). Since 1966 this publication has provided reliable scholarly information on the Pacific. The volume XXI 3-4, 1986 issue includes several scholarly articles on recent events in Polynesia. Outstanding.

Journal of the Polynesian Society. Department of Anthropology, University of Auckland, Private Bag, Auckland, New Zealand. Established in 1892, this quarterly journal contains a wealth of specialized material on Polynesian culture.

NFIP Bulletin. Jan Symington, 52 Salisburg Road, Crookes, Sheffield S10 1WB, England (ten pounds sterling a year). This bulletin of Women Working for a Nuclear Free and Independent Pacific appears six times a year.

Pacific Islands Monthly. GPO Box 1167, Suva, Fiji Islands (annual subscription A$30 to Australia, US$45 to North America, and A$63 to Europe). Founded in Sydney by R.W. Robson in 1930, PIM is the granddaddy of regional magazines. In June, 1989, the magazine's editorial office moved from Sydney to Suva. The articles by PIM's Tahiti correspondent, Al Prince, are highly informative.

Pacific Issues. Social Responsibility and Justice, Uniting Church in Australia, 130 Little Collins St., Melbourne, Victoria 3000, Australia (A$20 a year in Australia). Photocopies of significant articles from other publications on regional, social, and political problems.

Pacific Magazine. Box 25488, Honolulu, HI 96825 U.S.A (every other month; US$15 annual subscription). This business-oriented magazine published in Hawaii since 1976 will keep you up to date on what's happening around the Pacific. An excellent means of keeping in touch.

Pacific News Bulletin. Pacific Concerns Resource Center, Box 489, Petersham, NSW 2049, Australia (A$12 a year in Australia, A$25 a year elsewhere). A 16-page monthly newsletter for use worldwide by members of the Nuclear Free and Independent Pacific Movement.

Réalités du Pacifique. Editions de l'Echiquier, B.P. 557, 75026 Paris Cedex 01, France. This serious bimonthly newsletter (in French) carries analytic features on the situation in the French Pacific territories. Overseas subscriptions are US$60, within France F500.

Tahiti Sun Press Magazine. Tahiti Publications Touristiques, B.P. 887, Papeete, Tahiti (US$50 a year to North America, A$65 to Australia, NZ$75 to New Zealand, US$58 to Europe). A subscription to this monthly magazine edited by Al Prince is the best way to keep up with what's happening in the islands.

The Contemporary Pacific. University of Hawaii Press, 2840 Kolowalu St., Honolulu, HI 96822 U.S.A. (published twice a year, annual subscription US$25). Publishes a good mix of articles of interest to both scholars and general readers; the country-by-country "Political Review" in each number is a concise summary of events during the preceding year. Those interested in current topics in Pacific Island affairs should check recent volumes for background information. Recommended.

The Surf Report. Box 1028, Dana Point, CA 92629 U.S.A ($35 a year). A monthly summary of worldwide surfing conditions with frequent feature articles on the islands.

Third World Resources. 464 19th St., Oakland, CA 94612-9761 U.S.A (two-year subscription $35 to the U.S. and Canada, US$50 overseas). A quarterly review of books, articles, and organizations involved with development issues in the Third World.

Tok Blong SPPF. South Pacific Peoples Foundation of Canada, 415-620 View St., Victoria, B.C. V8W 1J6, Canada ($25 a year). This quarterly of news and views focuses on regional environment, development, human rights, and disarmament issues. Recommended.

Wellington Pacific Report. Box 9314, Wellington, New Zealand (10 issues NZ$14 in N.Z., US$14 elsewhere). An incisive newsletter with startling revelations of covert U.S. activities in the Pacific.

AN IMPORTANT MESSAGE

Authors, editors, and publishers wishing to see their publications listed here should send review copies to:

David Stanley
c/o Moon Publications Inc.
722 Wall St.
Chico, CA 95928 U.S.A.

GLOSSARY

ahimaa—Tahitian underground or earth oven; called an *umu* in Samoa

ahu—a Polynesian stone temple platform

aparima—a Tahitian hand dance

archipelago—a group of islands

arii—a Polynesian high chief

Arioi—a pre-European religious society which traveled among the Society Islands presenting ceremonies and entertainments

atoll—a low-lying, ring-shaped coral reef enclosing a lagoon

bareboat charter—chartering a yacht without crew or provisions

barrier reef—a coral reef separated from the adjacent shore by a lagoon

bêche-de-mer—sea cucumber; trepang; an edible sea slug; in Tahitian, *rori*

blackbirder—European recruiter of slave labor during the 19th century

breadfruit—a large, round fruit with starchy flesh grown on an *uru* tree *(Artocarpus altilis)*

cassava—manioc; the starchy edible root of the tapioca plant

CEP—Centre d'Expérimentations du Pacifique; the Moruroa nuclear test zone

ciguatera—a form of fish poisoning caused by microscopic algae

CMAS—Confédération Mondiale des Activités Subaquatiques

coir—coconut husk sennit used to make rope, etc.

confirmation—A confirmed reservation exists when a supplier acknowledges, either orally or in writing, that a booking has been accepted.

copra—dried coconut meat used in the manufacture of coconut oil, cosmetics, soap, and margarine

coral—a hard, calcareous substance of various shapes comprised of the skeletons of tiny marine animals called polyps

coral bank—a coral formation over 150 meters long

coral head—a coral formation a few meters across

coral patch—a coral formation up to 150 meters long

cyclone—Also known as a hurricane (in the Caribbean) or typhoon (in the north Pacific). A tropical storm which rotates around a center of low atmospheric pressure; it becomes a cyclone when its winds reach 64 knots. In the Northern Hemisphere cyclones spin counterclockwise, while south of the equator they move clockwise. The winds of cyclonic storms are deflected toward a low-pressure area at the center, although the "eye" of the cyclone may be calm.

DGSE—Direction Générale de la Sécurité Extériere; the French CIA

direct flight—a through flight with one or more stops but no change of aircraft, as opposed to a nonstop flight

dugong—a large plant-eating marine mammal; called a manatee in the Caribbean

EEZ—Exclusive Economic Zone; a 200-nautical-mile offshore belt of an island nation or seacoast state which controls the mineral exploitation and fishing rights

endemic—native to a particular area and existing only there

fafa—a "spinach" of cooked taro leaves

farani—French; *français*

FIT—foreign independent travel; a custom-designed, prepaid tour composed of many individualized arrangements

fringing reef—a reef along the shore of an island

gendarme—a French policeman on duty only in rural areas in France and French overseas territories

guano—manure of sea birds, used as a fertilizer

lagoon—an expanse of water bounded by a reef

leeward—downwind; the shore (or side) sheltered from the wind; as opposed to windward

le truck—a truck with seats in back used for public transportation

LMS—London Missionary Society; a Protestant group which spread Christianity from Tahiti (1797) across the Pacific

maa Tahiti—Tahitian food

mahimahi—dorado, Pacific dolphin fish (no relation to the mammal)

mahu—a male transvestite, sometimes also a homosexual

makatea—an uplifted reef around the coast of an elevated atoll

mama ruau—actually "grandmother," but also used for the Mother Hubbard long dress introduced by missionaries

mana—authority, prestige, virtue, "face," psychic power, a positive force

manahune—a commoner or member of the lower class in pre-Christian society

mangrove—a tropical shrub with branches that send down roots forming dense thickets along tidal shores

manioc—cassava, tapioca, a starchy root crop

maohi—a native of Tahiti-Polynesia

marae—a Tahitian temple or open-air cult place, called **meae** in the Marquesas

Melanesia—the high island groups of the western Pacific (Fiji, New Caledonia, Vanuatu, Solomon Islands, Papua New Guinea)

Micronesia—chains of high and low islands mostly north of the Equator (Carolines, Tungaru, Marianas, Marshalls)

monoi—perfumed coconut oil

motu—a reef islet on an atoll

Oro—the Polynesian god of war

ORSTOM—Office de la Recherche Scientifique et Technique d'Outre-Mer

otea—a ceremonial dance performed by men and women in two columns

overbooking—the practice of confirming more seats, cabins, or rooms than are actually available to ensure against no-shows

pa—ancient stone fortress

PADI—Professional Association of Dive Instructors

pandanus—screw pine with slender stem and prop roots. The sword-shaped leaves are used for plaiting mats and hats. In Tahitian, *fara*.

parasailing—being carried aloft by a parachute pulled behind a speedboat

pareu—a Tahitian sarong-like wraparound skirt or loincloth

pass—a channel through a barrier reef, usually with an outward flow of water

passage—an inside passage between an island and a barrier reef

pelagic—relating to the open sea, away from land

peretane—Britain, British

pirogue—outrigger canoe, in Tahitian *vaa*

poe—a sticky pudding made from bananas, papaya, pumpkin, or taro mixed with starch, baked in an oven, and served with coconut milk

poisson cru—raw fish marinated in lime, in Tahitian *ia ota*, in Japanese *sashimi*

Polynesia—divided into Western Polynesia (Tonga and Samoa) and Eastern Polynesia (Tahiti-Polynesia, Cook Is., Hawaii, Easter I., and New Zealand)

pupu—traditional dance group

raatira—chief, dance leader

reef—a coral ridge near the ocean surface

scuba—self-contained underwater breathing apparatus

sennit—braided coconut-fiber rope

shareboat charter—a yacht tour for individuals or couples who join a small group on a fixed itinerary

shoal—a shallow sand bar or mud bank

shoulder season—a travel period between high/peak and low/off-peak

subduction—the action of one tectonic plate wedging under another

subsidence—geological sinking or settling

tahua—in the old days a skilled artisan; today a sorcerer or healer

tamaaraa—a Tahitian feast

tamure—a new name for Ori Tahiti, a very fast erotic dance

tapa—a cloth made from the pounded bark of

the paper mulberry tree *(Broussonetia papyrifera)*. It's soaked and beaten with a mallet to flatten and intertwine the fibers, then painted with geometric designs; called *ahu* in old Tahitian.

tapu—taboo, sacred, set apart, forbidden, a negative force

taro—a starchy tuber *(Colocasia esculenta)*, a staple food of the Pacific islanders

tavana—the elected mayor of a commune (from the English "governor")

tifaifai—a patchwork quilt based on either European or Polynesian motifs

tiki—a humanlike sculpture used in the old days for religious rites and sorcery

tinito—Tahitian for Chinese

toere—a hollow wooden drum hit with a stick

tradewind—a steady wind blowing toward the equator from either northeast or southeast, depending on the season

trench—the section at the bottom of the ocean where one tectonic plate wedges under another

tridacna clam—eaten everywhere in the Pacific, its size varies between 10 centimeters and one meter

tropical storm—a cyclonic storm with winds of 35 to 64 knots

tsunami—a fast-moving wave caused by an undersea earthquake

vigia—a mark on a nautical chart indicating a dangerous rock or shoal

windward—the point or side from which the wind blows, as opposed to "leeward"

zories—rubber shower sandals, thongs, flip-flops

CAPSULE TAHITIAN VOCABULARY

ahiahi—evening
aita—no
aita e peapea—no problem
aita maitai—no good
aito—ironwood
amu—eat
ananahi—tomorrow
arearea—fun, to have fun
atea—far away
atua—god
avae—moon, month
avatea—midday (1000-1500)

e—yes, also *oia*
e aha te huru?—how are you?
e hia?—how much?

faraoa—bread
fare—house
fare iti—toilet
fare moni—bank
fare rata—post office
fenua—land
fetii—parent, family
fiu—fed up, bored

haari—coconut palm
haere mai io nei—come here
haere maru—go easy, take it easy
hauti—play, make love
he haere oe ihea?—where are you going?
hei—flower garland, lei
here hoe—number-one sweetheart
himene—song, from the English "hymn"
hoa—friend

ia orana—good day, may you live, prosper
i nanahi—yesterday
ino—bad
ioa—name
ite—know

maeva—welcome
mahana—sun, light, day
mahanahana—warm
maitai—good, I'm fine; also a cocktail
maitai roa—very good
manava—conscience
manu—bird
manuia—to your health!
mao—shark

mauruuru—thank you
mauruuru roa—thank you very much
miti—salt water
moana—deep ocean
moemoea—dream
moni—money

nana—goodbye
naonao—mosquito
nehenehe—beautiful
niau—coconut palm frond
niu—coconut tree

ora—life, health
ori—dance
oromatua—the spirits of the dead
otaa—bundle, luggage
oti—finished

pahi—boat, ship
pape—water, juice
parahi—goodbye
pia—beer
pohe—death
poipoi—morning

popaa—foreigner, European
potii—teenage girl, young woman

raerae—effeminate
roto—lake

taata—human being, man
tahatai—beach
tamaa maitai—bon appetit
tamarii—child
tane—man, husband
taofe—coffee
taote—doctor
taravana—crazy
tiare—flower
toetoe—cold
tupapau—ghost

ua—rain
uaina—wine
uteute—red

vahine—woman, wife
vai—water
veavea—hot

NUMBERS

hoe—one
piti—two
toru—three
maha—four
pae—five
ono—six
hitu—seven
vau—eight
iva—nine
ahuru—ten
ahuru ma hoe—11
ahuru ma piti—12
ahuru ma toru—13
ahuru ma maha—14
ahuru ma pae—15
ahuru ma ono—16
ahuru ma hitu—17

ahuru ma vau—18
ahuru ma iva—19
piti ahuru—20
piti ahuru ma hoe—21
piti ahuru ma piti—22
piti ahuru ma toru—23
toru ahuru—30
maha ahuru—40
pae ahuru—50
ono ahuru—60
hitu ahuru—70
vau ahuru—80
iva ahuru—90
hanere—100
tauatini—1,000
ahuru tauatini—10,000
mirioni—million

CAPSULE FRENCH VOCABULARY

bonjour—good day
bonsoir—good evening
salut—hello
Je vais à . . .—I am going to . . .
Où allez-vous?—Where are you going?
Jusqu'où allez-vous?—How far are you going?
Où se trouve . . . ?—Where is . . . ?
C'est loin d'ici?—Is it far from here?
Je fais de l'autostop.—I am hitchhiking
À quelle heure?—At what time?
horaire—timetable
hier—yesterday
aujourd'hui—today
demain—tomorrow
Je désire, je voudrais . . .—I want . . .
J'aime . . .—I like . . .
Je ne comprends pas.—I don't understand
une chambre—a room
Vous êtes très gentil.—You are very kind.
Où habitez-vous?—Where do you live?
Il fait mauvais temps.—It's bad weather.
gendarmerie—police station
Quel travail faites-vous?—What work do you do?
la chômage, les chômeurs—unemployment, the unemployed
Je t'aime.—I love you.
une boutique, un magasin—a store
pain—bread
lait—milk
vin—wine
casse-croûte—snack
conserves—canned foods
fruits de mer—seafood
café très chaud—hot coffee
eau—water
plat du jour—set meal
Combien ça fait?—How much does it cost?
   Combien ça coûte?
   Combien? Quel prix?
auberge de jeunesse—youth hostel
la clef—the key
la route, la piste—the road
la plage—the beach
la falaise—the cliff
cascade—waterfall
grottes—caves

Est-ce que je peu camper ici?—May I camp here?
Je voudrais camper.—I wish to camp.
le terrain de camping—campsite
Devrais-je demander la permission?—Should I ask permission?
s'il vous plaît—please
oui—yes
merci—thank you
cher—expensive
bon marché—cheap
merde—shit

un—1
deux—2
trois—3
quatre—4
cinq—5
six—6
sept—7
huit—8
neuf—9
dix—10
onze—11
douze—12
treize—13
quatorze—14
quinze—15
seize—16
dix-sept—17
dix-huit—18
dix-neuf—19
vingt—20
vingt et un—21
vingt-deux—22
vingt-trois—23
trente—30
quarante—40
cinquante—50
soixante—60
soixante-dix—70
quatre-vingts—80
quatre-vingt-dix—90
cent—100
mille—1,000
dix mille—10,000
million—million

INDEX

Page numbers in **boldface** indicate the primary reference. *Italicized* page numbers indicate information in captions, callouts, charts, illustrations, or maps.

THE METRIC SYSTEM

1 inch = 2.54 centimeters (cm)
1 foot = .304 meters (m)
1 mile = 1.6093 kilometers (km)
1 km = .6214 miles
1 fathom = 1.8288 m
1 chain = 20.1168 m
1 furlong = 201.168 m
1 acre = .4047 hectares (ha)
1 sq km = 100 ha
1 sq mile = 2.59 sq km
1 ounce = 28.35 grams
1 pound = .4536 kilograms (kg)
1 short ton = .90718 metric ton
1 short ton = 2000 pounds
1 long ton = 1.016 metric tons
1 long ton = 2240 pounds
1 metric ton = 1000 kg
1 quart = .94635 liters
1 US gallon = 3.7854 liters
1 Imperial gallon = 4.5459 liters
1 nautical mile = 1.852 km

To compute centigrade temperatures, subtract 32 from Fahrenheit and divide by 1.8. To go the other way, multiply centigrade by 1.8 and add 32.

ABOUT THE AUTHOR

A quarter-century ago, David Stanley's right thumb carried him out of Toronto, Canada, and onto a journey which has so far wound through 138 countries, including a three-year trip from Tokyo to Kabul. His travel guidebooks to the South Pacific, Micronesia, Alaska, and Eastern Europe opened those areas to budget travelers for the first time.

During the late 1960s David got involved in Mexican culture by spending a year in several small towns near Guanajuato. Later he studied at the universities of Barcelona and Florence before settling down to get an honors degree (with distinction) in Spanish literature from the University of Guelph, Canada.

In 1978 Stanley linked up with future publisher Bill Dalton and together they wrote the first edition of *South Pacific Handbook* (now in its fifth edition). Since then Stanley has gone on to write additional definitive guides for Moon Publications, including *Fiji Islands Handbook, Micronesia Handbook, Tahiti-Polynesia Handbook,* and *Alaska-Yukon Handbook.* His books informed a generation of budget travelers.

From his base in Amsterdam Stanley makes frequent research trips to the areas covered in his guides, jammed between journeys to the 83 countries and territories worldwide he still hasn't visited. To maintain his independence, Stanley does not accept subsidized travel arrangements or "freebies" from any source. In travel writing, David Stanley has found a perfect outlet for his restless wanderlust.

David Stanley atop Tahiti's Mt. Aorai

Moon Handbooks—The Ideal Traveling Companions

Open a Moon Handbook and you're opening your eyes and heart to the world. Thoughtful, sensitive, and provocative, Moon Handbooks encourage an intimate understanding of a region, from its culture and history to essential practicalities. Fun to read and packed with valuable information on accommodations, dining, recreation, plus indispensable travel tips, detailed maps, charts, illustrations, photos, glossaries, and indexes, Moon Handbooks are ideal traveling companions: informative, entertaining, and highly practical.

To locate the bookstore nearest you that carries Moon Travel Handbooks or to order directly from Moon Publications, call: (800) 345-5473, Monday-Friday, 9 a.m.-5 p.m. PST

The Pacific/Asia Series

BALI HANDBOOK by Bill Dalton
Detailed travel information on the most famous island in the world. 12 color pages, 29 b/w photos, 68 illustrations, 42 maps, 7 charts, glossary, booklist, index. 428 pages.   **$12.95**

BANGKOK HANDBOOK by Michael Buckley
Your tour guide through this exotic and dynamic city reveals the affordable and accessible possibilities. Thai phrasebook, 16 color pages, 55 b/w photos, 30 maps, 19 illustrations, 9 charts, booklist, index. 214 pages.   **$10.95**

BLUEPRINT FOR PARADISE: How to Live on a Tropic Island by Ross Norgrove
This one-of-a-kind guide has everything you need to know about moving to and living comfortably on a tropical island. 8 color pages, 40 b/w photos, 3 maps, 14 charts, appendices, index. 212 pages.   **$14.95**

FIJI ISLANDS HANDBOOK by David Stanley
The first and still the best source of information on travel around this 322-island archipelago. 8 color pages, 35 b/w photos, 78 illustrations, 26 maps, 3 charts, Fijian glossary, booklist, index. 198 pages.   **$8.95**

INDONESIA HANDBOOK by Bill Dalton
This one-volume encyclopedia explores island by island the many facets of this sprawling, kaleidoscopic island nation. 30 b/w photos, 143 illustrations, 250 maps, 17 charts, booklist, extensive Indonesian vocabulary, index. 1,000 pages.   **$19.95**

MICRONESIA HANDBOOK:
Guide to the Caroline, Gilbert, Mariana, and Marshall Islands by David Stanley
Micronesia Handbook guides you on a real Pacific adventure all your own. 8 color pages, 77 b/w photos, 68 illustrations, 69 maps, 18 tables and charts, index. 300 pages.   **$11.95**

NEW ZEALAND HANDBOOK by Jane King
Introduces you to the people, places, history, and culture of this extraordinary land. 8 color pages, 99 b/w photos, 146 illustrations, 82 maps, booklist, index. 546 pages.   **$14.95**

OUTBACK AUSTRALIA HANDBOOK by Marael Johnson
Australia is an endlessly fascinating, vast land, and *Outback Australia Handbook* explores the cities and towns, sheep stations, and wilderness areas of the Northern Territory, Western, and South Australia. Full of travel tips and cultural information for adventuring, relaxing, or just getting away from it all. 8 color pages, 39 b/w photos, 63 illustrations, 51 maps, booklist, index. 355 pages.   **$15.95**

PHILIPPINES HANDBOOK by Peter Harper and Evelyn Peplow
Crammed with detailed information, *Philippines Handbook* equips the escapist, hedonist, or business traveler with thorough coverage of the Philippines's colorful history, landscapes, and culture. 8 color pages, 2 b/w photos, 60 illustrations, 93 maps, 30 charts, index. 587 pages.
$12.95

SOUTHEAST ASIA HANDBOOK by Carl Parkes
Helps the enlightened traveler discover the real Southeast Asia. 16 color pages, 75 b/w photos, 11 illustrations, 169 maps, 140 charts, vocabulary and suggested reading, index. 873 pages.
$16.95

SOUTH KOREA HANDBOOK by Robert Nilsen
Whether you're visiting on business or searching for adventure, *South Korea Handbook* is an invaluable companion. 8 color pages, 78 b/w photos, 93 illustrations, 109 maps, 10 charts, Korean glossary with useful notes on speaking and reading the language, booklist, index. 548 pages.   **$14.95**

SOUTH PACIFIC HANDBOOK by David Stanley
The original comprehensive guide to the 16 territories in the South Pacific. 20 color pages, 195 b/w photos, 121 illustrations, 35 charts, 138 maps, booklist, glossary, index. 740 pages.
$15.95

TAHITI-POLYNESIA HANDBOOK by David Stanley
All five French-Polynesian archipelagoes are covered in this comprehensive guide by Oceania's best-known travel writer. 12 color pages, 45 b/w photos, 64 illustrations, 33 maps, 7 charts, booklist, glossary, index. 235 pages.   **$11.95**

THAILAND HANDBOOK by Carl Parkes
Presents the richest source of information on travel in Thailand. Color and b/w photos, illustrations, maps, charts, booklist, glossary, index. 600 pages **$16.95**

TIBET HANDBOOK by Victor Chan
This remarkable book is both a comprehensive trekking guide and a pilgrimage guide that draws on Tibetan literature and religious history. Color and b/w photos, illustrations, maps, charts, booklist, glossary, index. 1,200 pages. **$24.95**

The Hawaiian Series

BIG ISLAND OF HAWAII HANDBOOK by J.D. Bisignani
An entertaining yet informative text packed with insider tips on accommodations, dining, sports and outdoor activities, natural attractions, and must-see sights. 12 color pages, 72 b/w photos, 73 illustrations, 22 maps, 5 charts, booklist, glossary, index. 347 pages. **$11.95**

HAWAII HANDBOOK by J.D. Bisignani
Winner of the 1989 Hawaii Visitors Bureau's Best Guide Book Award and the Grand Award for Excellence in Travel Journalism, this guide takes you beyond the glitz and high-priced hype and leads you to a genuine Hawaiian experience. 12 color pages, 86 b/w photos, 132 illustrations, 86 maps, 44 graphs and charts, Hawaiian and pidgin glossaries, appendix, booklist, index. 879 pages. **$15.95**

KAUAI HANDBOOK by J.D. Bisignani
Kauai Handbook is the perfect antidote to the workaday world. 8 color pages, 36 b/w photos, 48 illustrations, 19 maps, 10 tables and charts, Hawaiian and pidgin glossaries, booklist, index. 236 pages. **$9.95**

MAUI HANDBOOK: Including Molokai and Lanai by J.D. Bisignani
"No fool-'round" advice on accommodations, eateries, and recreation, plus a comprehensive introduction to island ways, geography, and history. 8 color pages, 60 b/w photos, 72 illustrations, 34 maps, 19 charts, booklist, glossary, index. 350 pages. **$11.95**

OAHU HANDBOOK by J.D. Bisignani
A handy guide to Honolulu, renowned surfing beaches, and Oahu's countless other diversions. 12 color pages, 93 b/w photos, 67 illustrations, 18 maps, 8 charts, booklist, glossary, index. 354 pages. **$11.95**

The Americas Series

ALASKA-YUKON HANDBOOK by Deke Castleman and Don Pitcher
Get the inside story, with plenty of well-seasoned advice to help you cover more miles on less money. 8 color pages, 26 b/w photos, 95 illustrations, 92 maps, 10 charts, booklist, glossary, index. 384 pages. **$13.95**

ARIZONA TRAVELER'S HANDBOOK by Bill Weir
This meticulously researched guide contains everything necessary to make Arizona accessible and enjoyable. 8 color pages, 194 b/w photos, 74 illustrations, 53 maps, 6 charts, booklist, index. 505 pages. **$14.95**

BAJA HANDBOOK by Joe Cummings
A comprehensive guide with all the travel information and background on the land, history, and culture of this untamed thousand-mile-long peninsula. 8 color pages, 40 b/w photos, 28 illustrations, 41 maps, 29 charts, booklist, index. 356 pages.   **$13.95**

BELIZE HANDBOOK by Chicki Mallan
Complete with detailed maps, practical information, and an overview of the area's flamboyant history, culture, and geographical features, *Belize Handbook* is the only comprehensive guide of its kind to this spectacular region. 8 color pages, 65 b/w photos, 43 illustrations, 25 maps, 30 charts, booklist, index. 212 pages.   **$11.95**

BRITISH COLUMBIA HANDBOOK by Jane King
With an emphasis on outdoor adventures, this guide covers mainland British Columbia, Vancouver Island, the Queen Charlotte Islands, and the Canadian Rockies. 8 color pages, 56 b/w photos, 45 illustrations, 66 maps, 4 charts, booklist, index. 381 pages.   **$13.95**

CANCUN HANDBOOK and Mexico's Caribbean Coast by Chicki Mallan
Covers the city's luxury scene as well as more modest attractions, plus many side trips to unspoiled beaches and Mayan ruins. 12 color pages, 76 b/w photos, 25 illustrations, 24 maps, 12 charts, Spanish glossary, booklist, index. 257 pages.   **$10.95**

CATALINA ISLAND HANDBOOK: A Guide to California's Channel Islands
by Chicki Mallan
A complete guide to these remarkable islands, from the windy solitude of the Channel Islands National Marine Sanctuary to bustling Avalon. 8 color pages, 105 b/w photos, 65 illustrations, 40 maps, 32 charts, booklist, index. 245 pages.   **$10.95**

COLORADO HANDBOOK by Stephen Metzger
Essential details to the all-season possibilities in Colorado fill this guide. Practical travel tips combine with recreation—skiing, nightlife, and wilderness exploration—plus entertaining essays. 8 color pages, 92 b/w photos, 15 illustrations, 57 maps, 10 charts, booklist, index. 422 pages.   **$15.95**

IDAHO HANDBOOK by Bill Loftus
A year-round guide to everything in this outdoor wonderland, from whitewater adventures to rural hideaways. 8 color pages, 35 b/w photos, 21 illustrations, 42 maps, booklist, index. 275 pages.   **$12.95**

JAMAICA HANDBOOK by Karl Luntta
From the sun and surf of Montego Bay and Ocho Rios to the cool slopes of the Blue Mountains, author Karl Luntta offers island-seekers a perceptive, personal view of Jamaica. 8 color pages, 21 b/w photos, 35 illustrations, 16 maps, 7 charts, booklist, glossary, index. 213 pages.   **$12.95**

MONTANA HANDBOOK by W.C. McRae and Judy Jewell
The wild West is yours with this extensive guide to the Treasure State, complete with travel practicalities, history, and lively essays on Montana life. 8 color pages, 62 b/w photos, 43 illustrations, 49 maps, 10 charts, booklist, index. 393 pages.   **$13.95**

NEVADA HANDBOOK by Deke Castleman
Nevada Handbook puts the Silver State into perspective and makes it manageable and affordable. 34 b/w photos, 43 illustrations, 37 maps, 17 charts, booklist, index. 400 pages. **$12.95**

NEW MEXICO HANDBOOK by Stephen Metzger
A close-up and complete look at every aspect of this wondrous state. 8 color pages, 85 b/w photos, 63 illustrations, 50 maps, 10 charts, booklist, index. 375 pages. **$13.95**

NORTHERN CALIFORNIA HANDBOOK by Kim Weir
An outstanding companion for imaginative travel in the territory north of the Tehachapis. 12 color pages, 200 b/w photos, 54 maps, 36 illustrations, booklist, index. 759 pages. **$16.95**

OREGON HANDBOOK by Stuart Warren and Ted Long Ishikawa
Brimming with travel practicalities and insider views on Oregon's history, culture, arts, and activities. 8 color pages, 113 b/w photos, 26 illustrations, 28 maps, 20 charts, booklist, index. 422 pages. **$12.95**

TEXAS HANDBOOK by Joe Cummings
Seasoned travel writer Joe Cummings brings an insider's perspective to his home state. 8 color pages, 79 b/w photos, 60 maps, 45 illustrations, 18 charts, booklist, index. 483 pages. **$13.95**

UTAH HANDBOOK by Bill Weir
Weir gives you all the carefully researched facts and background to make your visit a success. 8 color pages, 102 b/w photos, 61 illustrations, 30 maps, 9 charts, booklist, index. 452 pages. **$12.95**

WASHINGTON HANDBOOK by Dianne J. Boulerice Lyons and Archie Satterfield
Covers sights, shopping, services, transportation, and outdoor recreation, with complete listings for restaurants and accommodations. 8 color pages, 92 b/w photos, 24 illustrations, 81 maps, 8 charts, booklist, index. 433 pages. **$13.95**

WYOMING HANDBOOK by Don Pitcher
All you need to know to open the doors to this wide and wild state. 16 color pages, 30 b/w photos, 42 illustrations, 64 maps, 19 charts, booklist, index. 427 pages. **$12.95**

YUCATAN HANDBOOK by Chicki Mallan
All the information you'll need to guide you into every corner of this exotic land. 8 color pages, 154 b/w photos, 55 illustrations, 57 maps, 70 charts, appendix, booklist, Mayan and Spanish glossaries, index. 391 pages. **$12.95**

The International Series

EGYPT HANDBOOK by Kathy Hansen
An invaluable resource for intelligent travel in Egypt. 8 color pages, 20 b/w photos, 150 illustrations, 80 detailed maps and plans to museums and archaeological sites, Arabic glossary, booklist, index. 510 pages. **$14.95**

MOSCOW-LENINGRAD HANDBOOK by Masha Nordbye

Provides the visitor with an extensive introduction to the history, culture, and people of these two great cities, as well as practical information on where to stay, eat, and shop. 8 color pages, 36 b/w photos, 20 illustrations, 16 maps, 9 charts, booklist, index. 205 pages. **$12.95**

NEPAL HANDBOOK by Kerry Moran

Whether you're planning a week in Kathmandu or months out on the trail, *Nepal Handbook* will take you into the heart of this Himalayan jewel. 16 color pages, 76 b/w photos, 45 illustrations, 46 maps, 9 charts, booklist, glossary, index. 378 pages. **$12.95**

NEPALI AAMA by Broughton Coburn

A delightful photo-journey into the life of a Gurung tribeswoman of Central Nepal. Having lived with Aama (translated, "mother") for two years, first as an outsider and later as an adopted member of the family, Coburn presents an intimate glimpse into a culture alive with humor, folklore, religion, and ancient rituals. 67 b/w photos. 165 pages. **$13.95**

PAKISTAN HANDBOOK by Isobel Shaw

For armchair travelers and trekkers alike, the most detailed and authoritative guide to Pakistan ever published. 28 color pages, 86 maps, appendices, Urdu glossary, booklist, index. 478 pages. **$15.95**

Moonbelts

Made of heavy-duty Cordura nylon, the Moonbelt offers maximum protection for your money and important papers. This all-weather pouch slips under your shirt or waistband, rendering it virtually undetectable and inaccessible to pickpockets. One-inch-wide nylon webbing, heavy-duty zipper, one-inch quick release buckle. Accommodates traveler's checks, passport, cash, photos. Size 5 x 9 inches. Black. **$8.95**

Travel Matters

Travel Matters is a biannual newsletter for travelers, containing book reviews, practical travel news, articles, and humorous essays. For a free copy, call Moon Publications toll-free at (800) 345-5473.

**New travel handbooks may be available that are not on this list.
To find out more about current or upcoming titles,
call us toll-free at (800) 345-5473.**

IMPORTANT ORDERING INFORMATION

FOR FASTER SERVICE: Call to locate the bookstore nearest you that carries Moon Travel Handbooks or order directly from Moon Publications:
(800) 345-5473 · Monday-Friday · 9 a.m.-5 p.m. PST · fax (916) 345-6751

PRICES: All prices are subject to change. We always ship the most current edition. We will let you know if there is a price increase on the book you ordered.

SHIPPING & HANDLING OPTIONS:
1) Domestic UPS or USPS first class (allow 10 working days for delivery):
   $3.50 for the first item, 50 cents for each additional item.

Exceptions:
· **Moonbelt** shipping is $1.50 for one, 50 cents for each additional belt.
· Add $2.00 for same-day handling.
2) UPS 2nd Day Air or Printed Airmail requires a special quote.
3) International Surface Bookrate (8-12 weeks delivery):
   $3.00 for the first item, $1.00 for each additional item. Note: Moon Publications cannot guarantee international surface bookrate shipping.

FOREIGN ORDERS: All orders which originate outside the U.S.A. must be paid for with either an International Money Order or a check in U.S. currency drawn on a major U.S. bank based in the U.S.A.

TELEPHONE ORDERS: We accept Visa or MasterCard payments. Minimum order is US $15.00. Call in your order: 1 (800) 345-5473. 9 a.m.-5 p.m. Pacific Standard Time.

WHERE TO BUY THIS BOOK

Bookstores and Libraries:
Moon Publications Handbooks are sold worldwide. Please write our sales manager for a list of wholesalers and distributors in your area that stock our travel handbooks.

Travelers:
We would like to have Moon Publications Handbooks available throughout the world. Please ask your bookstore to write or call us for ordering information. If your bookstore will not order our guides for you, please write or call for a free catalog.

**MOON PUBLICATIONS INC.
722 WALL STREET
CHICO, CA 95928 U.S.A.
tel: (800) 345-5473
fax: (916) 345-6751**

ORDER FORM

Be sure to call (800) 345-5473 for current prices and editions or for the name of the bookstore nearest you that carries Moon Travel Handbooks · 9 a.m.-5 p.m. PST
(See important ordering information on preceding page)

Name:_____ Date:_____

Street:_____

City:_____ Daytime Phone:_____

State or Country:_____ Zip Code:_____

Quantity	Title	Price

Taxable Total	
Sales Tax (7.25%) for California Residents	
Shipping & Handling	
TOTAL	

Ship: ☐ 1st class   ☐ UPS (no P.O. Boxes)   ☐ International Surface

Ship to: ☐ address above   ☐ other_____

_____

_____

Make checks payable to:
Moon Publications Inc., 722 Wall Street, Chico, California 95928 U.S.A.
We Accept Visa and MasterCard
To Order: Call in your Visa or MasterCard number, or send a written order with your Visa or MasterCard number and expiration date clearly written.

Card Number: ☐ Visa   ☐ MasterCard

☐ ☐ ☐ ☐   ☐ ☐ ☐ ☐   ☐ ☐ ☐ ☐   ☐ ☐ ☐

Exact Name on Card: ☐ same as above   expiration date:_____

☐ other_____

signature_____

3-87-5

Capt. Cook's 1769 map of Tahiti and Moorea

CHART
OF THE ISLAND
OTAHEITE,
BY
LIEUT. J. COOK
1769.

Scale of Miles.